Letters to

Pastors' Wives

Letters to Pastors' Wives

WHEN SEMINARY ENDS
AND MINISTRY BEGINS

EDITED BY

CATHERINE J. STEWART

P&R PUBLISHING
P.O. BOX 817 • PHILLIPSBURG • NEW JERSEY 08865-0817

Unless otherwise indicated, Scripture quotations are from *ESV Bible* ® (*The Holy Bible, English Standard Version* ®). Copyright © 2001 by Crossway Bibles, a publishing ministry of Good News Publishers. Used by permission. All rights reserved.

Scripture quotations in chapter 10 are from the King James Version.

Italics within Scripture quotations indicate emphasis added.

"Depression: A Dark Valley" is taken from *Women Counseling Women: Biblical Answers to Life's Difficult Problems* © 2010 by Elyse Fitzpatrick. Published by Harvest House Publishers. Used by permission.

ISBN: 978-1-59638-700-3 (pbk)
ISBN: 978-1-59638-701-0 (ePub)
ISBN: 978-1-59638-702-7 (Mobi)

Postage stamp © istockphoto.com / traveler1116

Printed in Canada

Library of Congress Cataloging-in-Publication Data

Letters to pastors' wives : when seminary ends and ministry begins / edited by Catherine J. Stewart.
     pages cm
  Includes bibliographical references.
   ISBN 978-1-59638-700-3 (pbk.)
   1. Spouses of clergy. 2. Wives--Religious life. I. Stewart, Catherine J., 1974- editor of compilation.
   BV4395.L48 2013
   253'.22--dc23
                    2013017933

To the professors' wives who faithfully mentored the seminary wives at Reformed Theological Seminary, Jackson, during the years of 1999–2002.

Contents

Preface

It's Not Good for a Pastor to Be Alone

A wife can make or break a man's ministry. Her influence is felt everywhere. It begins behind the front door as she turns a house into a haven and a home. Without her, there will almost always be something "not good" about the man. Even for Adam in the garden—a perfect man, in perfect paradise, in perfect relationship with God—there was a jarring want about him before Eve came into the picture. How could he image the triune God by himself (Genesis 1:27)?[1]

As an anecdotal statement of this, I once heard Dr. Martyn Lloyd-Jones tell the story of a minister in London during the 1920s. He was of an extremely liberal theological bent and went from one conflict to another in his ministry. Yet, more than anything else, this minister was known for his cheerful, happy disposition. When asked about the source of this joy, he replied, "My wife loves me, and when I go home at night, I close the door on all my troubles and open a door into a realm of peace and rest." Of course, the true Christian needs a deeper source of joy than a good marriage, and we must not lean on our spouses in the way that we should lean only on God. With that said, however, the Puritan Thomas Gataker was surely onto something when he noted, "A good wife is the best companion in wealth; the fittest and readiest assistant in work; the greatest comfort in crosses and griefs; and the greatest grace and honor that can be, to him that hath her!"[2]

9

Her presence also has a way of brightening the church and balancing her husband's ministry. In God's kind providence, opposites have a way of attracting one another in marriage. How many times has the tender, personable, winsome, sincerely interested wife served to take the edge off an overly bookish, at times insensitive, and naturally introverted minister? Think of the absentminded professor type. How often has this forgetful soul found himself joined to a highly disciplined and organized helpmeet! Were it not for the safety net afforded by her watchful eye, how many pastoral lunches might this dear man have missed? And we have all met the highly organized, ducks-in-a-row, "Don't interrupt me; can't you see I am pursuing my number-one priority for the morning?" type of preacher. He wouldn't have lasted five minutes in the church were it not for the Abigail-like graces of his wife, who gently reminds him that he is a shepherd of sheep by calling—not a butcher of interruptions!

Writing this the week that Stephen Covey died, I think it is fair to say that marrying such a balancing influence is perhaps the first habit of highly successful ministers! In that regard, have you never noticed that the book of Proverbs—a book designed for fathers who teach wisdom to their sons—ends with the subject of the excellent wife? For the longest time, I used to think that this was Solomon's instruction to the fairer sex—too little and too late, perhaps, but at least he didn't forget women altogether. Then it hit me. The passage isn't directed at women in order that they might become such wives but directed to men in order that they might find them. Remember how King Lemuel started his description: "An excellent wife who can find? She is far more precious than jewels" (Prov. 31:10)? Isn't it also interesting to note that one of the marks of this woman is that her husband is known in the gates, where the elders sit governing the city's affairs? In light of this, could it be that the book ends on this note to teach the son the last great lesson of wisdom: "Son, when it comes to being wise and having a voice that carries weight in society, whom you choose to marry matters a very great deal indeed"?

A wife has a way of shining as a beacon in the community. Ministers by the very nature of their task are always on the run. I sometimes feel that

I am always going from home to study to pulpit to parlor to hospital and back to home again. I don't get much time with my neighbors. Catherine has proved invaluable to me over the years. She jogs in the morning and stops to talk to all the neighbors as they take out the trash and do their yard work on the weekends. She knows the names of the cashiers and baggers at our local grocery store. She takes time with people whom few others ever stop to notice. She stands behind me like the welcoming glow of a sunset in a Thomas Kinkade painting, where even the snow looks warm! I always appear much kinder when she's near me. Many in our community who think well of me actually hardly know me, but they know Kate, and the favor reflects on her husband.

All this to say, while I suppose it is possible for a man to be an effective minister without a godly wife to help him, it will be very difficult, and for the most part, it will be impossible. May God use this book to help our wives to help us, so that more and more we might all have cause to say with old Mr. Cotton: "Women are creatures without which there is no comfortable living for man. . . . They are a sort of Blasphemers then who despise and decry them, and call them a necessary evil, for they are a necessary good!"[3]

REV. DR. NEIL C. STEWART
July 2012

Acknowledgments

"The steadfast love of the LORD never ceases; his mercies never come to an end; They are new every morning; great is your faithfulness."

LAMENTATIONS 3:22–23

There are a few people who did not contribute to this book but whose time undergirded it. I would like to thank Linda Breen, Kate Dyer, Camille Hebert, Dorsey Ketcham, Lee Ann Koon, Tracey Shannon, and Ellen Smith for their help when my eyes became glazed over! These women have given freely and without complaint to this project.

My dear mother spent her vacation time with our family while I worked on this book. Thank you for flying thousands of miles to visit us and watch your daughter bury herself in a project!

I am indebted to Terry Johnson for his time and wise counsel. Only a man of seasoned experience in ministry could have afforded the insight he provided for this book.

For our five children, Hannah (my tireless assistant), Benjamin, Eleah Marie, Josiah, and Samuel—you are the ones who gave of yourselves sacrificially for this book. You sacrificed a mommy more than a few times. May countless lives be helped because of your selflessness.

Finally, and most importantly, my dear husband, Neil, who shares my zeal to see pastors' wives equipped to serve their husbands—your sacrifice at every level is a further demonstration of a man devoted to Christ's cause. This book would not be in existence without you. You gave me the privilege of being a pastor's wife. Thank you.

Introduction

A Journey into Ministry Life

*A*s you enter a new season of life, I want to remind you that the Lord has bestowed a rare privilege on you. It is my prayer that as you read through these letters you will find friends, sisters, and mentors in the dear women who have contributed to this book. They have not yet arrived at their final destination, but they are well-seasoned pilgrims who have trod the path as ministry wives. They can wholeheartedly testify to the Lord's never-failing mercies along the way. I know that I speak for all the women writing to you when I say, "We write as beggars showing another beggar where God has so graciously fed us along the ups and downs of our own lives immersed in Christian ministry."

Let me first of all give you a whistle-stop tour of my journey into ministry life and the circumstances that led to the writing of these letters. I was, by today's standards, a young bride. At the age of twenty-one, I had completed my degree in theology and found a young, earnest Christian husband. He had just completed medical school, and I was embarking on postgraduate studies. While we had discussed the probability of a call to the ministry, its reality always seemed a long way off. With both our families living nearby, we established our baby daughter and ourselves in a comfortable little home in Northern Ireland. Life seemed to be rolling along quite nicely.

Suddenly, one spring day, the peace was shattered. My husband arrived home from work and announced that the call to preach was fast becoming an irrepressible burden on his soul. I can openly admit that although we both shared a desire to engage in full-time Christian ministry, I was not prepared for the break from our earthly home, from our families, or indeed from the security of a physician's paycheck.

In God's kind providence, he brought us to a seminary all the way across the Atlantic Ocean. There in Mississippi we were surrounded by people in similar circumstances who were seeking to faithfully obey a call to ministry life. For our husbands, this was the first exciting step in fulfilling God's divine purpose as instruments in spreading the Word. We women, however, saw these same events from an entirely different perspective. While we all recognized God's call in our husbands' lives, we were much more prone to place our focus on the everyday practicalities of student life.

Mercifully, this tendency had not gone unnoticed by the wives of the Reformed Theological Seminary (RTS) faculty. And so, when we arrived on campus, we found ourselves surrounded by an established network of support, intended to equip the wives of ministry students. Every Thursday night, several godly, mature pastors' wives mentored us. Their persistent desire to teach and equip the young women provided us with some of the finest wisdom imaginable.

At the time, we probably didn't realize the full extent of what we were receiving, but we all look back to each of those women with deep gratitude for their sacrificial example to us. This book is largely born out of a desire to impart this same wisdom to other wives sharing our calling and to assure you that there really is nothing new under the sun, not even to the wife of a pastor!

Over the years of being a pastor's wife, I have had the joy of meeting countless women who share the same privileged lot in life that I have. The one enduring lesson that has been embedded in my mind is that there is no right "type" of pastor's wife, only the one whose heart is wholly set on serving Christ. In this book you will find the beauty of various personalities, character types, and giftedness interweaving the pages of these letters. We are not called to fit into a certain mold but to be helpmeets to our husbands, helpmeets who enable them to serve God more effectively with us at their side than they ever could alone.

I would like to point out that the views expressed in these letters are the authors' own and may not be representative of the other contributors' opinions. May the Lord use the words of these women as a channel of his grace to equip you for a life of ministry.

CATHERINE J. STEWART
July 2012

Part 1

The Piety of the Pastor's Wife

CHAPTER ONE

Priorities: Putting First Things First

Catherine J. Stewart

A pastor's wife must be both efficient and effective in her work. She must be efficient in her ability to stay on task and get a never-ending list of chores done on schedule. Even more importantly, however, she must be effective: she must get the right list of chores done on schedule. To do this, she will need priorities.

Catherine grew up around horses, and in Ireland you spell horse "w-o-r-k." From her earliest days, she was trained to work, and work she does, with proficiency and with pleasure! I often stand amazed at her ability to plan and prioritize and simply get things done. Over the years, I have come to the conclusion that she might actually be a machine—a beautiful, blue-eyed machine, but a machine nonetheless. She is to chaos what magnets are to heaps of iron filings, yet she is no neatnik! The order she brings to our home glows with the glory of Christ, reflecting his mind, obeying his Word, serving his glory. Of all the virtues I cherish about Kate, I think this is the one I admire most of all: she keeps first things first. I can think of no one better equipped to write this chapter.

Rev. Dr. Neil C. Stewart

Dear sister in Christ,

From the very outset of this letter, I want you to know that the life you now possess as the wife of a pastor is the most privileged life you could ever desire. It may not always seem that way, but God has cocooned you in a place where you will constantly be exposed to his Word. This is a manifestation of his love toward you in Christ. As the prophet once wrote, "I know the plans I have for you, declares the LORD, plans for welfare and not for evil, to give you a future and a hope" (Jer. 29:11).

With confidence of his never-failing goodness toward you, I want to help you to take a look at your life and be certain that you are putting first things first. During my college years, I had a dear friend who set me a wonderful example of a biblically prioritized life, and the lessons I gleaned from her still order my life today. As I sojourn through this passing world, those lessons continue to hold me in good stead. With God's help, I hope to be to you what my good friend was to me.

My husband loves to illustrate spiritual truth in an earthly way. He once came out with a statement that has always stuck with me: "Heart attacks don't just suddenly occur; they happen one hamburger at a time." My dear sister in Christ, this principle also holds true in the heart of our spiritual lives. Failure does not occur out of the blue but is the result of a lifetime of bad habits, putting off until tomorrow what we should have set in order today. Sadly, the wives of pastors are not exempt from this great threat. If we do the wrong things at the wrong time, they will come back to bite us. None of us wants failure to be our legacy. All of us want to reach the end of our lives in glorious victory. If we are to do this, if we are to avoid Satan's many "beautiful" but deadly daggers, then we will need to put on the whole armor of God and be strong with the strength that Christ provides. Only then will we reach the Celestial City when our earthly journey is done.

So where do we begin? First of all, we need to identify our current priorities. Whether we see it or not, our lives are already prioritized. The daily habits we establish, the manner in which we speak, the people with whom we spend time, and the places we go all indicate where we have placed the focus of our hearts. The habitual bent of our soul reveals where we look for satisfaction, security, and significance. Do we look to God for these things, or do we scatter our hopes elsewhere?

Think, for example, of the woman who finds her satisfaction, security, and significance in the fair opinion of others. She spends her life chasing people's smiles and fleeing their frowns. Her satisfaction is always fleeting, hanging insecurely on the good favor of those she really values. Likewise, her security is always crumbling, and her significance—the sense that she has lived a life worth living, a life that has counted for something—is always one faux pas away from evaporating. Such a woman knows no rest. Her life is like a line of dominoes. Once one falls, the others will soon follow.

Pastors' wives are perpetually surrounded by spiritual matters and submerged in the life of the church. These waters can be treacherous. Without a heart firmly rooted in Christ, we will drown in them. Christ alone can give us the satisfaction, security, and significance for which our hearts long. Our natural, idolatrous tendency is to look for these things in the broken cisterns of the world and all its empty promises. "Remember Lot's wife" (Luke 17:32). We must flee without looking back.

Search your heart. What do you want out of life? Where do you root your desire for satisfaction, security, and significance? Are you searching for it in the right place? What are the things you feel you need—the things without which you would feel life is not worth living? When do you tailspin into despair and panic? Only you and God know what your heart really wants. One local pastor put it well when he said, "What the heart wants, the heart gets"; i.e., whatever is most important to you will drive every moment of every day. Indeed, we all constantly pursue what our hearts want. It is an inevitable fact of life. The question is, are we pursuing God's priorities or only our own?

As you begin to organize your new life as a pastor's wife, more than anything else I want you to see that prioritizing is not organizing. Before you begin to organize your life, you must first address your priorities. As I try to help you in this regard, please be assured that I don't want to organize or control your schedule. I don't want to squeeze you into my mold. God knows my schedule is littered with the debris of human sin and frailty. Instead, I would like to point you to three sources that have proved vital in molding my thinking:

1. Christ: Our Ultimate Example
2. Women of the Word
3. Women of Piety throughout History

CHRIST: OUR ULTIMATE EXAMPLE

Looking at Christ's life, I have often struggled to know how to effectively apply his priorities to my life. After all, Jesus is a man; I am a woman. His earthly life was outside the home; mine is inside it. His primary calling was to bring the good news of the gospel to many; mine is to bring it to the little flock in our home. Our daily routines bear almost no resemblance to each other. Yet I am persuaded that the focus of my life must be derived from his example in the Word. In particular, three aspects of his life strike me as peculiarly relevant to our call as pastors' wives: his times of prayer, his obedience to the Father, and the relationships he cultivated with others.

A Life of Prayer

The book of Luke is replete with examples of Christ's prayer life. From the very outset, Christ's adult life was marked by the fact that he was a man of prayer: "When Jesus also had been baptized and was praying, the heavens were opened, and the Holy Spirit descended on him in bodily form, like a dove" (Luke 3:21–22).

In the next chapter, we find Jesus retreating to a desolate place to be alone with the Father. In Luke 6 we find him going out to the mountain to pray and "all night he continued in prayer to God" (v. 12). Before long we see him take Peter, John, and James up a mountain to pray, and it is the next day before they return (Luke 9). In Luke 11, Christ provides us with the pattern for intercession that we know as The Lord's Prayer. The list goes on and on.

My dear sister, one of the hardest things to do in the Christian life is pray. It is fairly easy to pick up the Word of God and read a chapter or two, but prayer is different. You see, when we get down on our knees before our Maker, our hearts are laid bare before his all-seeing eye. In the secret place of his presence, when we are alone with our Father, we realize the full extent of our desperate need of grace. Even in our best times, we are unworthy of mercy. Such moments bring a devastating clarity to the soul. They show us for who and what we really are. As Robert Murray McCheyne is said to have put it, "What a man is alone on his knees before God, that he is, and no more."

Yet in this place of emptiness and total frailty, we find Christ to be our only fullness. Here alone, in his loving embrace, we find satisfaction. No other relationship can ever fill the God-sized hole in our hearts. I feel sure you know this already. The question is, have you experienced it? Remember that what the heart wants, the heart gets. Do you treasure your relationship with your Father enough to pursue him at the cost of every other fleeting pleasure? Oh, how I have struggled in this area. I imagine you do too. How easy it is to pick up the telephone to call a friend, to convince ourselves that our daughter really does need that new dress for Sunday, that we really must bake that cake for a neighbor, or that the shoes needing to be re-heeled can't wait until a later time. How easy it is to forget God in

25

the clamorous crowd of second-place things. How lethally simple it is to major on the minors!

So when it comes to putting God first, where do we start? For me, the only time when I can be certain of stillness and solitude is early in the morning before our children arise. This is the time for me to fill my mind with the Divine Majesty. Does that mean that I am up at 4:00 a.m. praying every day? I wish it did. In fact, there are days when I would need to be up at that time in order to beat our five children out of bed! However, it is my testimony that when I am diligent in rising early to spend time on my knees, the Lord deals closely with my soul. In a strange but happy contradiction, he satisfies my deepest longings while leaving me still hungering for more.

You will undoubtedly have a different schedule from mine, but when you are planning out your day, put your personal time with the Lord on the schedule. Consider it a nonnegotiable. As pastors' wives we are in no less need of private fellowship with the Lord than other women are. At times I have found myself depending on the spiritual conversation of our home, the discussion of sermons, and the cocoon of ministry life as a crutch for my soul. In such times my soul emaciates; I become a spiritual anorexic. This is a common trap for pastors' wives. At one time or another, we have all fallen into it. As a great hymn of old so aptly states, I have tried the "broken cisterns," and I can testify that they fail—every time. Do not feed your soul on the run. Do not substitute spiritual snacks for unhurried time before God in private prayer and devotion every day.

Obedience to the Father

Second, Christ's life is distinctly set apart from others through his obedience to the Father. Every day we find him doing his Father's will and fulfilling his Father's plan for his life: "I have come down from heaven, not to do my own will but the will of him who sent me" (John 6:38).

Such obedience extended far beyond Satan's temptations, far beyond the extremity of physical exhaustion and the constant desire to stop and rest amidst the unceasing pressures of life. Christ's obedience extended all the way to the cross. He obeyed God through the gates of hell because he loved us and was determined to do anything and everything to save us. "Going a little farther he fell on his face and prayed, saying, 'My Father, if it be possible, let this cup pass from me; nevertheless, not as I will, but as you will'" (Matt. 26:39).

We could discuss Christ's remarkable obedience forever. Permit me to root his example in your life with a question: "Is the general tenor of your heart marked by a conscious obedience to the revealed will of God?" Be honest with your reply, and repent of any habitual sin that may be inhibiting your walk with Christ. What weights hinder you as you climb Jacob's ladder? Some weights are lead, others are gold, but if they hold us back, we must cut them loose (Heb. 12:1–3). May the Lord help us both to pursue a life of obedience to his will.

Relationships with Others

Third, I am struck by Christ's earthly relationships with other people. He ministered to many, yet he kept a small cadre of close friends with whom he enjoyed the closest and deepest intimacy. Despite spending three years in public ministry, he spent most of his time in close proximity to the twelve men he wanted to influence most of all. Christ devoted his efforts to teaching, eating, sleeping, and fellowshipping with these twelve disciples. Among them, he treasured three men more than the others.

We need to consider the focused impact that our Savior had on a few souls and its subsequent widespread effects. Just like Christ, we must focus on the few we most need to influence. As with all charity, this effort begins at home with the little flock God has entrusted to our care. Never forget that we are wives and mothers before we are anything else. No amount of success in the church and in the world can ever make up for failure in the home.

We must remember that our children are natural-born sinners. By default, their hearts are wayward and full of folly. If they are ever to be salt and light in this dark world, they will need the love and compassion of

Christ to penetrate their souls with saving mercy. It is our role to tenderly teach and apply the Word of God to their hearts and minds on a daily basis. If they do not hear and see it from us, from whom will they ever hear it? The way we live before them, the habits we cultivate, the priorities we exemplify, and the identity we have in Christ all leave a never-ending impact on their never-dying souls. Our children are covenant children, and while the responsibility of teaching the Word to them lies primarily with our husbands, we are the ones with whom they will spend the most time.

When I come to die, I am quite sure that I will not look back over my life and wish I had poured more time into the tangibly attractive distractions of the world. My greater concern will be that I influenced my children for the kingdom of God with all my heart, soul, mind, and strength. When I consider the far-reaching implications of the time Christ spent with the twelve disciples, I am reminded that the gospel has subsequently been brought to millions of lost sinners. Though we may become caught up in the minuteness of the seemingly small realm of influence currently before us, a family well raised will be a mighty weapon in the hand of Christ. It will reap fruit forever.

There will come a time when your little ones are up and gone and your primary sphere of influence will change. But when your children are young, try not to be distracted from first things. If you get this right, you will be well set by God's grace to become a Titus 2 role model in the years to come. Too many pastors' wives forsake their primary calling in order to become a Titus 2 woman before their time. Little do they know it, but their best efforts disqualify them before they even begin.

WOMEN OF THE WORD

Now that we have spent some time reflecting on the priorities of Christ, it seems a natural progression to consider some women of biblical times whose lives exemplify their priority choices. There are many women whose lives are marked by these choices, yet only a handful of them are directly related to men who were used as either prophets or ministers of God's Word.

Examples to Avoid

Let's begin with some examples we would do well to avoid. Though some of our priorities as pastors' wives are apparent to the public eye, others will remain hidden. The manifestation of our real priorities will sometimes become more apparent when we are faced with trials of varying degrees.

You have often heard mothers warn their children of the consequences of disobedience and the painful results of acting without thinking. One of our children has a delightful passion for all things adventurous, hesitating at almost nothing! We warn him of the consequences that will befall him, but he invariably ends up learning the hard way!

God has graciously supplied us with a few scattered examples of women whose choices reflect a similar immaturity. These examples warn of the consequences that invariably fall to those who live with a careless disregard of what really matters. For the most part, these tragic examples are a direct result of women forgetting their place and the role God has assigned to them in the church and in the home. I think you will agree with me that when we find ourselves willfully engaged in compromising situations, it is generally because we have made a similar mistake.

Consider Numbers 12:2, where Miriam, the sister of Moses, while standing alongside her brother Aaron, seeks preeminence for herself. "'Has the LORD indeed spoken only through Moses? Has he not spoken through us also?' And the LORD heard it."

Miriam stands as a solemn warning to us of a woman's natural propensity to disregard God-given male authority. We all know that our sinful natures incline our hearts to usurp male leadership—some to a greater degree than others—but nonetheless, we all too often find ourselves with the mumblings of Miriam's heart. No doubt, my sister, you desire to be submissive to your husband, but there will be times when you will think you know better than him. There will be occasions when you will want some of the credit for his labors. You will want your opinions to be heard. After all, you are his "better" half.

29

My sister, do not be deceived. At such times we must remind ourselves of the dire consequences of speaking without thinking. Miriam paid dearly for her presumption. She became a leper and for a season was cast out of the camp. Imagine the shame that must have filled her heart. All this befell her because she lost sight of her calling to serve, entertained delusions of grandeur, and despised the man God had set in charge over her and the people of God.

We women thrive best when we embrace the place and the ministry God has entrusted to us, not when we reach for positions of authority God never intended for us to occupy. We must take heed to our hearts. Lest we despair, though, we must not forget the Lord's kindness in his dealings with Miriam. Mercifully, his chastening hand relented. Miriam's season as an outcast lasted only seven days. This should comfort us in our repentance. His mercy really does endure forever.

Martha is, of course, another woman who allowed her priorities to slip out of place. As pastors' wives, we can easily fall into the same trap. Our home serves as a place of grace to others, and we often have much work to do in terms of preparation. The work doesn't stop there! We want the time spent by guests in our home to be pleasant, so we carefully attend to all practical needs to make that possible. It is a joy to prepare for God's people. It is good and noble to make our guests feel welcome and comfortable. However, the simple mistake of placing the emphasis in the wrong place at the wrong time can have long-term consequences on our souls.

Remind yourself of the parable of the sower. One of the weeds that can choke out the Word is busyness. Sometimes our family home seems to have a steady stream of guests coming and going, and it always delights me to open our home to any folks who wish to stay with us. However, on more than one occasion, I have missed the blessing of getting to know our guests because I have been too busy attending to the "next thing." Busyness can seem so very necessary, yet it can be a huge hindrance to cultivating true fellowship. Actively seize as many opportunities as you can to listen to the words of wise guests, and be assured that if their meal is a little late due to your interest in their conversation, they are unlikely to complain!

I would encourage you to read further into the lives of other women whose misplaced priorities bore bitter fruit. Sarah's desperate attempt to have children through Hagar produced a whole nation of godless people. Job's wife was a snare to his soul. Indeed, the damage we can do to our husbands in private is immeasurable. Let us not serve as a Mrs. Job, discouraging our husbands at every juncture, but rather let us radiate Barnabas's perpetual efforts to serve as an encourager.

Examples to Embrace

In 1 Samuel, we find Hannah on her knees in prayer. She is barren and brokenhearted, yet while many a woman would have grumbled at her husband or lashed out in vindictive malice at her rival (in this case, Peninnah), Hannah takes herself to a better sanctuary. She pours out her heart to God. Should we not follow her up to the throne room of heaven? Yet, if we are honest, when it comes to responding to the difficulties of life, this is the road less taken. I find it much easier to take my problems to my husband. This, of course, is perfectly appropriate, but not as a first port of call. Many times God has used Neil's absence to remind me that the first ear I should approach is that of my heavenly Father. After all, he tells us, "I, the LORD your God, hold your right hand; it is I who say to you, 'Fear not, I am the one who helps you' " (Isa. 41:13).

How easy it is instead to put my trust in the hands of a man who knows the Word of God and whose life is marked by holiness, almost as if he has the power to aid me. Paul Miller recently wrote a book titled *The Praying Life*. In it he repeatedly illustrates the power of prayer over the frailty of human conversation. Whenever anything comes into your mind that causes you to flee to a human being for help, view it instead as an opportunity to draw near to God. Hannah is a delightful example of this.

No doubt it may be a great challenge to you, but as pastors' wives we cannot run to others with our concerns. We cannot pick up the phone and discuss the trying times of ministry with friends in the congregation. In fact, without our husbands' prior approval, we are not at liberty to discuss any church problems with anyone. This may well be one of the hardest things about a life in full-time ministry. We have fewer earthly bolt-holes to which we can run when times are hard. Unexpectedly, however, this has been one of the greatest blessings in my spiritual life, and my soul has been deeply nourished by the need for verbal restraint. The lack of an ever-present human ear has ultimately led me to my knees in prayer, driving me to cultivate a deeper relationship with the One whose ears are always open, whose heart is always warm, and whose hand is always ready (Ps. 34:15).

The godly woman of Proverbs 31 remains our richest example of a perfectly prioritized life, both spiritually and practically. If you and I could implement everything this woman did, we would be pillars both to the church and to society. There are exhaustive Bible studies on this paradigm of a pious woman, but for now I would ask you to reflect on just one verse: "The heart of her husband trusts in her, and he will have no lack of gain" (Prov. 31:11).

The rest of chapter 31 is an unfolding of verse 11, providing us with an explanation of why this woman's husband can safely trust her. She is described as a very organized woman of great practical effort. While her personal devotion to God is not mentioned, it is certainly assumed, and her acts of great piety are an outward reflection of a heart devoted to him. If your husband can safely trust you, his ministry will never have the unnecessary burden of a constantly frenetic, tumultuous home life. Neil and I have always sought to establish regular communication in our home over everyday practicalities. It has proved invaluable. I know the things that make our home a haven for my husband, and my endeavors to fulfill his desires bring a degree of harmony that allows us to enjoy our home life to the full. While it may seem rather elementary, one of the greatest services you can offer to your husband is to make your home a refuge of peace amidst the storms of life. When he returns from a hard day, he can close the door on conflict and rest in a little harbor of peace. The reverse is also the case: few things are more debilitating for your husband than to open the front door and walk into another world of conflict. Hitler learned this lesson the hard way: no one can fight a war on two fronts.

WOMEN OF PIETY THROUGHOUT HISTORY

Mary Love

As a young pastor's wife, I was eager to find women from previous generations who had exemplified remarkable piety. There are few who stand out like Christopher Love's wife, Mary.

Christopher Love was born in Cardiff in 1618. From the earliest years of his conversion, he pursued a call to the ministry. After receiving a bachelor's degree from Oxford in 1639, he became the chaplain to a sheriff in London by the name of John Warner. It was through the sheriff that he first met his future wife, Mary Stone. Love is perhaps best known for his strong advocacy of Presbyterianism during the English Civil War. Following his death, Mary wrote a 140-page memoir of her husband, giving us a glimpse of his humble piety.

In all my years of reading, Mary's calm repose of soul and steadfast spirit remain an unparalleled example of Christian fortitude under pressure. Her piety shines brightest in the days leading up to her husband's execution. During the days of Oliver Cromwell, the British Parliament sentenced Love to death for his involvement in a conspiracy to establish Charles II on the throne. On July 14, 1651, Mary wrote a final farewell to her prison-bound husband. It drips with the assurance of faith and the deep contentment of soul that one can learn only from long experience of reposing in the arms of God.

> O that the Lord would keep thee from having one troubled thought for thy relations! I desire freely to give thee up into thy Father's hands, and not only to look upon it as a crown of glory for thee to die for Christ, but an honor to me, that I should have an husband to leave for Christ. . . . Thou leavest but a sinful, mortal wife, to be everlastingly married to

the Lord of Glory: thou leavest but children, brothers and sisters, to go to the Lord Jesus, thy eldest brother.[1]

Were we to find our husbands in a modern-day parallel predicament, I wonder if we would empathize with such sentiments. Would we willingly deny our own desires? Are you and I giving our husbands the liberty to have a heart wholly set on the glory of Christ? Mary Love's steadfastness of spirit is evidence of her trust in the sovereign hand of her heavenly Father. This, in turn, is evidence of a woman who spent much time on her knees and in the Word. This kind of firmly placed faith does not come easily but only through personal effort to spend time alone with Christ.

Margaret Baxter

As you walk through ministry life, you will find that your husband is naturally drawn to particular writers. There is one Puritan, however, who has had an almost limitless impact on the lives of Reformed pastors: Richard Baxter. He is the "pastor's pastor." During the times when you are unable to comfort your husband, those times when he needs a man to get alongside him who has walked in his shoes, Baxter is just the man to place before his weary soul. (His book, *The Reformed Pastor*, is probably sitting on your husband's bookshelf.)

The Reverend Baxter chose to marry later in life, at the age of forty-six. His wife was younger than he, a mere twenty-three years of age. Margaret Charlton was the daughter of a landed proprietor and justice of the peace. She grew up in a home of considerable wealth where her parents were renowned for their piety and devotion to Christ. Margaret received theological instruction as part of her education and was urged to consider her need for a personal relationship with Christ.

Despite her privileged instruction, Margaret was better known for her social life and flighty frivolity. Initially she sat under Baxter's ministry out of a sense of duty to her mother rather than from an earnest desire for Christ. Baxter's preaching, however, proved attractive to Margaret's intellectual mind. She began to listen attentively to his sermons. He put a stone in the shoe of her heart. A deep conviction of sin began to grip her soul, and it was not long before she came to a solid and saving knowledge of Christ.

The story of the events leading to their marriage is well worth a read—a veritable feast for the soul. For the purpose at hand, however, I would like to focus your attention on her priorities as a pastor's wife. Despite the fact that Margaret remained unconverted in her youth, the Lord used her mother's religious instruction to mold her character for her future role as Mrs. Baxter. In a sense, Margaret's conversion put living, loving flesh on those bones. We might compare her experience to the apostle Paul's voluminous knowledge of the Old Testament. While he was Saul, this knowledge lay dormant, dead, and devoid of spiritual usefulness. But once the lights came on, this lifeless, legalistic bookishness became a lively library of earth-shattering power. So it was with Margaret. She never knew it at the time, but in her heady days of girlish silliness, the Almighty was equipping her to be a remarkable woman of God.

Once converted, Margaret devoted considerable earthly resources to further her husband's work. She did this initially by freeing him from the need to accept a salary. Within the church, she helped those who were in some measure of financial strain. It seems that the pleasure she discovered through such generosity entirely replaced her former desires to live in affluence. Despite significant limitations of space, services were held at the Baxters' new home. News of Margaret's kind, charitable manner spread like wildfire through the parish of Kiddeminster. Her presence by Baxter's side made him stronger and more effective for Christ than he ever could have been alone.

She thus became a great favorite in the parish. Helping to gain for Baxter a firmer hold on the respect and affection of the people, she much contributed to the popularity and success of his ministrations among them, thus becoming his fellow helper in the work of the Lord.[2]

Margaret's piety found a much more private outlet after her husband's imprisonment. Baxter was arrested after refusing to swear under oath that it was unlawful to take up arms against the king. Margaret's response? In joyful submission, she followed him to prison. There she maintained her famously happy disposition! In fact, Baxter found her companionship to be more cheerful in prison than at any other time in their lives. She made the very prison cell a place of great comfort for them both.

To bring this romantic ideal down to you and me in our modern-day setting, I want to draw the main priority of Margaret's life to the fore. Some years ago, a young man asked a seasoned pastor what a pastor's wife should be like. The older pastor's instinctive reply was, "She must not be a hindrance; anything else is a bonus!" While I don't know what gave rise to this answer, I am quite certain that neither of us wants to be remembered for "not being a hindrance." (I would prefer to be remembered as a helpmeet suitable for my husband!) So what does that really look like? What was it about Margaret's life that enabled her to behave with such composure?

I am first reminded of the apostle Paul's words:

> I have learned in whatever situation I am to be content. I know how to be brought low, and I know how to abound. In any and every circumstance, I have learned the secret of facing plenty and hunger, abundance and need. I can do all things through him who strengthens me. (Phil. 4:11–13)

Paul's response to life is not one that we are naturally endowed with, nor do we all possess Margaret Baxter's happy disposition. However, we do have the same claim on Christ's strength that Paul had. When faced with the daily duty of prioritizing, we must seek to be what Margaret was to her husband; a Barnabas. Our husbands daily encounter the attack of the Evil One, accompanied by the immense mess of a flock of sinful sheep. You and I are generally sheltered from such extremities of Satan's attacks, thus providing us with the privilege of making our husbands' calling a pleasant one.

This is where Margaret Baxter's example should hit home to our souls. Remember how she made the prison cell a palace, both physically and relationally? What was her focus in doing this? Did she sit on the pity pot and put on a forlorn face, declaiming her miserable lot in life? No, she had spent too much time on her knees for such self-pity to take over her soul. She had learned to trust her Father's plans above her own. She had learned that God's purposes for his people ripen best in the soil of trials. She had learned to be a rose among the thorns, and I want to exhort you to do likewise. Ask the Lord to show you the greatness and wisdom of his ways, especially when they lead you through the vale of tears. Plead with him for wisdom to know how you can bring joy to your husband in his difficult days. Ask the Lord for opportunities to show your husband kindness.

When I encourage you to make such a request, I don't mean that you need to spend hours preparing a gourmet meal, starching his shirts one by one, or lavishing him with the latest piece of technical gadgetry. (Of course husbands love these things too, but that isn't where you will reap long-term fruit for your efforts.) The long-term impact that you will have on your husband's ministry will be largely an effect of your character. You are familiar with the old saying, "If momma ain't happy, ain't nobody happy." Well, that same principle applies to us as wives. If you aren't happy in your soul, your outward disposition will reflect discontentment. You will have a complaining spirit and perpetually whine in your husband's ear. Your grumbling heart will wear him out, and ultimately it will weaken his effectiveness for ministry. Remember Solomon's wisdom: "A joyful heart is good medicine, but a crushed spirit dries up the bones" (Prov. 17:22).

Such joy doesn't come naturally. Paul had to learn it. He testifies, "I have learned in whatever situation I am to be content" (Phil. 4:11).

This joy can come only as we learn to do all things through Christ who strengthens us. As you approach the daily ins and outs of ministry life, put on a spirit of holy joy in Christ. Rejoice in the hand God deals you, not the one you wish he'd given! Mary and Margaret found joy living beyond this life. They knew this world was not their home, and this knowledge gave them stability to enjoy good times without needing them and to endure hardship without despair.

It is my prayer that you will be just the kind of helpmeet your husband needs and that the Lord will be your refuge and strength. If our paths should never cross on this earth, I will look forward to the day when we will stand together before our Savior and rejoice in the privileged earthly life he gave us as wives whose husbands were called to be pastors.

Your sister in Christ,

CATHERINE

STUDY QUESTIONS

1. What is the difference between organizing and prioritizing?

2. On notebook paper, draw up two lists: one to identify your current priorities and one that reflects biblical priorities. Make a plan to replace any current, sinful priorities with biblical priorities.

3. Read Job 2:7–10. Contrast Mrs. Job's response to adversity with Hannah's in 1 Samuel 1:1–11. What habits of life lead to the individual responses of these two women?

4. Consider the lives of Mary Love and Margaret Charlton. What aspects of their characters do you most admire? How can you cultivate similar attitudes?

5. Read Isaiah 26:3–4. What steps will you take to keep your mind stayed on God? Why should we keep our eyes upward (Col. 3:1–4)?

RECOMMENDED RESOURCES

Anderson, James. *Memorable Women of the Puritan Times*. 2 vols. Morgan, PA: Soli Deo Gloria Publications, 2001.

James, John Angell. *Female Piety*. Pittsburgh: Soli Deo Gloria Publications, 1994.

Prentiss, Elizabeth. *Aunt Jane's Hero*. Amityville, NY: Calvary Press, 2007.

Personal Devotions: The Heart before the Actions

Margy Tripp

It is of great benefit to a pastor for his wife to possess a thorough knowledge of the Scripture. While it is natural for the women of the church to desire friendship and support from the pastor's wife, it is the Word of Christ dwelling in her richly that enables a pastor's wife to truly minister to other women. They will not be sustained and nourished by her sympathy and understanding, as important as those are, but by the Word of God. Of course, as with any area of ministry, the ability to feed oneself from the Word and to experience its callings and comforts is what enables a pastor's wife to bring it powerfully to others. Margy's ability to bring this sort of biblical counsel has been a great encouragement both to me in ministry and to the women who have received her counsel.

REV. DR. TEDD TRIPP

Dear sister in Christ,

I am always thankful for the privilege of corresponding with women who are assuming their new role as a pastor's wife. It is daunting to dive into a new church community while supporting your husband in his new role and finding your niche as the pastor's wife. You can feel overwhelmed. Every pastor's wife is concerned over whether she is sufficiently prepared.

You have probably been asking yourself, "How will I minister to women in the church who know the Scriptures better than I do, to women who are older and more experienced than I am? Most of them have much more experience juggling their devotional life with other responsibilities." This is a natural question for women with a humble spirit and a deep desire to serve Christ.

I think there are actually two important considerations raised by this question. First, how should I think about my spiritual ministry to other women in the body? Second, with all my other responsibilities, how can I have an effective devotional life and memorize the Scriptures?

In answer to the first question, remember that your husband has been called as the pastor. Your role is that of wife and mother in your home. Your role as wife and mother, as well as your own spiritual gifts, will shape any ministry you have in the body. This is true of every married woman in the body. I am not denying the natural expectations that attach themselves to being the pastor's wife. I *am* saying that those expectations should not shape your role—rather, your calling as wife and mother, along with the prayerfully considered use of your gifts, should determine your ministry in the body.

There is not a one-size-fits-all pastor's-wife job description. I personally know pastors' wives who have had very little "public" role in the body but who have had an incredible influence because of their personal devotional life, prayer life, and godly example. Others have had much more visibility in women's and children's ministry because that's where their gifts and interests lie. Their godly contribution has been a blessing to the body of Christ as well.

Of course, you must also remember that there are seasons of life. In these early years as a mother and wife, your primary calling will be obvious as your days are filled with the nurture and care of your family. In later seasons of life, you will have time to serve outside the home in ways that aren't possible now. I recommend that you start slowly, get settled, adjust to your husband's schedule and your family's needs, and get to know the folks in the body. Time and prayer will help to shape the ministry you will have as a support to your husband.

The second question is more comprehensive: With all your other responsibilities, how can you have an effective devotional life and memorize the Scriptures? This is a very busy time of life for you, but there will always be more things to do than are doable. I have often told myself in the last thirty-five years, "Things will settle down as soon as . . . and there will be more time for this or that." But there will always be something new to take the place of each finished task. Rather than waiting for circumstances to change, plan your daily routine in ways that reflect your spiritual goals. I'm not suggesting that you neglect the practical daily routines of life but rather that you imbed the tangible duties of daily life in spiritual routines that are essential for your soul's well-being.

Let me share a different perspective on Scripture memorization and personal devotions, more than just memorization techniques and schedule or organizational tips. Have you ever been to the local county fair where the kitchen gadget salesman is huckstering the slicer-dicer-corer of your dreams? He regales you with descriptions of its benefits with such panache that you can hardly wait to get your hands on the limited supply! Now imagine that we are at the Scripture memorization and devotional booth at the Bible Fair. I want to tell you about the benefits of God's Word until you can hardly wait to get your heart to that endless supply of truth and nourishment for your soul! Delight in God's Word will grease the wheels of devotional life and Scripture memorization. Vivid recollections of the Spirit's blessing of your devotional times will warm your cold heart when your daily devotional schedule and spiritual fervor are not in sync!

Personal devotions and Scripture memorization are often regarded as a spiritual duty or a means of gaining God's approval and good graces. Perhaps you've heard someone say, "I won't be able to get there until 9 o'clock. I have to have my devotions early today if I'm going to fit them in." It sounds like our children calling to their friends with resignation, "I can't come over until my homework is done." Personal devotions and Scripture memorization are precious means of grace and growth ministered by a loving heavenly Father.

Rather than trying to find time for these spiritual activities, we should consider them an irresistible respite for our weary and troubled souls in the battle with sin and the ravages of a fallen world. Let me acknowledge here that spiritual disciplines are not convenient or easy. Even if I get a "renewed mind" as to their precious value to my soul, it doesn't change the fact that my soul will often lie to me and try to persuade me that more sleep and leisure are what I really need. Why is it that when I'm hungry, chips are more enticing than a hearty salad? It is because cuisine is just one of the vast number of life issues that were affected by the fall. The bent of our hearts, apart from redemption, is to please ourselves with sensory delights, regardless of the implications for our physical and spiritual well-being.

I struggle with arthritis. I know that exercise has both the immediate benefit of strengthening my muscles and joints for daily work and the long-term benefit of prolonged mobility, but that knowledge doesn't make it any easier for me to drag myself out of bed at 6:00 a.m. to get to the YMCA for a swim and exercise. I get up to do what is contrary to my immediate gratification because I believe that the benefits are real and of greater value than another hour of sleep. This truth is demonstrated to me every time I leave the YMCA. My body is strengthened, and my mobility is eased. Each time I enter the pool, I remember that the water provides respite for my weary joints as I feel relief from the harsh impact of weight bearing. I am doing battle with the ravages of arthritis, and the water makes me somewhat weightless, allowing me to achieve needed exercise without further damage to those arthritic joints.

If you will allow the analogy, the Scriptures are to our needy souls what exercise is to my arthritis. Communion with the Lord brings comfort and solace to the trials and challenges of life. They are like the relief and comfort that pool water brings to my inflamed, aching joints.

I'm sure that you love the Scriptures as I do. I do not offer these thoughts as admonishment for your lack of spiritual fervor. Rather, I write them as an encouragement to revel in the precious provision of God's Word, which will enhance your desire to draw near to your Savior.

Many passages highlight the precious qualities of God's Word. If our hearts are convinced of the life-giving qualities of God's Word, we will find time for it. Remember Moses' words to the Israelites after he recited the law of God in their hearing: "Take to heart all the words by which I am warning you today, that you may command them to your children, that they may be careful to do all the words of this law. For it is no empty word for you, but your very life, and by this word you shall live long in the land that you are going over the Jordan to possess" (Deut. 32:46–47).

The words "your very life" strike me as dramatic, but we often don't grasp the reality of those words in our daily Bible reading habits. I was surprised by a recent conversation with a sister as we began a Bible study. She was looking for her Bible and acknowledged, "I leave it here at church since that's the only time I need it." *Yikes!* I thought. *How do I graciously get her to Moses' words to the Israelites?*

Poorly nourished people don't eat once a week to remedy their weakened condition. They eat often and with great care for the quality of their diet. So it is with spiritual food. Think of the pictures God uses to describe his Word: pure spiritual milk, meat, the richest of fare, honey from the rock. It is no mistake that God uses an analogy of something without which we cannot sustain life—food—to alert us to our need for regular and conscious consumption of his revelation. The connection between the food that nourishes our bodies and the Word that nourishes our souls is just such an example. I'm afraid, however, that a malnourished body is more readily detected and corrected because the physical effects are dramatic and immediate, while spiritual anemia can slip by unnoticed until the soul is in danger of being ravaged and left unprotected from the attacks of the enemy.

Someone has said, "We do what we want to do." I know that there are times when the demands of the moment encroach on our regular schedule, but generally we follow a pattern that reflects our preferences. We also find that Scripture memorization becomes a byproduct of devotional life when it is fueled by our passion to draw near to God, rather than just another spiritual duty, especially for those of us who cannot memorize easily.

God's Word is a centerpiece of our relationship with God. We are in danger of spiritual anemia when we neglect personal devotions in deference to busy lifestyle choices. Serious study of God's Word is so susceptible to the pressure of immediate needs that we are often tempted to put off devotional times until later—and often *later* never comes because of the press of time and responsibilities.

It falls to us to graciously and lovingly encourage one another to recognize the relationship between the study of Scripture and God's purposes for our growth in grace. Let me illustrate.

Paul reminds the Thessalonians, "When you received the word of God . . . you accepted it . . . [as] the word of God, which is at work in you believers" (1 Thess. 2:13). What a radical view! The Scriptures are not an external resource for refueling or for help in trouble. They are planted in us to give courage, perseverance, and hope.

I like to think of the Bible as my spiritual family album. It is not a book about "them" way back "then." It is about my own sisters and brothers in the faith. The people and events of the Bible are as relevant to my experience each day as a child of God as my nuclear family is to me. The patriarchs are as real as Aunt Tilly and Uncle George at the family reunion, because those historic figures bring the Scriptures to life. They help me to interpret and respond to the people and circumstances of my life. That's what they're there for (1 Cor. 10:11)!

Paul warns the Hebrew Christians at the end of the first century, "The word of God is living and active, sharper than any two-edged sword, piercing to the division of soul and of spirit, of joints and of marrow, and discerning the thoughts and intentions of the heart" (Heb. 4:12). God's Word helps me to know myself. It is my counselor. It exposes my heart. All this has great import for daily living. The desires, expectations, longings, and leanings of my heart drive my interpretation of and interaction with everything that happens to me all day. My responses to all these things are prompted either by the Spirit through the Word planted in me or, in the absence of God's Word, by the ways and thoughts of the world.

Paul is acutely aware of our weakness and tendency to unbelief and despair. His encouragement for the Roman Christians regarding relationships in the body highlights the place of the Scriptures in church life: "Whatever was written in former days was written for our instruction, that through endurance and through the encouragement of the Scriptures we might have hope" (Rom. 15:4).

Peter exhorts the elect, "Conduct yourselves with fear throughout the time of your exile, knowing that you were ransomed . . . with the precious blood of Christ, like that of a lamb without blemish or spot. . . . so that your faith and hope are in God" (1 Peter 1:17–21). And further, "Love one another earnestly from a pure heart, since you have been born again, not of perishable seed but of imperishable, through the living and abiding word of God" (1 Peter 1:22–23).

The Word of God is not only the instrument of new birth. It is God's chosen ingredient, along with his Spirit, for the work of sanctification. How can we do without it?

Probably the most familiar New Testament passage that extols the qualities of Scripture is 2 Timothy 3:16–17:

> All Scripture is breathed out by God and profitable for teaching, for reproof, for correction, and for training in righteousness, that the man of God may be complete, equipped for every good work.

What a mouthful! Look at all the benefits highlighted in this passage. We want our lives and efforts to be useful—*profitable*. The Scriptures are, for fallen humanity, the equivalent of the Creator's walk and talk in the cool of the day with Adam and Eve in the garden of Eden. God "breathed into [Adam's] nostrils the breath of life" (Gen. 2:7).

The same anthropomorphism is used in 2 Timothy 3:16 to describe God's mercy in delivering revelation to fallen humanity. Remember that Adam and Eve required instruction and direction in Paradise. They were perfect but not infinite. How much more do we—fallen and desperate—need daily instruction and direction? It is a great blessing that God has revealed himself to us in his Word. Only arrogance allows me to think that I can navigate the waters of life without the benefits described in Paul's counsel to Timothy. Adam and Eve neglected truth with devastating results. Even as God's redeemed child, I cannot neglect God's revelation without spiritual harm. Think of the incredible benefits packed into the words of 2 Timothy 3:16–17.

Teaching is the function of Scripture. Just as surely as our young children need to be taught the basic issues of physical life through our care, nurture, and example, so we need spiritual instruction to understand the basic issues of spiritual life. In fact, the general teaching of Scripture is essential before the benefits of a particular passage can minister to our hearts.

Reproof serves as admonishment when we are wayward. You would think that the strong reproofs of the Epistles would be reserved for unbelievers. Not so. Believers are targeted in the letters to the churches! In James 4, James refers to "brothers" as he brings harsh admonishment to the Jews scattered among the nations for their spiritual adultery. "Do you not know that friendship with the world is enmity with God?" (James 4:4). But I love James's direction in the reproofs of James 4:1–6. He moves from stern rebuke for waywardness to topics of repentance and restoration! This is not a legalistic message: "This is the law, and you had better get it right or else." Rather, James opens his readers' eyes to their departure from truth and calls them to repent in verses 7–10. He ends with words of hope: "Humble yourselves before the Lord, and he will exalt you" (James 4:10).

Correction reminds me of making right what is wrong. It identifies what needs to change. Writing to his "beloved brothers" (James 1:19) who are tempted with sin, James encourages them to "receive with meekness the implanted word, which is able to save your souls" (v. 21). James declares that the Word of God has power to correct us and keep us safe.

Training in righteousness, or *instruction in righteousness,* is the regimen for correction. James goes on to remind us that the "one who looks into the perfect law, the law of liberty, and perseveres, being no hearer who forgets but a doer who acts, he will be blessed in his doing" (James 1:25). Training in righteousness that takes us to the cross is the remedy for our struggle with sin. We need constant correction and redirection through God's chastisement and his ensuing grace. We quickly get "out of plumb." We lose our direction. Scripture and its call to prayer and repentance set our feet on the path of life once again.

Before we leave 2 Timothy, let me underscore something that is significant for ministry. This passage is a double blessing. The Scriptures are a means of personal spiritual growth *and* preparation for ministering to others. The result of God's powerful revelation, in addition to the teaching, reproof, correction, and training in righteousness that change us personally, is "that the man of God may be competent, equipped for every good work" (v. 17).

Our ability to minister does not come from our role or title or even our gifts and abilities. Spiritual ministry to others, in our home, the church, and the community, is an extension of the ministry of God's Word by his Spirit to our own hearts. When devotions and Scripture memorization are an arduous duty to us, we will not display an irresistible gospel message to others. We will produce legalistic replicas of ourselves. When we delight in the life-giving qualities of the Word, we will "shine as lights in the world, holding fast to the word of life" (Phil. 2:15–16). Tedd always says, "You can't give away what you don't have." That is certainly true regarding spiritual fervor.

This might be a good time to pick up an earlier thought about Scripture memorization. I have never found memorization easy. I admire Tedd's ability to remember long passages of Scripture with, relative to me, little work. But over the years I have found that I memorize more easily those verses and passages that the Spirit has used to bring conviction, reproof, comfort, promise, and hope to my soul. This makes perfect sense. Things that are specific to our circumstances or relationships stick to the brainpan better than unrelated things. What a marvelous impetus to be in God's Word and committing it to memory.

God's Word speaks with power and precision to all the needs of your life. *Nothing else* will meet your deepest need except the living, active Word of God that leads to Christ, the cross, and your loving heavenly Father. As you access God's precious Word for the circumstances and relationships of your life again and again, the Spirit seals the words to your heart. I have found that my most successful Scripture memorization follows my spiritual journey from my needs to the cross of Christ. I need the passages that describe my sin and my need, but I also need the glorious promise and hope of the Savior's work accompanied by God's great purposes for me now and for eternity. From the cross there flows a fountain of Christ's blood-bought provision for all the needs of my soul—for love, forgiveness, hope, comfort, strength, friendship, protection, courage, direction, healing . . . and my resources in him are never ending!

Here's the amazing thing. Your greatest ministry to others, to your husband, to your children, and to your sisters and brothers in Christ will flow from the passages of Scripture that have brought help and hope to you. We can talk and talk to others with our wisdom and counsel, but nothing has the power or impact of the Scriptures.

Of course, it is always good to strive to commit passages to memory as a family, with our husbands, or with other believers. All God's Word is profitable and worthy of our attention. But I want to encourage you to use the challenges, struggles, disappointments, hurts, grief, joys, and triumphs of daily life to "store up [God's] word in [your] heart" (Ps. 119:11) and to have God's Word be "a lamp to [your] feet and a light to [your] path" (v. 105).

Perhaps the most lovely and thorough expression of the delights of Scripture for our souls' regular consumption is found in Psalm 119. Let me suggest that you read this psalm one section at a time and find all the benefits of God's Word. They create in my soul a longing for devotional time. After all, time in the Word is time with the Lord.

The last stanza of Psalm 119 is a fitting conclusion to the treasures of God's Word described throughout the chapter.

> Let my cry come before you, O LORD;
>> give me understanding according to your word!
> Let my plea come before you;
>> deliver me according to your word.
> My lips will pour forth praise,
>> for you teach me your statutes.
> My tongue will sing of your word,
>> for all your commandments are right.
> Let your hand be ready to help me,
>> for I have chosen your precepts.
> I long for your salvation, O LORD,
>> and your law is my delight.
> Let my soul live and praise you,
>> and let your rules help me.
> I have gone astray like a lost sheep; seek your servant,
>> for I do not forget your commandments. (Ps. 119:169–76)

Psalm 42 beautifully captures the spiritual rapture of time with the Lord,

> As a deer pants for flowing streams,
>> so pants my soul for you, O God.

49

My soul thirsts for God,
>   for the living God.
When shall I come and appear before God? (Ps. 42:1–2)

There may be no more important expression of the sufficiency of the Scriptures than from the psalmist David in Psalm 19:7–11. Think of these wondrous ministries of God's Word for us.

"The law of the LORD is perfect, reviving the soul" (v. 7). I am always looking for perfection. It doesn't exist anywhere except in spiritual realms and is always attached to God. His law is a perfect revelation. Let your mind expand on the wonder of a place to go for direction, comfort, help, counsel, everything, in fact, that is perfect—nothing lacking, nothing marred! And this perfect revelation has restorative power. The King James Version translates this verse using the word *converting* instead of *reviving*. The concept here is transformation. The law of the Lord revives the soul in the sense that it is powerful and comprehensive enough to totally convert an individual's entire life and conduct.

"The testimony of the LORD is sure, making wise the simple" (v. 7). The Scriptures are our trustworthy, immovable, solid, unwavering guide. They provide a sure foundation for building our lives. They make the simple person wise. The word *simple* here means, literally, *open door*. A simple person lacks discernment to know when to shut the mind's door. The Scriptures direct the heart to open or close the mind. The Scriptures make the simple person wise. They give her discernment and enable her to apply the law of God to her life.

"The precepts of the LORD are right, rejoicing the heart" (v. 8). The Word of God directs life along the righteous path of blessing. God's Word enables us to live and be productive for his glory. We have all we need for life and godliness in his precious promises. To walk in his paths is to know true joy and blessing. When God's sheep are depressed, despondent, anxious, fearful, or doubting, we may flee to God's counsel and find joy and happiness in the Lord. In God's truth there is lasting joy and satisfaction.

"The commandment of the LORD is pure, enlightening the eyes" (v. 8). The divine mandates of the Word of God are authoritative and binding. The commandments of the Lord are clear; they are lucid; they speak with clarity that sheds light and brings eternity into focus. In that sense they give light to the eyes. As David writes, "With you is the fountain of life; in your light we see light" (Ps. 36:9). This light, which exposes darkness and points the way to light, is the monopoly of the Scriptures. Human minds are clouded and muddled. The Scriptures are light for dull eyes.

"The fear of the LORD is clean, enduring forever" (v. 9). The Scriptures are clean. There is no impurity or defilement in the Scriptures. They are pure. Because they are flawless, they endure forever. God's truth has relevance for all times and all places because it endures forever.

"The rules of the LORD are true, and righteous altogether" (v. 9). God's words are sure. They are true. All God's verdicts, all his judgments, are holy and just. Therefore, if we walk in his ways and his precepts, we are led down the path of righteousness.

"More to be desired are they than gold, even much fine gold; sweeter also than honey and drippings of the honeycomb" (v. 10). The qualities of the Word make them more precious than any temporal treasure and sweeter than any temporal sensation to the palate.

"Moreover, by them is your servant warned; in keeping them there is great reward" (v. 11). David does not say one is rewarded for keeping the law of God, but that keeping the law of God is great reward. To be empowered to keep the law of God by grace—that same power that raised Jesus Christ from the grave—is itself great reward. To be known and loved by the Creator of the world and the Architect of our salvation is great reward. Our souls must feast on the Word as if our lives depended on it, because they do. Because we are made for God, because he is ultimate, because we are restless until we find our rest in him, because he is the fountain of life, and because in his light we see light, we will find our greatest freedom, our greatest joy, in finding God the Father, Jesus

Christ the Son, and God the Holy Spirit displayed in all majesty and sufficiency in the Scriptures.

Dear sister, I'm afraid that this has been a lengthy letter. I have enjoyed sharing my heart with you and hope you will delight in the passages I have suggested for your consideration. God's words have far greater worth than my own—in fact, infinite worth! My words and counsel have weight and merit only as they reflect God's truth. May God grant you courage and faith on your journey through life with your husband in ministry for Christ's kingdom.

Your sister and fellow traveler,

MARGY

STUDY QUESTIONS

1. How does Titus 2:4–5 speak to your primary calling (ministry) as a pastor's wife?

2. How does 2 Timothy 3:16–17 show that being equipped to serve is more a function of Scripture dwelling in you richly than of natural gifting?

3. Deuteronomy 32:45–47 says that God's Word is "your very life." Think of the many ways that the Scriptures are not just idle words but your life. Write them down and thank God for his Word.

4. How does the Scripture work within us so that "we might have hope" (Rom. 15:4)?

5. How does the grace of the gospel—Christ's life, death, and resurrection in your behalf—affect your longing for the Word (Col. 1:3–14)?

RECOMMENDED RESOURCES

Edwards, Brian H. *Nothing But the Truth: The Inspiration, Authority and History of the Bible Explained.* Darlington, England: Evangelical Press, 2006.

McQuilkin, Robertson. *Understanding and Applying the Bible.* Chicago, IL: Moody Press, 1992.

Robertson, O. Palmer. *The Final Word.* Edinburgh, Scotland: Banner of Truth, 1993.

Ryle, J. C. *A Call to Prayer.* Laurel, MS: Audubon Press, 1996.

Stott, John R. W. *God's Book for God's People: Why We Need the Bible.* Carmel, NY: Guidepost, 1982.

CHAPTER THREE

Humility: The Only
Way Up Is Down

Lynn Crotts

Humility is the most elusive virtue in the world. Pride lurks at the core of everyone's being. As Christians we are no longer slaves of pride, and by God's grace we have new eyes to begin to see God and ourselves in proper perspective. Even so, pursuing humility must be our constant quest.

I thank God for my wife Lynn. He has given her new eyes (beautiful blue ones, in her case) and given her a heart to pursue humility. It is wonderful to see her serve the Lord, our church, and our family for his glory. This letter is a glimpse into the grace he is giving her to humbly pursue him.

REV. JOHN CROTTS

Dear sister in Christ,

I am glad that you and I can now relate to one another as pastors' wives. People have many different ideas of what it is like to be married to a pastor. I consider it a wonderful privilege, and I hope you will always be thankful for the life of ministry that God has planned for you. Life in the sphere of Christian ministry entails many blessings and challenges along the way. Even though we have the title "pastor's wife" (but not an official church office such as elder or deacon), we are in some respects very similar to all members of the church family: we need wise, loving leadership from our elders, we need to be patiently taught God's Word, we need to serve one another and be served. Yet in other ways our situation is very different because our husbands are the pastors.

Every wife who is trying faithfully to serve her husband will make adjustments and sacrifices in order to accommodate what is best for her family. Every husband's job has effects on his family and his marriage. The same is certainly true for a pastor's wife. When we first began life in the ministry, I didn't really think that being married to a pastor would make much difference to our family life. Over the years, however, more and more things that are quite obviously the result of my husband's ministry have come to my attention. Most of these things have been great blessings to us as a couple and to our children. It is a great comfort to know that God's plans are always best for us and that he goes before his people in all life's changes and challenges!

Pastors' wives can struggle with all sorts of issues, even when we wholeheartedly support our husbands' calling. Perhaps we compare our situation to others' and wish for a different financial status or a nicer home or more time with our husbands. When my husband first became a pastor, I became increasingly unhappy that he did not have "normal" office hours, often working on Saturdays.

It will be no great surprise to you that pastors' wives tend to see the best and the worst of people. We see faithful Christians sacrifice and persevere through difficult days, giving us strength and inspiration. We also see hearts and lives utterly ruined by the darkness of sin. We are shocked by how generous people can be, and at other times we are equally shocked by their miserliness. We see our husbands misunderstood and attacked and consequently feel very hurt, confused, and overwhelmed. (I have felt all these things.)

I often sit in wonder at how different God's plans for each of us can be, yet how very similar we all are in terms of our sin and need. Of course there is no way that I can know what lies ahead of you—the joys and sorrows that will fill your heart and your home. However, there is a foundational virtue that is relevant to every situation. It is something to which I did not pay careful attention until recent years.

Each day that I live, I become more convinced of my need to cultivate an attitude of humility. Humility means possessing a mindset that sees God in his rightful place and us in ours. Stuart Scott has written that humility is the mindset of a servant as opposed to the mindset of a master.[1] I would encourage you to seek growth in this virtue, which is sadly a foreign concept to our minds and society. The reason we need to cultivate humility is not because we are married to a pastor, nor is it because it is a good virtue in and of itself. Rather, it is because we are naturally proud and given to thinking all too highly of ourselves. As pastors' wives, we have many opportunities to help others through our humility or to hurt them through our pride.

The Lord regularly provides opportunities to grow in humility by presenting us with situations that necessitate self-denial. This reminds me of James 4, where James describes how conflict and turmoil are caused when we don't get what we want. "What causes quarrels and what causes fights among you? Is it not this, that your passions are at war within you? You desire and do not have, so you murder. You covet and cannot obtain, so you fight and quarrel" (James 4:1–2).

Each time our plans are frustrated, our desires are unfulfilled, or our resources are taxed, we should view it as an opportunity to cultivate humility. The goal of my life, and therefore of each individual day, should not be to accomplish all my will, but all God's will. He reveals his plans for us as his providence unfolds in our lives, and we should always be ready and willing to submit our will to his. God's Word (not the to-do list) should be our guiding principle. I once heard a friend say that we should not be trying to rule our own little kingdom, but we should be thrilled to be a servant in God's big kingdom! This is, as you know, an impossible attitude to adopt if we seek to do it in our own strength. James encourages us: "God opposes the proud, but gives grace to the humble" (4:6).

LAYING THE FOUNDATION

In my experience, several patterns of thought have led me to have the mind of Christ in my efforts to pursue humility. The first and foremost way is to intentionally focus on the gospel as the main theme of my life. What I mean by this is that I must specifically take time each day to meditate on the gospel and its redemptive effect on my life. It all begins with God and his divine character. Contemplating his greatness and limitless attributes enables me to have a right view of who he is. Passages in the Bible such as Isaiah 40 and 41 remind me of my rightful place before an awesome God whose mercy led Christ all the way to the cross.

Despite God's majesty, our natural state as sinners has led us to rebellion against him. In pride we raise ourselves up in defiance, seeking to usurp his place on the throne. Paul reminds us,

> As it is written,
>> "None is righteous, no, not one;
>>> no one understands;
>>> no one seeks for God.
>> All have turned aside; together they have become worthless;
>>> no one does good,
>>> not even one." (Rom. 3:10–12)

Christ took the suffering that we deserved, and we become the recipients of what he deserved. The reason God loves us and blesses us each day is that Jesus traded places with us. He was punished, and we are blessed! In my safe, comfortable surroundings, it is hard to remember that all I have ever deserved from God is punishment. Each day that I enjoy good health, a happy family, or pleasant circumstances, I am receiving gifts that I do not deserve. Any tragedy that does *not* happen to me is an example of God's undeserved kindness. I often enjoy reading the prayers found in *Valley of Vision* and have been particularly humbled by the reminder of the words, "My trials have still been fewer than my sins."[2] What a humble response to life's difficulties! Trials are what I deserve (though now God sends even those for my benefit), yet I enjoy countless blessings every day. Reminding myself of this helps me to cultivate a humble heart.

Setting my mind on the grace of the gospel and disciplining my thoughts to stay there enables me to be characterized by humility as opposed to pride. The longer I go without standing in awe of the redemptive work of Christ, the more likely I am to forget my place before him. When thoughts of the gospel are forgotten or crowded out, my responses are more likely to be full of pride. (This is why I must never be "too busy" to spend time in God's Word and prayer.) Throughout each day, when things don't go quite as we planned, we must turn our thoughts back to the gospel. When people cause us pain (intentionally or otherwise), we must think of our Lord, who deserved everything good, yet chose to lay aside the riches of glory and subject himself to abhorrent treatment so that he could rescue us! Surely we don't deserve better than he did! Yet despite our fallen state, we receive much comfort, being assured of the promise that he has given us: "I will never leave you nor forsake you" (Heb. 13:5)!

His omnipresence frees us from the burden of having to pursue our personal agenda in matters of this life. We can trust his wisdom, humbly admitting that the way that seems best to us may not be best at all. We can humbly accept that our strength and knowledge are extremely limited and always imperfect. This kind of trust protects us from prideful sins like anger, complaining, and even self-pity.

Peter writes,

Clothe yourselves, all of you, with humility toward one another, for "God opposes the proud but gives grace to the humble."

Humble yourselves, therefore, under the mighty hand of God so that at the proper time he may exalt you, casting all your anxieties on him, because he cares for you. (1 Peter 5:5–7)

Let us consider an example of how this might work. Suppose for a moment that regular visitors in your church family decide to leave in order to pursue another church. Suppose also that someone declares that you are to blame for their departure because you didn't reach out to them. The person infers that you are selfish with your time or implies that you don't really care about people outside your own family. Our natural reaction to such accusations is generally either defensiveness or discouragement, or perhaps a combination of both. You might be fully convinced that it is not your fault and quite probably resent the suggestion that it is! You may be certain that it *is* your fault and feel no hope that you will ever sufficiently reach out to others.

Our minds tend to overanalyze these kinds of situations, and Satan uses our negative thinking for his ends. The lie we so easily believe is that somewhere in this mess there is a standard that we can keep on our own. "If only I weren't so busy, I could reach out to people more often." "If only I felt less tired, I could serve better." "If only people knew how much I already do, they wouldn't expect more!" "The people who are fussing at me should be reaching out more!"

The truth is that none of us have anything to offer people except the good that God has imputed to us. The truth is that any time we *have* displayed kindness or been of help to others is not because we are great, but because God is working through us. It shouldn't surprise us that some people leave our fellowship; it should pleasantly surprise us that anybody stays! All our failures and successes are evened out at the foot of the cross. Jesus must be given all the credit for any good that we have done, yet he takes all the punishment for all our sin. How grateful and humble we ought to be! With this kind of attitude, we can hear accusations against us without being destroyed by them. We can answer graciously and ask the Lord to help us to see if we bear any blame or if we need to change our conduct. And, though we don't behave with humility in order that we might receive any personal benefit, God may use our biblical response as an opportunity to share his Word with those who have wronged us. Giving careful thought and attention to the character of God and the gospel of our Lord Jesus Christ is the foundational step in cultivating humility. It is a mindset that we must train ourselves to exercise and for which we must pray. According to Isaiah 66:1–2, it is a mindset that draws God's attention and favor.

> Thus says the LORD:
> "Heaven is my throne,
>   and the earth is my footstool;
> what is the house that you would build for me,
>   and what is the place of my rest?
> All these things my hand has made,
>   and so all these things came to be,
> declares the LORD.
> But this is the one to whom I will look:
>   he who is humble, and contrite in spirit
>   and trembles at my word."

FOUR PRACTICAL STEPS

When we have actively disciplined ourselves to think right thoughts about God, we put ourselves in a place where we can focus on the practical steps of pursuing humility. Let me share four of those practical steps with you.

The first one almost goes without saying. Time spent alone with God in Bible study, meditation, and prayer is essential. A prayer for humility is certainly a desire that God delights to answer, but it is important to bear in mind that the way he answers might not always be the way we would choose. John Newton said, "Above all things we must pray for humility. It may be called the guard of all other graces, and the soil in which they grow."[3] The memorization of specific verses about humility and pride are vitally important elements of prayer when we seek to bring this matter before the Lord.

The second practical step that helps us to curb pride is confession of our sins. Confession is an act of obedience and a necessary ingredient for a right relationship with God, but it is my personal testimony that when I purposely look for opportunities to admit my wrongs and resist the urge to minimize my own guilt, I find myself on my knees repenting of my pride. I always taught my children when they were little that "whoever conceals his transgressions will not prosper, but he who confesses and forsakes them will obtain mercy" (Prov. 28:13). Resolve to make yourself say, "I was wrong; you were right," as often as possible. Humble people are quick to admit their mistakes, and they are easy to approach and correct.

A third element in training ourselves in humility is learning to submit to our husbands. In several places the Bible makes it clear that the husband is the head of his wife and family. Living life in a role of submission is a daily training course in humility! Even when we outwardly obey our husbands' instructions, it is all too easy to have a prideful attitude on the inside. It is always more pleasing in God's sight to earnestly seek to respect our husbands. Of course this includes making our wishes and plans subordinate to, or at least correspondent to, theirs. This attitude goes directly against the ideals of the world around us and directly against our own natural inclinations. It reflects a heart that is submissive to our Lord Jesus, laying our desires at his feet.

To cultivate humility we must cultivate gratitude. Discipline yourself to say thank you as often as you can, even for little things. Unmet expectations are a disguised way for pride to control us. Whenever you notice that things are not turning out quite the way you expected, try to stop and identify exactly what you were expecting. Remember that God doesn't owe us anything and is not obligated to meet our expectations. Try being thankful, whatever circumstance you find yourself in. Counting our blessings, listing answered prayers, and remembering what we really deserve from God will fill us with reasons to be thankful!

My personal experience is that opportunities to grow in gratitude particularly arise during holidays or vacations—times that we expect to entail earthly perfection! It is times of high expectations or excitement that often prove to be fertile ground for disappointment and ingratitude. Of all the "special" yearly holidays, I try to set aside the Christmas season as a time to express my gratitude to the Lord. Each year it is a precious privilege to focus on the humility of Christ's birth, life, and death. Paul reminds us, "You know the grace of our Lord Jesus Christ, that though he was rich, yet for your sake he became poor, so that you by his poverty might become rich" (2 Cor. 8:9).

PERSONAL ILLUSTRATION

Throughout my life, pride has caused me several problems. There will be many situations where your pride will find room to manifest itself too.

Let me give you a specific example relating directly to the ministry. There was a man in our church who had expressed considerable unkindness to my husband, and when it came to my attention, I found an ever-growing sense of bitterness and anger creeping into my heart, mingled with unkind thoughts toward him. Initially he had been an extremely kind man who was enthusiastic about my husband and his ministry. But when my husband didn't live up to his expectations and expressed differing views from his own, his attitude changed. He quickly became critical and accusing. Eventually it became impossible for my husband to minister to him. Because this man had initially been *so* friendly and encouraging, we considered him a personal friend, someone who loved us. When his behavior changed so drastically, we felt very hurt, betrayed, and possibly even set up!

It was very clear to me at that time that my husband and I were in the right and the other man was in the wrong. He had wrong doctrine, wrong attitudes, and wrong conclusions. He had quite suddenly made our lives very difficult. As I considered the situation, my thoughts and prayers were all based on the assumption that God, my husband, sympathetic friends, and I were all on one side (the right side), while this man and anyone who agreed with him were on the other side (the wrong side). But one day as I was driving and using the time to meditate on God's Word, I became convicted that my heart was not pure. My thoughts were not right. God was opening my eyes to my sin. I realized what you have probably already realized as you read this. In looking down on this man, my embittered heart was oozing with pride.

The Lord used the parable about the Pharisee and the tax collector (Luke 18:9–14) to convict me. Both a self-righteous Pharisee and a humble tax collector went to the temple to pray. The first compared himself to others and felt a great sense of superiority. The second man compared himself to God and knew that he was terribly sinful. God saw into their hearts and showed favor to the tax collector, the one who had begged for mercy, knowing he didn't deserve it. When I thought about this parable, I realized that the man who had sinned against us—and indeed everyone else in the world, including my husband and me—were all in one category: the wrong one! Only God was in the right, only God was worthy, and only God had been justly offended. As you can imagine, I was convicted to the core of my soul. God led me to full repentance, and I asked him to forgive me for my ugly, blinding pride. My heart is still filled with remorse for those sinful days and weeks, but I remain very grateful for the many times over the years when God has used that lesson to keep me on guard against the damaging effects of pride. (I look back on it as a pride vaccination to protect me from a more deadly case in the future.)

You, I, that man, and the best and worst people you can think of—we are all on equal ground, fellow sinners in need of a Savior. The good news of the gospel is that a Savior was provided for us, a humble one whose power sanctifies us every day in order that we might be more like him. So let me encourage you to be committed to the Word and to prayer. Be thankful, be submissive, and don't shy away from confession of sin. But above all, and undergirding all, preach the gospel to yourself every day. If you pay close attention to this lesson early in your life and early in the ministry, you will avoid many sins and heartaches, both for yourself and for God's people.

I can't say it better than Paul did in Philippians 2:3–9:

Do nothing from selfish ambition or conceit, but in humility count others more significant than yourselves. Let each of you look not only to his own interests, but also to the interests of others. Have this mind among yourselves, which is yours in Christ Jesus, who, though he was in the form of God, did not count equality with God a thing to be grasped, but emptied himself, by taking the form of a servant, being born in the likeness of men. And being found in human form, he humbled himself by becoming obedient to the point of death, even death on a cross. Therefore God has highly exalted him and bestowed on him the name that is above every name, so that at the name of Jesus every knee should bow, in heaven and on earth and under the earth, and every tongue confess that Jesus Christ is Lord, to the glory of God the Father.

May we follow his example as we live out this life, humbly seeking to serve him and his people.

Your sister in Christ,
LYNN

STUDY QUESTIONS

1. List three (or more) characteristics of God followed by three Scripture verses that demonstrate these characteristics.

2. How does our view of God affect our view of ourselves? How does that relate to humility?

3. How can we train ourselves to accept God's will when it is contrary to our will?

4. What are some ways we can remind ourselves of the gospel?

5. Name four practical steps we can take to help us to cultivate humility.

RECOMMENDED RESOURCES

Mahaney, C. J. *Humility: True Greatness*. Sisters, OR: Multnomah Publishers, 2005.

Pink, Arthur W. *The Attributes of God*. Grand Rapids, MI: Baker Books, 1975.

Stuart, Scott. *From Pride to Humility: A Biblical Perspective*. Benidji, MN: Focus Publishing, 2002.

CHAPTER FOUR

Tongue and Thumb: Guarding the Ways We Communicate

Barbara Davis

I was attracted to Barbara originally because she didn't talk much. It was difficult to divine just what she was thinking, and there was something terribly tantalizing about that. I have since come to realize Barbara simply has a "gentle and quiet spirit" (1 Peter 3:4)—except when watching college football. In our pastoral ministry she never made messes that I had to clean up. Whenever we left a congregation, it's no wonder they were sad to see her leave.

REV. DR. RALPH DAVIS

Dear sister in Christ,

I was recently asked in a conversation how I guarded my tongue in all spheres of my life, especially as a minister's wife in the ups and downs and knocks and bounces of church life.

As I consider my speech, I agree with James when he said, "No human being can tame the tongue" (James 3:8). Words are formed on the tongue, but they originate in the heart. Our words are like a barometer of our hearts. We need to plead with the Lord for cleansing of our hearts, so that our speech is profitable to others and acceptable to him.

Of course, James's description is simply scary; the tiny tongue exerts huge power, the way a bit in a horse's mouth controls the whole animal or a small rudder directs a massive ship. It reminds me of one of my banana cake failures. One day I thought I had put in all the ingredients, but the cake turned out completely flat. Suddenly I realized I had forgotten the baking soda. It was only one teaspoon, but it affected the whole cake. Our tongue is like that: it is small but can leave a real mess.

Let's begin with some very ABC-level matters. First, commit yourself to be candid and open about speaking the truth, even if it makes things sticky for you. I remember when an emergency once arose in our congregation. My husband was away, speaking at a conference. One of the staff was expected to cover for him during the time. When I heard of the emergency, I called the staff member's home. I asked to speak with him, but his wife seemed evasive about his whereabouts. I eventually discovered that her husband was out of town, interviewing for another church position! Nothing wrong with that, except he hadn't requested the time away. His wife was in a difficult position, yet she was not straightforward and tried to cover his tracks. One can be tempted to shade the truth and tell a "white lie"—whatever that is. Much better simply to be candid, no matter the consequences. We are often only a step away from our own Ananias-and-Sapphira situations (Acts 5:1–11); ours may not be immediately fatal, but they can be just as devious.

Being careful about confidences is a second basic in our use of the tongue. Since I didn't blab about situations and people, others in time had confidence to come to me with confidential matters. What was spoken to me in confidence stayed with me. Only if necessary did I ask permission to share the matter with my husband or the session. Women will feel at ease in seeking you out when they come to realize that you will not discuss their problems with others.

Be sure to respect your husband's need to be confidential with the difficulties of people and the decisions of the session. Occasionally the elders may have to deal with a very tense discipline case. Your husband will not be able to (or should not) discuss this with you. Sometimes I have found myself in awkward positions because of what I didn't know, but I trusted the Lord to make known his ways to my husband and the session.

I would also suggest a third basic guideline: if in doubt (and even if not in doubt), follow a principle of restraint. There is a time to speak and a time to be silent, and it takes wisdom to know one time from the other. Some women need to give their tongues a rest. As Proverbs 17:28 says, "Even a fool who keeps silent is considered wise; when he closes his lips, he is deemed intelligent." Did the wise man wink when he wrote those words? Some women, including pastors' wives, can be dominating, obsessive talkers at social gatherings. Even if the talk is informed and knowledgeable, it is still voluminous and wearies long-suffering hearers. In short, limit your words. This advice includes not offering advice when advice is not asked for!

Because the tongue can involve us in so many pitfalls, we can easily accentuate the negative. But we must remember the positive—the tongue's finest opportunities. One of these is weekly public worship. Naturally that carries its own set of cautions: each Sunday I have to be alert about how I use my tongue to assent to the congregational liturgy; to pray with my mind on the Lord; to sing truthfully the words of a hymn; and to accept the preaching of God's Word into my life. Yet for all the care it involves, what a joy and delight! With all the saints I get to "proclaim the excellencies of him who called [me] out of darkness into his marvelous light" (1 Peter 2:9). Every Lord's Day I get to do what I was made and called to do!

Your home is a second arena of opportunity for you. This is primarily positive, but it also entails its share of cautions. Your tongue and heart will be most tested within your home. It is there that you need to demonstrate proper use of the tongue. I remember a time when our boys visited another

69

church family's home. They were blown away by the yelling, squabbling, and turmoil there—a domestic war zone. Both the father and the mother were in positions of leadership in the church. So show honor and respect in your speech toward your husband and children. May they in turn "rise up and call [you] blessed" (Prov. 31:28).

Speaking of your husband, give special thought to how you can encourage him in his ministry. Some of this is verbal and some not. Try, for example, to express how a point or illustration in his sermon proved helpful to you. Yet much encouragement will not be verbal at all. My husband has told me that my taking on all the washing, ironing, and food preparation in our home frees him up from such matters to concentrate on his ministry. He finds that encouraging.

While I am thinking of speech in the home, let me add a plea for consistency. Some mothers repeatedly tell a child not to do something and threaten punishment. The child still does whatever "it" is, but nothing happens. This is deceptive! It is right to warn verbally, but if action is promised, the promise should be kept. Is it not lying on our part to tell a child not to do something and state consequences, then fail to carry out what we have promised?

I should perhaps say something about "hard cases"—times when you are convinced that you should speak but are unsure of what the response may be. Let me give an example or two.

It is a risk to exhort another person, and we may be tempted to think we've been wrong to say anything when a person doesn't take our remarks the right way. I once made a personal phone call during the week to remind a church volunteer to be on time for Sunday school nursery. I did this because visitors' children often arrived before anyone was there to welcome them. The following Sunday the woman publicly remarked that she'd gotten a bad report card on nursery duty! My attempt to amend the situation had not been received in the way I'd intended.

Another occasion brought quite a different response. Once I heard a woman express her opinion about some church repairs at a women's function. To give credence to her statement, she quoted her husband. Another woman heard and took the comments in a very personal way, for her husband had been doing the repairs. I thought about the episode for a few days, and then I asked the first woman to come by my house so I could discuss something with her. She came, and I told her how her remarks had come across to me as an observer. This woman was receptive to my counsel and immediately recognized her inappropriate comment, especially in quoting her husband who was in a position of leadership. She made a point to call the other woman and apologize. This woman is still a close friend of mine.

Let me switch to another piece of anatomy as I close. In our day, not only is the tongue a symbol of communication but the thumb is also. I am using *thumb* as a figure for the current texting craze—and indeed for the whole gamut of electronic communication.

Like the tongue, the thumb poses its own set of problems. Our thumb is busy texting in the home—which often leads to our ignoring other family members; in the car—waiting for an accident to happen; in the church—at a Wednesday night prayer time or in the church pew so that messages can be checked often during a worship service.

I do see many benefits of technology, especially e-mail, skyping, and so on. I love to e-mail an "adopted" daughter in a foreign country. My brother and his wife greatly enjoy skyping with their daughter and family in Spain. It is great to keep up with missionaries by quickly responding to their prayer requests or needs. Counseling can be done from a distance via Skype. All of the above can be used properly.

But our "techy" tools can be misused. They can be terribly depersonalizing. Have you ever been engaged with someone in a useful conversation when that person feels compelled to look at a text or take a call? It lets you know where you stand in her list of priorities!

I have seen this kind of thing again and again. Just days ago we were in a restaurant ordering lunch. A married couple was sitting at the table next to us; the wife was speaking to the husband, who never looked at her but occupied himself with receiving and sending text messages. On another occasion we noticed a woman texting while her three children ran wildly throughout the restaurant. We heard her daughter try twice to ask her mommy a question—with no attention given to the young child. We seem to embrace our toys but ignore persons.

Even social media pose their own dangers. So many "friends" can be indiscreetly informed of personal problems or deluged by a litany of your children's achievements. The principle of restraint that I mentioned earlier surely applies here.

In the face of all our gadgets, a pen and stationery seem so passé. However, I find that writing a personal note or letter shows a personal touch and a willingness to spend money on stationery and a stamp. I am investing myself in that person. Please understand. I am not antitechnology as such, but I think believers can often be blind to its pitfalls.

Well, I have tried to pass on what I *think* I have learned about proper use of the tongue. It's a frightening thing to be a Christian with a body part that is a "restless evil" (James 3:8)—even more frightening to be a pastor's wife with such an unruly piece of anatomy. Perhaps we can pray for each other that the Lord will sanctify both of us in tongue and thumb.

Your sister in Christ,
BARBARA

STUDY QUESTIONS

1. How have you guarded your tongue in the past week at home and in the church?

2. We often think the speech of pastors' wives should be characterized by restraint, but what situations call for some sort of assertiveness in our use of speech (Gal. 2:11–14; 1 Cor. 11:17)?

3. What rules of thumb should guide our use of electronic devices in order that we might keep ourselves from sabotaging the attention we should give to people?

4. Aside from requests for confidentiality, what are other wisdom areas in which we should keep matters confidential (Prov. 11:12–13; 13:3)?

5. What key steps do you take in curtailing gossip?

RECOMMENDED RESOURCES

Proverbs (for the blessings and the pitfalls of the tongue)

James 3 (on the power of the tongue)

Prentiss, E. *Stepping Heavenward*. Uhrichsville, OH: Barbour Publishing, 1988.

Part 2

Practical Counsel for Us All

CHAPTER FIVE

Expectations: God-centered or Self-imposed

Donna Ascol

Donna is a wonderful gift of God to me. She faithfully, humbly, and joyfully helps me to remember the grace that is in the Lord Jesus. Her devotion to Christ, continued growth in his grace, and devotion to his kingdom have encouraged me to persevere in pastoral ministry for more than three decades. Her example and wisdom have been used by our Lord to challenge and motivate me to mortify sin and pursue holiness. I am a much better pastor because of her than I otherwise would have been.

Donna fully embraces her calling to be not only my wife but also my sister in the Lord. In so many ways she is my superior, yet she joyfully finds contentment in serving as my helper, enabling me to give myself to the work of the pastorate. The grace that she has ministered to her family has resulted in our children already rising up and calling her blessed.

Donna's faithfulness to Christ also strengthens and blesses the church. Our members know that she is a fully devoted wife and mother, but

they also see her developing and using her gifts to encourage, teach,
evangelize, and disciple young people and women as she has opportunity.
Her life commends the gospel. I love her dearly and thank God that she
is willing to share biblical wisdom she has learned by enduring that
uniquely challenging crucible that goes with being "the pastor's wife."

REV. DR. THOMAS ASCOL

Dear sister in Christ,

What an exciting time this is as you begin a new season of life and ministry as the wife of a pastor. Marrying a man who has been called to ministry necessitates that life will never be the same for you. There will be blessings and rewards in ministry that you cannot now imagine. There will also be unique challenges and struggles that come with being a ministry wife.

One of my biggest challenges was the effort to be "real" while fulfilling the role to which God had called me as a wife and helpmeet in marriage and ministry. I felt overwhelmed by the various expectations facing me as the pastor's wife that had the potential to make me into something or someone unfamiliar to myself. As a young pastor's wife, you also are facing those expectations. There will be a standard of conduct anticipated from you by everyone you know and many you have never met. Because you are married to a pastor, your congregation, community, parents, siblings, children, and even your husband may expect you to think, feel, dress, and behave in a particular way. You too will expect certain things of yourself in this new role. It seems that anyone who is vaguely familiar with church culture has an opinion about what a "typical pastor's wife" is to be, do, and look like. With input from such a variety of sources, these opinions are often in conflict with each other and may or may not line up with the expectations that God has of you. Certainly you feel the weightiness of all this. I hope that, by sharing with you some of what God has taught me regarding expectations in my many years of being a pastor's wife, I will strengthen and encourage you in the work that God has called you to do.

"So you're the pastor's wife?" When I was a young pastor's wife, those words created a flood of pressure that washed over me as I tried to imagine the woman I was expected to be. Just hearing my new title caused my mind to formulate images of the ideal wife and mother, perfect homemaker, gracious hostess, gifted ministry leader, competent Bible teacher, engaging speaker, chief counselor for women in the church, and capable piano player. You get the picture!

Regardless of the intention of the speaker, that statement was loaded with implications for me as a pastor's wife. I felt the pressure of those high expectations. But while none of those expectations were sinful and all were commendable, the way I often responded to them revealed a heart full of pride. Desires to feel good about myself and to be esteemed by others consumed my thoughts and motivated my actions. My motivation was not gospel driven, nor did it reflect a desire to glorify God. As an immature and inexperienced pastor's wife, my misguided assumptions, coupled with self-absorption, proved to be a source of anxiety and discouragement for me for years. I spent far too much time and energy trying to force myself into a role God had never intended for me—one that would glorify me rather than him. Thankfully, God did not leave me there. He was faithful to reveal that area of sin in my life and to call me to a higher expectation, one that originated and culminated in his Word.

Dealing with my own expectations was only one part of the solution. I also had to learn to deal with what others expected of me. Many church members often have strong opinions about what their pastor's wife should be and do. While being the "first lady of the church" carries no job description, it comes with high expectations to which you may feel pressed to conform. Sometimes those expectations will be biblically correct and wise; sometimes they will be unbiblical, unhelpful, and undeserved. Too often they will be based on subjective thinking shaped by societal norms mixed with cultural and geographical biases. There will be a degree of pressure to conform to an expected image or, more typically, images tailored to individual members' needs, opinions, and ideas (which will inevitably conflict with the expectations of others in the congregation). When those varying expectations become excessive, demands, conflict, and difficulties will soon arise.

As long-time pastor's wife Gail McDonald noted, "At best, people are seeking us out as models of Christian grace and maturity. At worst, people are watching with an intent to critique anything that is out of alignment with what they think are the highest standards of Christian behavior."[1] To be the "model of Christian grace and maturity" is a daunting undertaking for any Christian, much less a young pastor's wife. It is inevitable that, in an effort to please all, you will disappoint some.

Wherever you and your husband serve, you will bring expectations with you, and you will be met with expectations within the church you serve. Trying to conform to everyone's expectations is an unachievable task. You will never please everyone. This thought can be extremely discouraging, particularly if your sense of well-being is attached to the approval of others. It would be naive to assume that you will not come under a certain amount of scrutiny and criticism. Life in a fishbowl, as some refer to it, often means that your words, actions, attitude, fashion, and so on will be more closely observed and evaluated than that of other Christian women in the church. If all things were considered equal and you could function in the church as any other Christian, much of the scrutiny would cease. However, as a pastor's wife you are in a position that is more visible and therefore more vulnerable. While others could be criticized in the same way, when it is directed at the pastor's wife, it has a heightened sense of weightiness (e.g., "Can you believe that, and she's the *pastor's wife!*").

This scenario produces both a challenge and a burden and can be a major source of anxiety for ministry wives. In the midst of this, God has not left you on your own but has given you his Word to help you discern what your ministry is to be and whose expectations you are to fulfill. You need not carry the weight of everyone's expectations. There is only *one* whose expectations should drive your motives and your actions. The bottom line is this—what does God expect? What has God called you to be?

When Scripture informs our way of thinking about God's expectations and calling for us, we will be guided by our Servant-King, Jesus Christ, who has given us an example of how to live and conduct ourselves in this broken world. The familiar passage in Philippians 2:3–8 describes Jesus' humility in giving up his own rights in order to humbly serve others, even to the point of death. His example of loving and ministering to people in order to bring glory to God should be our example. In living his life of service, he met God's expectations, which meant that he often did not meet the expectations of others. His service to others was always motivated by a deeper purpose.

Consider his example:

- When people were clamoring for his attention and even demanding it, Jesus often walked away. He could have chosen to stay; however, for his own welfare, for his Father's purposes, and for the ultimate good of his people, he made the choice to separate himself from the crowds (Matt. 14:22, Mark 3:7–9).
- Jesus did not always give the answers that people wanted to hear, even to the point of offending some by his words. He was not being offensive in a sinful way but was always speaking the truth in redemptive ways (John 6:60–61, 66).
- When pressured by his brothers to do ministry their way, Jesus resisted their attempts to manipulate the situation (John 7:3–9).
- Martha was disappointed when Jesus tarried rather than hurry to rescue her brother. What she expected of him was not in keeping with God's purposes for her or her brother, and Jesus understood that. Though he was moved by the situation, Jesus refused to be motivated by her emotional outcry and "if only" expectations (John 11:6, 21).

- On another occasion, when falsely accused, Jesus declined to defend his innocence or answer his critics, though they expected him to respond. His reputation was of no concern, but rather he trusted himself to the one who judges righteously (Mark 15:3–5, 1 Peter 2:22–23).
- Herod expected Jesus to "perform" according to his abilities and Herod's expectations, but he refused to do anything outside his Father's will (Luke 23:8–9).
- Even those closest to him challenged Jesus' actions when he did what was not expected or understood. However, he did not shrink from doing his Father's will, even in the face of "friendly" opposition (John 13:3–17).

In order to serve a greater, redemptive purpose, Jesus intentionally disregarded expectations that were not in keeping with his Father's will. He did not change his methods to suit others but rather always did the things that were pleasing to God (John 8:29). To him, nothing else mattered. He is our example of following his Father's expectations in spite of what everyone else around him thought. He was rejected, doubted, ridiculed, misunderstood, lied about, betrayed, scorned, beaten, and ultimately killed, yet he stayed the course with a single passion to live up to the expectations of the Father who had sent him, confident in who he was and what he came to accomplish: "I glorified you on earth, having accomplished the work that you gave me to do" (John 17:4).

Early in our ministry, as I looked to Jesus as my example and guide, God gave me these verses in Romans 12 that have had a profound effect on me as I have sought to discern what God would have me to be and to do and have helped to shape my thinking about his expectations and my calling.

I appeal to you therefore, brothers, by the mercies of God, to present your bodies as a living sacrifice, holy and acceptable to God, which is your spiritual worship. Do not be conformed to this world, but be transformed by the renewal of your mind, that by testing you may discern what is the will of God, what is good and acceptable and perfect. (Rom. 12:1–2)

In the first eleven chapters of Romans, the apostle Paul lays down the foundation of Christian belief and living and then says, "therefore . . . sacrifice." Sacrifice indicates that something must die (Gal. 2:20; Col. 3:3); being a living sacrifice means that I am willing to completely put myself at God's disposal. I am called to live in such a way that my life is a reflection of a sacrificial love for God and a desire to do his will. All my service is to be done for the One who knows me best, loves me most, and has rescued me from death.

Because of his mercies, I want to do those things that please him. In order to know what pleases him, I must renew my mind and reset my way of thinking so that I will no longer take my cues from the world's way of thinking. As Elisabeth Elliot reminds me, I am to

> pray for a clear eye to see through the fog of popular opinion, and a will strong enough to withstand the currents—a will surrendered, laid alongside Christ's. He is my model. This means a different set of ambitions, a different definition of happiness, a different standard of judgment altogether. Behavior will change, and very likely it will change enough to make me appear rather odd—but then my Master was thought very odd.[2]

You and I, as pastors' wives, must strive not to be molded into any image that is of the world's making but rather to shape our thinking to do our Father's will. In doing so, you will have to sort out the expectations and make hard decisions that will affect your ministry as a pastor's wife.

FOUNDATIONAL PRINCIPLES

Here are some foundational principles that may help to discern God's will for you as a pastor's wife and free you from mere duty-driven service in the church.

Be Confident in Christ Jesus

Before discovering who you are as a pastor's wife, you must discover who you are in Christ. Understanding this will be the foundation on which your life and ministry is built. Your identity is not based on what people expect or who they say you are but rather on what Scripture says is true of you in Christ.

In Christ:

- You have been rescued—Colossians 1:13
- You are blessed with spiritual blessings—Ephesians 1:3
- You are forgiven—Ephesians 1:7
- You are a new creation—2 Corinthians 5:17
- You are chosen and accepted (blessed) by God—Ephesians 1:3–6
- You are justified—Romans 3:23–24
- You are full and complete—Colossians 2:9–10
- You are loved—1 John 3:1
- You are adopted—John 1:12
- You are no longer a slave to sin but are now a slave to righteousness—Romans 6:17–18
- You are a joint heir with Christ—Romans 8:17

To be "in Christ" means that all the things listed above, and more, are now true about you. They are realities that should fuel your present and future ministry. Our service to our husbands, our families, and our church should be a natural spring flowing from our love and devotion to Christ. Being confident in Christ means that you will no longer be enslaved to anyone's expectations or good opinion of you, because your loyalty will be to him (Gal. 5:1).

Rather than striving to be the very best pastor's wife, be devoted to being the very best Christian you can be because your desire is to honor and obey Christ in all things. John Piper describes this radical freedom we have in Christ: "You are free in Christ, because when you do from the inside what you *love* to do, you are free, if what you *love* to do is what you *ought* to do. And that's what transformation means: when you are transformed in Christ you *love* to do what you *ought* to do. That's freedom."[3]

Recognizing your standing in Christ frees you to love people rather than be concerned with whether or not they love and accept you. This also keeps you from being a people-pleaser. If you are committed to pleasing others, you are not committed to pleasing Christ. Being free in Christ, being confident in him and devoted to him, creates a desire in you to please him. That should be your aim (2 Cor. 5:9)!

Be Focused on Your Ultimate Purpose

Every Christian has a divine purpose to be the image bearer of God. In our various roles we represent God on earth. We have this glorious goal, and it involves being more than doing. As we determine how to live our lives as ministry wives, at the heart of our doing is glorifying God and enjoying him forever (as the Westminster Catechism says). We must first focus our minds on the fact that we exist only to glorify God. In doing so, our focus becomes him rather than ourselves.

Be Mindful of Your Calling and Careful in Your Commitments

As you think about the expectations you will face, it is important that you filter all of them through the grid of God's Word so that you can respond to them in truth. When you face the question of whose expectations matter, you must come back to the Author of truth and Creator of your life. His expectations matter! Any decisions you make should line up with his expectations of you. But what does God expect of you as a pastor's wife? Does your husband's call come with a job description for you? If you are thinking biblically, you will realize that God has given you a calling that is far greater than being a pastor's wife. With the glory of God foremost in our minds (1 Cor. 10:31), we are called, first and foremost, to be genuine Christians, presenting our lives as living sacrifices in service to him. Beyond that, there are also distinctive duties that are attached to specific roles.

As a Christian wife, your first calling, beyond your devotion to Christ, is to your husband. Through our years of ministry, whenever my husband and I would evaluate my role in the church, he would affirm that my most important (and difficult) job was to "keep him in the ministry." That is an enormous task that I do not take lightly.

With all the stress and discouragement that can come to my husband, I realize that he needs someone he can trust who will speak truth to him and minister love and grace to him. My role as a means of grace to my husband includes encouraging him, counseling him, praying for him, and speaking the gospel to him in much the same way as he does for the members of the congregation.

If you are a mother, your next calling is to be the very best mother you can be for your children. Solomon says,

> Behold, children are a heritage from the LORD,
>   the fruit of the womb a reward.
> Like arrows in the hand of a warrior
>   are the children of one's youth. (Ps. 127:3–4)

As Christian mothers, we must, by the grace of God and by the power of his Spirit, be actively engaged in intentionally raising our offspring with eternal purposes in mind. They are like arrows that need to be prepared for launch so that God's purposes will be fulfilled in their lives for the advancement of his kingdom here on earth. With the added pressures that come with being in a ministry family, your children will need a mom who is fully engaged, strong in her faith, and prepared to guide them through their formative years. If you and I neglect this calling, we are doing a disservice to our Lord and to his church.

In pursuing those callings it might feel like you are neglecting your service in the church, but that investment is a *great* service to the church because of the unusual demands on ministry families. The strength and stability of your home is essential to your husband's ministry and, as his wife, your faithful ministry in the home is crucial and immeasurable. While other people may not appreciate it, you must focus on its value. As your husband begins his ministry in a church, you may quickly feel the pressure of expectations that, if fulfilled by you, will render it nearly impossible for you to thrive in your calling as a wife and mother. You may also discover that serving Christ by being a godly wife and mother will not bring the accolades that might otherwise come by serving those in the church, and it may even invite criticism from those who feel neglected because of your priority to serve your family. However, if you are negligent in this calling, it will reflect poorly on the gospel of the Savior whom you love and serve.

As you make decisions regarding your service in the home and in the church, you will want to do so with the help and counsel of your husband. He has been given to you as a protector and leader and is one of the chief means of grace that God has provided for you as a wife. Together you must learn to resist the temptation of being swept along by the tide of expectations that tend to draw you away from your primary calling as a wife and mother.

Be Realistic about Your Limitations

Wisdom demands that you acknowledge the truth about yourself. You are not God. You cannot meet everyone's expectations. You were not fashioned or designed by God to be gifted in all things and able to meet everyone's needs. Because you are finite, you will naturally be limited, both in scope and purpose, based on your giftedness as well as your season of life.

How you minister in the church as a pastor's wife will look different from how I minister in the church. Your gifts may not resemble the giftedness of the pastor's wife before you. Being truthful about who you are and what God has gifted you to do will enable you to serve others in the church while enabling them to use the gifts that God has given to them. If you act as if you are the only one or the best one to minister in certain areas of the church, you may actually be crippling the body. Because of your reticence to step back due to misguided guilt or undue expectations, others may not see needs they are suited to meet or be open to being stretched beyond their comfort zones. This is contrary to what Scripture teaches in 1 Corinthians 12:18–20:

> But as it is, God arranged the members in the body, each one of them, as he chose. If all were a single member, where would the body be? As it is, there are many parts, yet one body.

Once you have discovered your areas of giftedness, you will need to be wise in how you exercise those gifts. You may have gifts that you are unable to use because of the limitations that come during certain seasons of life. When my own children were younger, my hands were full with ministering to them and training them in worship. Obviously their preacher-father could not train them while leading the worship service. Because of that, for many years I was unable to use my gift of playing the keyboard during our times of congregational worship. Once my children were old enough to know what was required of them in worship and to exercise some self-control and measure of attentiveness, I could once again serve in that way.

There may be ministries in the church that you would like to partici-pate in, however, because of the ebb and flow of life (family limitations, health issues, working outside the home, and so on) you are unable to pursue them. Your situation and circumstances will be constantly changing. Your children will not always be small. If you are homeschooling, your time will be freed once your children are grown. There may be times when you must focus most of your time and energy in pursuits outside the church. One older and wiser pastor's wife once shared with me how this phrase, "and it came to pass," served as a constant reminder to her that the seasons of life are fluid. On this side of eternity, no circumstance is forever as you grow and mature in the Lord.

There may also be gifts that are latent in you now but that will develop as you mature in the faith. As a young pastor's wife, I was very comfortable working with and teaching younger children and was intimidated by the thought of teaching anyone old enough to read! Today I regularly teach our high-school Sunday school class (the most intimidating class of all)! What happened? While I was absorbing gospel preaching and teaching and as I became more comfortable in my skin and more confident in Christ, God was maturing me as a woman and as a Christian. He was working to create in me a desire to do harder things. It did not happen overnight. It did not happen because everyone expected it. It certainly did not happen simply because I married a pastor. God brought me along gradually. He knew my frame and remembered that I was dust (Ps. 103:14). You may feel very intimidated now at the thought of counseling other women or speaking at a parenting seminar. That is understandable. It is a season of life. As you prepare yourself to serve by living life, being a student of the Word, and maturing in the faith, God will begin to do a work in you to give you an increasing desire and ability to do those things you feel incapable of doing now. God is sovereign to fulfill his purposes in you. You are responsible to prepare yourself to be used by him.

Be Discerning in Dealing with Expectations

If you do not consider the truth about yourself and remember your personal limitations, the many expectations from various sources will conflict and collide with chaotic and often damaging results. The reality is that while not all expectations are sinful, some unhelpful and even harmful aspects shape them all. As a pastor's wife, you will have an almost endless list of expectations that you could potentially fulfill. What you will soon discover is that you have limited energy and resources within you to deal with the endless expectations you could meet. How you deal with them will have an impact on your family, your ministry in the church, and the kingdom of God. For instance, here is a representative list of a few of the choices I have had on any given Sunday:

- Play the keyboard
- Sing on the praise team
- Oversee the nursery workers (and fill in when they did not show)
- Teach Sunday school
- Welcome visitors
- Greet the other saints
- Train my young children to worship
- Counsel a hurting woman
- Get a message to the pastor
- Meet with the Women's Ministry Team
- Discipline my child(ren)

As you can see, none of these expectations are sinful, but it would be next to impossible to make them all happen and do them all well. In your strivings to please everyone and meet those expectations, the weightiness and guilt of unmet expectations can cripple you, keep you from being all you were meant to be in Christ Jesus, and ultimately hinder the work of God's kingdom in the church. Just because you *can* do something does not always mean that you *should*. Scripture teaches us that " 'all things are lawful,' but not all things are helpful. . . . not all things build up" (1 Cor. 10:23).

On any given Sunday, the previous list of expectations could and has been expected of me and, sadly, even attempted by me. I had to learn to gauge my limited energy and resources in light of their potential kingdom value as I determined which expectations to satisfy.

For instance, when my children were small, I was often the only one qualified to play the keyboard in worship. People enjoyed the keyboard and expected to hear it during worship. To complicate matters, I was the one who had primary responsibility to care for my many small children and train them in worship. Obviously their father had pastoral responsibilities that occupied his time and energies on the Lord's Day, so he rightly entrusted me to care for them and train them in his absence. What then? Do I neglect the training of my children in order to play the keyboard?

What is the greater calling here? In a situation like this, my husband and I had to determine what was best for our family and had the greatest value in God's kingdom plan. The reality is that with every *yes* to one thing comes a *no* to something else.

Let me give another example. It was suggested, at one time, that if I would host some teas for the women, it would help them to connect with me and prevent them from feeling neglected by me. In consultation with the elders, it was determined that my time and energies would be better spent and the church would be better served if I would continue to invest in the lives of the young people as I had been doing for the past several years. There was not enough of me to give to both endeavors. A *yes* to one necessitated a *no* to the other. The *no* did not mean that I neglected ministry to other women. It simply meant that the expectation for me to host teas for the women would not be satisfied. I will always be grateful for the wisdom my elders displayed in their intervention and help with this process. They considered the suggestion made, while also considering my gifts and abilities, and ultimately determined what they felt would best serve me and my family as well as the church and the kingdom of God. They helped me to recognize my gifts and encouraged me to use them as I was able, recognizing my limitations and thereby relieving me of the guilt that can come from not doing it all.

Just as with me, God has called you and gifted you uniquely. You must recognize that you are finite and cannot do it all. Don't be pressured to perform duties that you are not equipped to handle or be loaded down with expectations that even those who hold them could not possibly fulfill. As you become increasingly discerning in dealing with expectations, God will help you to satisfy your responsibilities and use your gifts as you are able with a goal of glorifying him.

Be Hopeful in the Midst of Serving

As you navigate the choppy and unpredictable waters of expecta-tions and the circumstances surrounding them, it is helpful to assume that everyone has your best interest at heart and that everyone desires what is best for the kingdom. Generally speaking, people are not out to get you. Most members of the church body will not fully understand the pressure you are under as a pastor's wife or how their expectations might affect you. They probably never think about how the pressure to perform and the criticism of unmet expectations can feel very personal to the one who is supposed to meet their many expectations.

Scripture tells us that "love bears all things, believes all things, hopes all things, endures all things" (1 Cor. 13:7). In showing love to those whom God has placed in your sphere of life, you should believe the best about them, hoping all things, so that you can minister among them with joy. Time and energy spent questioning motives or looking for hidden meaning is unprofitable at best. Be who you are in Christ, believing that those he has placed in your life are for your good. You can care about those in your life and what they think without letting their opinions and demands define you.

BE GOSPEL-CENTERED AND GRACE-FILLED

Finally, as a child of God and as a pastor's wife, you are positioned to be a conduit of the gospel and an instrument of grace to those whom Christ has placed in your circle of influence. As the "good news" is embedded deep into our hearts and bears fruit in us, our minds will continue to be renewed and our lives transformed as we minister to our families, to our brothers and sisters in Christ, and to an unbelieving world.

Living in the light of the gospel means remembering who Jesus is, what he has done, and why that matters to us. In short, the gospel is the story of Jesus' perfect, sinless life, purposeful death, and victorious resurrection to execute a rescue for sinners who were spiritually dead in their sin, without hope and help in this world. Sadly, many Christians believe that the gospel is essential only to obtain salvation; however, what God accomplished for sinners through Jesus Christ is not only crucial to who we are but also sufficient for all that we do. The gospel is not only what saves us. It is active and living, helping us to live godly lives, bear spiritual fruit, and renew our minds. Therefore it should be applied in every area of life.

As the gospel truths begin to shape your thinking, emotions, and will, you will be spared some of the heartache that comes from a life of bondage to the expectations of others. As you work at applying the gospel every day, especially in light of the many expectations you will face, you must remember that in Christ the cross both criticizes and justifies us.

In the cross, you must affirm God's criticism/judgment of you:

The wages of sin is death, but the free gift of God is eternal life in Christ Jesus our Lord. (Rom. 6:23)

Whoever keeps the whole law but fails in one point has become accountable for all of it. (James 2:10)

In the cross, you must also affirm and agree with God's justification of you:

All have sinned and fall short of the glory of God, and are justified by his grace as a gift, through the redemption that is in Christ Jesus, whom God put forward as a propitiation by his blood, to be received by faith. (Rom. 3:23–25)

In light of the cross, we do not have to fear human expectations, judgments, or criticisms because we have agreed with God's criticism of us. Likewise, we do not have to crave or seek human approval because we have God's approval. You are justified in Christ and are free to fulfill your primary responsibility, apart from anyone else's expectations, of being a disciple of Christ and growing in holiness.

In 1 Corinthians 4:1–4, the apostle Paul explains that his chief concern was not his personal reputation or people's good opinion of him, but rather his right standing before God. He was first and foremost a servant of Christ. Just like Paul, we must look on the judgment of human beings as a very little thing as we strive to live for Christ and do his will. Rather than being driven by the expectations that come from human sources or crushed by the condemnation of human critics, you are set free by the gospel to be a disciple of Christ, living to please, honor, and serve him.

There is much more that could be said about this topic, dear sister, from pastors' wives across time and around the world. Though our words and our stories might differ, I think we would all agree that our Father and Creator has uniquely fashioned you in ways that will further his kingdom, minister to his church, and bring him glory.

You are his special child, and he has equipped you to be and to do all that he requires of you and desires for you. Keep looking to Jesus.

As you grow spiritually and mature in Christ, you will not only gain spiritual strength to discern and to stand against unhealthy expectations, but you will also become a much-needed ally for your husband and your children in their own spiritual walk. The deeper you plunge into the depths of God's grace and the more you access the gospel each day, the better equipped you will be to serve Christ in the church. As you faithfully serve him, you will become a source of spiritual strength and blessing for those in your sphere of influence.

With much love and prayers,

Your sister and fellow servant of Christ Jesus,

DONNA

STUDY QUESTIONS

1. "Rather than striving to be the very best pastor's wife, be devoted to being the very best Christian you can be because your desire is to honor and obey Christ in all things." What are some of the marks of a life transformed by Christ (Luke 6:43–45; Rom. 12; 2 Cor. 5:17; Gal. 5:22–23; Eph. 4:32)?

2. In our various roles (as wives, mothers, daughters, friends, ministry wives, and so on), we represent God on earth. We have this glorious goal, and it involves being more than doing. Why is it sometimes

easier for us to focus on "doing" rather than "being"? What is the relationship between "doing" and "being" for the Christian (Gal. 2:19; 5:22–23—the fruit of the Spirit are "being" qualities that lead to "doing" actions; Titus 2:11–14)?

3. God has revealed in his Word a magnificent plan and design for us as ministry wives that must be kept in the right order and with the right perspective. As a woman who desires to bring glory to God, you have a first calling, beyond your devotion to Christ, to your husband and children.

   a. What are practical ways you can minister grace to your husband in the home (Col. 3:18; Titus 2:5; 1 Peter 3:1–7; cf. 1 Cor. 7:5; Gal. 5:13; Eph. 5:22–24; 1 Thess. 5:11)?

   b. What are practical ways you can minister grace to your children in the home (Pss. 34:11; 78:5–7; 127:3–4; Prov. 14:26; 31:27–29; Luke 18:16)?

4. As you contemplate your role in the church, how does 1 Corinthians 10:23, 31 help you to discern what that role will look like for you?

5. In what ways is the gospel important in shaping the way you think and respond to the expectations of ministry (2 Cor. 4:7–18; Eph. 4:1–2, 25–32; Heb. 12:1–3)?

RECOMMENDED RESOURCES

Bridges, Jerry. *The Gospel for Real Life: Turn to the Liberating Power of the Cross.* Colorado Springs, CO: NavPress, 2002.

Greear, J. D. *Gospel: Recovering the Power That Made Christianity Revolutionary.* Nashville, TN: B&H Publishing Company, 2011.

Peace, Martha. *Attitudes of a Transformed Heart.* Bemidji, MN: Focus Publishing, Inc., 2002.

Tripp, Paul David. *Instruments in the Redeemer's Hands: People in Need of Change Helping People in Need of Change.* Phillipsburg, NJ: P&R Publishing, 2002.

CHAPTER SIX

Hospitality: Fellowship or Entertainment?

Shirley Rankin

Shirley and I go a long way back; we met on day one of Mrs. Windham's fourth-grade class. She was a Riley and I a Rankin, so the alphabetical seating order of grammar school generally meant the quiet blond girl was just a desk or two away. When we were thrown together again in high school, this good Presbyterian lad searched throughout our class of 650 for the Lord's perfect will for his life—and there she was! Shirley loved the Lord, and I admired her steady, solid walk with God. During our senior year, we lost our hearts over Swenson's ice cream and homemade Chef Boyardee pizza. In our Christian home together, we have shared our lives with countless church members and visitors who have passed through the front door on the way to the dining room table. It is no wonder

*that Shirley's experience provides helpful insight into the elixir to
the soul of true Christian hospitality.*

REV. DR. DUNCAN RANKIN

Dear sister in Christ,

You and your husband are about to embark on the adventure of a
lifetime. A call to the ministry translates into a parallel call of service involv-
ing both blessing and sacrifice. One of the most satisfying blessings is that
of hospitality. In retrospect there have been few times of greater sweetness
than those spent around a table sharing the joy of the Lord's grace with
new acquaintances or longtime friends. I pray that you too will grow to
cherish these opportunities.

This letter is not meant to be a hospitality manual; many books have
already been written on the subject. Rather it is to encourage you to have
people into your home on regular occasions. It is through these times of
fellowship that you will get to know individuals in your congregation
and often help them to cultivate friendships with one another. The work
involved in preparing for guests is more than made up for by the blessings
gained in Christian fellowship and conversation.

WHAT IS HOSPITALITY?

The word *hospitality* brings to mind many things: overnight guests,
supper clubs, elaborate dinner parties, a casual lunch in your home after
church, finger food and coffee, even offering the neighborhood children
a cool drink on a hot afternoon. A dictionary definition describes it as
"kindness in welcoming strangers or guests."[1] This is supported by several
examples in the Bible.

Consider Abraham's welcome to the three men standing near his tent (Gen. 18:1–8). On seeing the men, he ran from his tent with a friendly greeting and invited them to stop for refreshment. When they agreed, water was brought to wash their dusty feet (demonstrating Abraham's thoughtfulness), an abundance of bread cakes were quickly baked (using thirty-three quarts of fine flour!), and a tender choice calf was prepared. As the men ate this feast with curds and milk, their host stood nearby under a tree. Abraham's kindness far exceeded the men's need. He offered an abundance of his very best.

Rahab, a foreigner, offered hospitality to the two Israelites spying out Jericho. She took them in and hid them from the men who sought their destruction. She then helped them to escape (Josh. 2:1–16). In a desperate plea to have her family spared from the coming conquest, she reminded them, "I have dealt kindly with you" (v. 12).

Abigail offered hospitality to David and his men after her foolish husband, Nabal, spurned their humble request for food (1 Sam. 25:1–35). When she heard that her husband had acted so shamefully, she prepared bread, wine, roasted lamb, raisins, and figs. She then sent the food out to David on donkeys with her young servants, whom she had instructed, "Go on before me; behold, I come after you" (v. 19). Her generosity and humility toward these strangers turned back David's quest for vengeance on Nabal's household.

Jesus himself offered hospitality when he fed the multitudes on at least two occasions, recorded in Matthew 14–15, Mark 6, Luke 9, and John 6. Demonstrating compassion for the hungry crowds who had come out to hear him teach, Jesus declared that he was "unwilling to send them away hungry, lest they faint on the way" (Matt. 15:32). Jesus then blessed the meager quantities of fish and bread, feeding four thousand and five thousand on separate occasions. There were even baskets full of leftovers when the people were satisfied.

God's Word commands us to practice hospitality in such verses as "Contribute to the needs of the saints and seek to show hospitality"

99

(Rom. 12:13); "Welcome one another as Christ has welcomed you, for the glory of God" (Rom. 15:7); "Show hospitality to one another without grumbling" (1 Peter 4:9); and the well-known admonition to "show hospitality to strangers, for thereby some have entertained angels unawares" (Heb. 13:2). Remember, the Lord's commands are always for our good!

While the Bible supports the definition of hospitality and the Lord himself exhorts us to practice it, the thought of entertaining guests in your home may be intimidating when you consider what it entails. I will never forget the day my husband informed me that he was praying I would feel comfortable with having people into our home. We had small children at the time so I was paralyzed with fear at the thought of offering a satisfying meal to guests in a clean house with clean, well-behaved children! God's gracious leading has taught me that having people in our home does not require serving up perfection on all fronts. It is simply providing a welcoming, relaxed atmosphere of kindness without expecting anything in return.

THE PRACTICE OF BIBLICAL HOSPITALITY

Seize the opportunity as the new pastor's family to become acquainted with your congregation by inviting families, couples, and singles into your home. You will more quickly connect names with faces and members to their families than if you just see them on Sundays at church. Don't let the fact that you are new to the role of pastor's wife deter you in any way. You will find that many people have never been invited into a pastor's home and are thrilled to have such an opportunity.

After the morning worship service is an excellent time to have people in your home. If there are visitors at church, it is a very natural time to invite them to join you for a meal and Christian fellowship. Perhaps you could include another family from the church. Think ahead and invite one or two families or several single people (depending on family sizes and the size of your home) on a specific Sunday.

You might want to start with elders' and deacons' families, then gradually work through the congregation. When he is aware of a particular need,

I am sure your husband will have suggestions regarding families to invite. Another good opportunity is during holidays; plan ahead and invite those who otherwise find themselves alone or without family members. Widows or others who have lost loved ones may welcome an opportunity to spend the holiday at your home. If they would rather be alone, offer to deliver a plate of holiday food to their house but do not tire of inviting them, as they might want to be included at some point in the future.

When your invitation is accepted, make it a habit to ask if your guests have any food allergies or particular dislikes. On one occasion I failed to inquire. Regrettably, an allergy to onions prevented our guest from eating the homemade vegetable soup I had prepared. This man ate only bread at my table! My husband says, "Love thinks." Prior thinking tangibly communicates thoughtfulness. The people you invite, the food you serve, and the provision you make for small children and nursing mothers need careful forethought. The example you set may provide your guests with the encouragement they need to offer hospitality to others.

Once you have established dietary preferences, it is time to plan your menu. The first rule here is to keep it simple. Food that tastes good and is simply prepared will take the stress out of entertaining. Food that can be prepared the day before and reheated or placed in a slow cooker in the morning is ideal. It will significantly reduce kitchen time when your guests arrive.

The menu can be casual (a pot of chili or soup with cornbread) or more formal (pre-prepared chicken casserole and salad with crusty bread) with a simple dessert prepared the day before or ice cream with a choice of toppings. One of my favorites is a roast done in the slow cooker. The vegetables cooked along with the meat taste marvelous. You can serve it over minute rice or mashed potatoes. Both of these are easily stretched if you have some spur-of-the-moment guests. Accompaniments might include a salad and some rolls. Once you have identified menus that work well for you, stock up on the ingredients as you find them on special offer at the supermarket to save time and money.

Enlist your family to help in several aspects of the preparation, as well as in the hosting. Preschool youngsters can pick up toys, run a dust mop over the floors, and wipe down the bathroom counters and sinks. Older children can dust the furniture and help to prepare salads or desserts ahead of time. Someone can set the table and arrange a centerpiece (a basket of shiny apples, a bowl of lemons, a pot of ivy, or a vase of flowers from the garden are all inexpensive, easy ideas).

When your guests arrive, you might consider enlisting the help of your husband, the children, and even the people you have invited. You will find that delegation frees you up for last-minute food preparations. Someone can be in charge of answering the doorbell and taking the guests' coats. A child can pass the crackers and cheese around. Another person can take drink orders and prepare them. People love to help, especially when they are given a specific task, and conversation seems to be easier and less formal when people are working together.

I would encourage you to consider that your conversation can also benefit from forethought. Have in mind some topics to discuss, such as where your guests live and whether they have always lived in the area. How did they come to know the Lord? How long have they been associated with the church? What do they do during the week? How did the husband and wife meet? Do they have children? What ages are they, and where do they go to school? These get-to-know-you questions are perfect for first-time guests and can open many avenues of conversation. Keep in mind, however, that some topics are not welcomed by all guests. For example, be sensitive to cues that someone might not want to talk about his or her family or past and don't press too hard in those areas.

While much blessing comes through planning and preparing for your guests, sometimes you will find yourself hosting people at the last minute. Perhaps your husband comes home and announces that he has brought someone with him, or you bump into a friend at the mall and invite her over for coffee, or maybe there is a sudden crisis and someone needs your counsel. These times will obviously be less formal, since you have had no preparation time. However, you can still make these times special. Make it a policy to have coffee and tea on hand, as well as a packet of special crackers or cookies that can be opened for just that occasion. Do your best to focus on the guest and forget about the dust and the dishes in the sink. Guests might feel like they are intruding if they think you are uncomfortable with having them there. Above all else, you should endeavor to be welcoming!

Perhaps I could encourage you to keep a special journal where you can record the names of your guests, the date, the menu, and any particulars you wish to remember about them. These might include such things as allergies, notes for special care when a baby is due, or a special prayer need. You might also record conversational information you would like to remember in order to prevent repetitive conversation in the future.

PERSONAL REFLECTIONS

I would also like to share a few memories of times when our family has been on the receiving end of hospitality. Some of the best memories come from our time in Scotland when my husband was a student and I was a young new mother. We were often invited home after church by people of all ages: retirees, families, even young singles. We were made welcome, sitting in the living room with oatcakes and tea while the meal was prepared. The conversation started with the welfare of the guests and always turned to things of the Lord—something from the sermon or a story of how God had recently shown his grace to someone. When dinner was ready, we gathered around the table and feasted on whatever was set before us, sumptuous or simple. We then retired to the sitting room for more tea and conversation. I think those times were particularly dear to us because we were strangers in that land, yet we had true fellowship with our hosts in the bonds of Christ!

By the way, one of the practices we have imitated from our time in Scotland is keeping a little book which guests sign. Sometimes our hosts would wonder out loud about a person they knew and had not seen for a while. They would pick up their guest book to see when the person had last been in their home and reminisce fondly over the different people they had welcomed into their home throughout the years. Our guest book likewise allows us to look back at the people who have come through our door and to remember God's blessings of those special days.

Remember what Jesus said in Matthew 25:35–40:

"I was hungry and you gave me food, I was thirsty and you gave me drink, I was a stranger and you welcomed me, I was naked and you clothed me, I was sick and you visited me, I was in prison and you came to me." Then the righteous will answer him, saying, "Lord, when did we see you hungry and feed you, or thirsty and give you drink? And when did we see you a stranger and welcome you, or naked and clothe you? And when did we see you sick or in prison and visit you?" And the King will answer them, "Truly, I say to you, as you did it to one of the least of these my brothers, you did it to me."

I will pray for you and your husband as you begin this adventure together, that the Lord will bless you as you are a blessing to the congregation. I look forward to hearing how he leads and blesses you both in the years to come!

Your sister in Christ,
SHIRLEY

STUDY QUESTIONS

1. The fact that God's Son took on a human body and lived in our fallen world with all its needs and weaknesses (hunger, sickness, loneliness, and so on) should validate the importance of ministering to people's human needs. Does this fact affect the way you approach hospitality?

2. In Matthew 25:35–40, Jesus makes it clear that when we offer kindness and hospitality to brothers and sisters in Christ, we are offering them to him. What difference does that make in your attitude and actions

in offering hospitality? If, for instance, you had been Zacchaeus on the day that Jesus said he was going to his house (Luke 19:5), what kind of hospitality would you have shown to the Lord?

3. Romans 15:7 follows a passage on self-denial for others. The welcome that Christ extended to us meant self-denial for him. Are you willing to deny yourself to show kindness and welcome others? What might that self-denial look like?

4. In Romans 16:1–2, Paul urges the Christians in Rome to receive a woman named Phoebe "in a way worthy of the saints." What kind of welcome would be "worthy of the saints"? Are there newcomers in your church who should be able to expect a Christian welcome and help, and what have you done to make that happen?

5. If you are unaccustomed to practicing hospitality, start by choosing a time during your average week that would work well for you to invite people into your home. Think through the specific practical details, such as how many people you can comfortably host, what the focus of the gathering might be (a meal after a worship service, a game night, etc.), what food you might serve them, and the names of three people or families you could invite. Write down the specific details you thought about. They will be a starting point for your new adventure. Pray that God would give you a heart for hospitality and make you thoughtful of others!

RECOMMENDED RESOURCES

Mains, Karen Burton. *Open Heart, Open Home: The Hospitable Way to Make Others Feel Welcome and Wanted.* Wheaton, IL: Mainstay Church Resources, 1998.

Strauch, Alexander. *The Hospitality Commands: Building Loving Christian Community: Building Bridges to Friends and Neighbors.* Colorado Springs, CO: Lewis & Roth Publishers, 1993.

Friendships over the Long Haul: Our Need for Female Fellowship

Betty Jane Adams

Wives can make or break a man's ministry. I've seen both happen. Foolish wives who have not taken the time to think through and implement biblical principles that appertain to their relationship with their husbands and his congregation are perhaps the greatest hindrance to a pastor's effective ministry. Because Betty, my wife, has given much thought to such matters and has successfully incorporated them into her closest relationships, her friendships have been a boon rather than a hindrance during my years of pastoral work. I am thankful to God not only for her—and the close friendship that she has provided me in every kind of situation—but also for the way in which she has been a help and inspiration to others as well. Young couples just starting out in the ministry would do well to seriously consider and apply the thoughts she has penned in the following paragraphs!

REV. DR. JAY E. ADAMS

Dear sister in Christ,

It is my hope that as you read this letter, you will learn at a young age what has taken me a lifetime to fully grasp. There are many lessons that can be learned only through experience. The area of Christian friendship as a pastor's wife is no exception. Let me try to give you a foundation for your thinking as you consider how to build lasting friendships in the ministry. I hope to do that by first taking a look at the biblical roots for friendship. I will then walk you through the different seasons of my life and how I approached friendships during those various stages.

ROOTING FRIENDSHIP IN THE WORD

Our God is a Trinitarian God enjoying completeness, harmony, and communion, oneness in purpose, power, and perfection. Made in his image, we are created by God to be relational beings. First and foremost the human race was intended to have a close relationship with its Creator. Adam enjoyed sinless communion with God in the garden prior to the fall. God also graciously designed a human companion to complete Adam. The animal kingdom was not created to provide companionship to meet man's loneliness, so Eve was given to Adam, made like him but different. Theirs was a special relationship: intimate, enduring, and productive.

As a woman married to a pastor, you understand your relationship to him, knowing that it is to be held in the highest regard (second only to your relationship with the Lord), enduring throughout the years of ministry and into retirement. Yet it would be unusual if you did not long for friendships among your own gender.

WHAT IS BIBLICAL FRIENDSHIP?

You may ask the question, "What is friendship?" I would encourage you to consider that it is not merely fellowship with others, singly or as a group, in a Bible study, prayer meeting, social function, sewing circle, cooking class, concert, garden club, political rally, tour, or any event in which common interests are shared and enjoyed. Friendship takes fellowship to a deeper level. Scripture gives us two prominent examples.

The first is the friendship between David and Jonathan, two young men who could easily have been rivals, but Jonathan's soul was knit to that of David's, and he loved him as his own soul (1 Sam. 18:1). "Jonathan made a covenant with David, because he loved him as his own soul" (v. 3). "They kissed one another and wept with one another, David weeping the most. Then Jonathan said to David, 'Go in peace, because we have sworn both of us in the name of the LORD, saying, 'The LORD shall be between me and you, and between my offspring and your offspring, forever' " (1 Sam. 20:41–42).

A kiss was much like a handshake in our day. In the New Testament, Paul encourages believers to greet one another with a holy kiss (Rom. 16:16). This was an honorable alliance forged by Jonathan and David's common faith; a deep, intimate association between two people of the same sex without any sexual overtones.

The second biblical friendship is that of Ruth and Naomi. Ruth, whose very name means "friend," aligns herself with her mother-in-law. Her memorable words are often used in weddings between a wife and husband; "Where you go I will go, and where you lodge I will lodge. Your people shall be my people, and your God my God. Where you die I will die, and there will I be buried. May the LORD do so to me and more also if anything but death parts me from you" (Ruth 1:16–17). Here we have a story of a young woman and an older one sharing widowhood but moving forward together. The younger was stronger and able to glean wheat for food; the older one gave counsel and advice.

Two disparate friendships—but the common thread uniting them is not their circumstances, ages, or culture, but rather the intimacy, the heart to heart, the depth of feeling, and the mutual trust and accountability that David had with Jonathan and Ruth had with Naomi, all grounded in their faith in the Lord.

AN UNREALISTIC EXPECTATION IN THE MINISTRY?

Do you remember how easily you made friends as girlhood buddies, sharing secrets, playing house or school? Remember the high school confidantes, the college roommate? Now, in maturity and ministry, do you long for that closeness and joy? Do you wonder if such friendship is possible in this more public arena? You may be fortunate in retaining some of those early friendships, which are treasures, but what do you do about forming positive friendships within the church? Is it possible, practical, problematic, or even something worth pursuing?

My answer is *yes* to all these questions but with some reservations. First, you must recognize that you do need friends and that the Lord in his wisdom will meet that need but not necessarily in the time or way you may have anticipated. In your position you are required to be friendly to all, but it is impossible to be a friend to all. You must be as cordial to the young as to the old, to those who are pleasant as to those who are unpleasant. Some parishioners may be distant as a result of shyness, indifference, or fear. Some will be vocal in support; others will be slow to accept you. Some will even categorize you according to their formula of what makes a good pastor's wife. But every person in the church and every visitor should be warmly welcomed. It takes only a little effort to be thoughtful, caring, and sensitive to others, and it is especially important to make that effort with those who stand off, with those who are new to the church, and with those who are new to the faith.

It takes time to determine who is likely to need you as a friend or with whom you can establish rapport and trust. Friendships are not usually spontaneous, planned, or contrived. In Jay's first pastorate, the woman who initially visited us on our arrival seemed domineering, but over time she became a dear friend. The couple who appeared to have little in common with us became very dear to us throughout the years spent there.

SOME CONSIDERATIONS

Without children I could be actively involved in all the church activities, working with the teens, sewing with the seniors, and so on. I realized that the wife who followed me would not have the luxury of time to give to the scheduled church events if she had small children. In fact, I myself followed a much-loved pastor's wife who had left a wonderful reputation and hard shoes to fill. The friends that she had made might not be the same for me, and any friends that I made might not be the ones for the next pastor's wife. This is normal.

Since Jay and I were young in his first pastorate, I had to guard against letting the teenagers take advantage of us. I was careful around the young boys, not allowing them to call us by our first names or in any way to show disrespect to my husband. I would advise you never to cultivate a friendship with the opposite sex. Too many friendships that develop over common interests, even between believers, unintentionally end up in sexual alliance. A wise pastor or counselor never counsels the opposite sex without another person present. This is simply a wise precaution and protection for both parties.

You must be discreet about friendships within the church, never making a display or allowing others to brag about outings or time spent at your house. If parties are given, invite everyone in that group, class, or age bracket. Feelings are easily hurt if parishioners feel left out or if favoritism is shown. I once knew a wise young pastor's wife who met with her small circle of friends on a monthly basis but kept it very private.

It causes no problems when there are friends outside the church. From the earliest days, we enjoyed being with other ministerial couples— after all, we had much in common. Those were times of complete relaxation, times to let down our hair, with no gossiping about church problems. We gleaned wisdom from those who had more experience and varying types of ministry. However, those friendships were more as couples than as individuals.

When you develop friendships within the church, refrain from speaking about others in a negative way. No matter how close a friendship may be, never divulge intimacies or unflattering things about your husband. A friend once suggested that she thought that revealing things about her husband would make him seem more like a regular guy. Congregants, no matter how much they honor and respect their minister, are smart enough to discern his weaknesses, which they either choose to ignore or endure. No help is needed from his wife. Remember, you still love the man, but you may plant misgivings in your friend's mind that will affect her response to his preaching.

Proverbs 31:11–12 reminds us,

The heart of her husband trusts in her,
    and he will have no lack of gain.
She does him good, and not harm,
    all the days of her life.

CONTINUING FRIENDSHIPS

If you hang on to friends, you can make things difficult for the minister who follows you. Once we left a church, we let go of whatever friendships we had developed during a pastorate, with the exception of sending Christmas cards. I am not advising you to say good-bye and maintain no contact with the congregation, but it is important that you exercise wisdom and consider the future pastor's wife and her relationship with the people.

We did hold on to our friendship with two other couples we had befriended when my husband had gone to graduate school. After leaving school we settled in different states but purposefully sought to continue the closeness we had all enjoyed together. For over twenty-five years, we vacationed annually for a week. It was not our intention to pursue these friendships with such intensity, but after our first time together we gradually made it a yearly practice. At first we rotated the hosting of the week, renting a vacation home. Eventually, however, we decided that it was easier to host the vacation at our individual homes, particularly because our families were growing. These families have been our closest and dearest friends. Lasting memories were made for ourselves as well as for our children, and because we are believers we will one day enjoy even closer reunions with these people in our heavenly home.

Developing deep friendships takes time, which always seems to be at a premium in ministry. True friends understand the constraints of time, family, and business, and they stay true without pampering you or demanding constant attention. To be a friend requires energy, sometimes money, rearranged schedules, and much prayer, but the rewards are undoubtedly worth it.

During a period of about seven years when my husband wasn't in active ministry, I made friends, female friends. That was simply marvelous! It provided a new freedom that I had never experienced before. I made friends who were open, giving, and gracious, and we formed lasting bonds. They didn't whine, they didn't gossip, and I loved it.

FRIENDSHIP AS A YOUNG MOTHER

I have learned over the years that friendships have seasons that generally correspond to the seasons of one's life. As a mother with young children, you will find it easier to relate to other mothers. Babysitting for one another, exchanging recipes, discussing parenting skills, and having Bible studies all help to develop bonds. During the day, activities such as lunch at McDonald's, zoo trips, or simple play times may be arranged (shopping is a "no" except for brave mothers), but don't encourage this at the cost of over-tiring your children. During this particular season of life, time doesn't generally allow for deep personal friendships. Babies are demanding and happier in a regular schedule. Children thrive best on a predictable pattern. This is a good time for family friendships. E-mail and notes make it possible to keep in touch with former friends, but you must keep in mind that your husband and children need a wife and mother more than you need a friend.

I would also caution you not to chitchat regarding your children's character issues. You shouldn't hang out their dirty linen. If your children misbehave in public, acknowledge it and deal with it properly. Otherwise such issues are a family matter.

I was richly blessed at two different times in my life to have a prayer partner. We met almost weekly to pray exclusively about our children. It's amazing (or is it?) that I left such sessions exhilarated, thankful for my children, and motivated to be a better mother.

FRIENDSHIP DURING YOUR CHILDREN'S SCHOOL YEARS

As your children begin school or you start homeschooling them, you will find that there are new, but limited, opportunities for friendships. Children take time; their activities take lots of energy, not to mention logistic maneuvering. Your circle of contacts will widen with school activities, sports, music, projects, and field trips. Indeed, you may find your life to be even more demanding than you had previously thought possible, particularly as your children become more involved in both extracurricular and church activities.

When your children reach high school and beyond (especially college age), there will naturally be more time for cultivating new friendships or refreshing old ones. It is during this season of life that you may be surprised by an ever-growing friendship with your own children. They are not as apt to be embarrassed by you and your old ways. They are fun to be around with no pretension. You know each other well, share so much, and have learned a mutual respect for one another.

During these years we used the Christmas holidays as a family vacation to include the boyfriends and girlfriends of our children. It gave us opportunities to get acquainted with their potential future spouses, and more precious memories were made.

FRIENDSHIP IN THE "GRANDMOTHER" YEARS

Then come marriages and new families. These are the years when one is needed not merely for familial advice and counsel but for assistance. Help with babysitting, transportation, homeschooling, school projects, sickness, and physical and spiritual needs is gladly rendered. Being a grandmother is the icing on the cake, and I have savored it to the full!

It has been a joy and a privilege to consider my children as close friends while still retaining the role of a parent, yet they must pursue their own friendships and you must continue to hold on to yours. "Make new friends, but keep the old; / Those are silver, these are gold."[1]

As you proceed into retirement years, it is a rich blessing to recount the many and different types of friends: friends you have maintained for a lifetime, friends with whom you may only make contact at Christmas, and friends you see only at special times of celebration (and others at times of bereavement). Although they may be few in number, they are the ones who know you well and still love you. They come to your side and you to theirs in grave times of need; they are the ones you speak with face to face, heart to heart. Exodus 33:11 says, "The LORD used to speak to Moses face to face, as a man speaks to his friend."

As an aside, I want you to refrain from being distressed when those whom you considered to be your friends part ways with you. Perhaps you needed to be friends only for a brief time. Perhaps there is embarrassment, a difficult issue, or a disagreement that can't be resolved. Such difficulties can often lead to the severing of a friendship. Some friends are like butterflies, hovering over and around, then flitting off to the next person.

Be thankful that you could meet a need for a time. Keep your door and heart open, giving thanks for those special times when you enjoyed those particular friendships.

There were times when I sought friendship but there was no response. During those times the Lord was my portion, yet he provided the friends I wanted in his time.

My friends have enriched my life, taught me many things, cried with me, laughed with me, given me experiences beyond my imagination, inspired, motivated, and encouraged me; they have strewn my path with love, kindness, and thoughtfulness by giving of themselves. I hope I have returned in kind.

Now in our sunset years I am able to devote my energies completely to my husband, who is and always has been my best friend (next to my true best Friend, Jesus, friend of sinners).

> You are my friends if you do what I command you. No longer do I call you servants, for the servant does not know what his master is doing, but I have called you friends, for all that I have heard from my Father I have made known to you. (John 15:14–15)

Yes, it is possible to have lasting friendships. Yes, it is practical and not necessarily problematic to enjoy real friendships. Yes, it is desirable to pursue real friendships. May the Lord make you, dear sister, friendly to all who cross your path and a true friend to those who need refreshing, and may you in turn be refreshed by the friendship of others.

Your sister in Christ,
BETTY JANE

STUDY QUESTIONS

1. Think of a close personal relationship you currently have with another woman. What are the character traits in her that you admire? What

is the common thread that unites you? How can you further cultivate your friendship?

2. Reflect on the ways that friendships may change throughout the seasons of your life. How can you effectively glorify God in your present season of friendships?

3. Have you been wounded by a close friend? What steps did you take to forgive and restore the relationship?

4. Proverbs 31:11–12: "The heart of her husband trusts in her, and he will have no lack of gain. She does him good, and not harm, all the days of her life." Meditate on these verses and make them a matter of continual prayer.

RECOMMENDED RESOURCE

Adams, Jay. *Shepherding God's Flock: A Handbook on Pastoral Ministry, Counseling and Leadership*. Grand Rapids, MI: Zondervan Publishing House, 1975.

CHAPTER EIGHT

Respecting My Husband: The Foundational Principles

Noelle Wilkerson

My dearest Noelle is a grand expression of God's goodness and loving-kindness. She is humbly dependent on the grace of God. She does not pretend to be righteous when she is not, nor does she use her sin as an excuse. She lives by the marks of repentance and faith as she strains forward to take hold of all that God is for her in Christ. It is her grace-filled life that helps me to pursue God's glory. Noelle lives what she writes, and she does so in a quiet, humble manner, without any fanfare. She is an excellent wife whose heart is focused in a Godward direction. I love her, trust her, and am enriched by her.

REV. JIM WILKERSON

"I believe nature has assigned each sex its particular duties and sphere of action and to act well your part, there all the honor lies."[1] —Abigail Adams

Dear sister in Christ,

Do you respect your husband? I suspect you would answer without even thinking, "Yes, of course I do!" But do you really respect him? In recent weeks, the Lord has laid this question heavily on my heart. I would like to take this opportunity to share some of my reflections with you in writing.

Before we take a closer look at the whole area of respect, let me give you a glimpse into my own life in the context of this great subject.

I wish I could say I have always respected my husband. I also wish I could say that I respect my husband all the time now. The truth is that I have not always respected him nor do I always respect him now. The Lord has worked in my heart and changed me, and I know that the work he has begun he will bring to completion in Christ Jesus!

After our fourth child was born, my husband and I were required by a mission agency to go through marriage counseling. We both learned and grew during that time. One of the things that stood out in my mind (although it seems very small in light of all that we learned) was that Scripture called Jim and me "one flesh." Instead of looking at a situation from opposing sides, we were to stand and look at it together. I was no longer to fight for my rights because I was no longer an individual but rather one flesh with my husband.

I struggled with respecting my husband as one with me in Christ. But gradually this truth became a relief to my soul. I was comforted knowing that I had someone on my side and that I was not alone with any experience or problem. It became a relief because I no longer had any fear. Jim was mine, and I was his. I had nothing to lose and everything to gain because we were one in Christ. My responsibility was to respect him in my one-flesh relationship with him.

Life did not change overnight, but that one biblical truth took root, and the Lord used it to set me on the road to respecting my husband.

WHAT IS RESPECT?

I fear there is a great deal of confusion in the church on this issue. Have you ever considered that it is possible to love your husband, yet not respect him? You can think of him fondly, even intimately, yet still not respect him. You can talk warmly to others about how you both met or extol his virtues before the church, yet, having done all this, still not respect him.

What does it mean to respect someone? Webster defines respect as "an act of giving particular attention and high or special regard, esteem."[2] Let's see if we can flesh that out a little more, adding a specific Christian emphasis. A wife respects her husband when she treats him both publicly and privately as the living image and representative of Christ in her home. This respect will transform her attitude, body language, tone of voice, and treatment of him. It is especially the case in those moments when she finds herself either disagreeing with, or aggravated by, her husband.

With this in mind, you must ask yourself a number of searching questions: Do I roll my eyes at my husband when he says something that bothers me? Do I say things to others about conversations we have had in private? Do I belittle him in front of others, either in or out of the home? Do I snap orders at him—even if he hasn't noticed that I am carrying the baby, the bag, and the covered dish for after church? Do I treat him as if he is stupid or ignorant? Do I betray his secrets? Do I talk to my parents (or, for that matter, his parents) about his shortcomings—even if I say them empathetically or purely for prayer? Do I assume that he should jump in as soon as he arrives home because I feel I need a break—a "tag-team" approach to childrearing?

We are all familiar with Paul's teaching on marriage in Ephesians 5. Paul calls marriage a "profound mystery." God gave it to us in order to illustrate the parallel nature of Christ's covenantal union with the church and a husband's covenantal union with his wife. As wives in the church, we are accustomed to hearing Paul's repeated call to submit to our husbands' leadership.

> Wives, submit to your own husbands, as to the Lord. For the husband is the head of the wife even as Christ is the head of the church, his body, and is himself its Savior. (Eph. 5:22–23)

This submission of the wife to her husband should parallel the submission of the church, the bride of Christ, to her Bridegroom, the Lord Jesus Christ. Since we live in a culture soaked with ungodly egalitarianism, this emphasis on submission is vital; we need to hear it. Yet Paul not only commands us to submit to our husbands but also commands us to respect them.

I fear that much of our treatment of this great chapter neglects the following command. Note closely what the apostle says in verse 33: "Let each one of you love his wife as himself, and let the wife see that she respects her husband" (Eph. 5:33). Here, on two separate occasions, Paul calls the husband to love his wife as Christ loves the church (vv. 25, 33). Such loving leadership requires the husband to die to himself and live a life of sacrifice toward his wife, fulfilling his role as a prophet, priest, and king. On her part, the wife is called to reflect the church's submissive and respectful posture toward her Savior (vv. 22, 33). In some books dealing with Christian marriage and biblical womanhood, you will find chapters dealing with submission that are strangely silent on the subject of respect. Perhaps we falsely assume that these ideals are synonymous. How easy it is to submit to our husbands without showing biblical respect and reverence for them. The Scriptures require both.

AN EXAMPLE TO AVOID

What does such respect look like in your home? Thankfully, Scripture gives us many examples, both bad and good, to warn and direct us. Let's look at several together.

First, 2 Samuel 6 gives an example of disrespect with a consequence. The writer tells us, "As the ark of the LORD came into the city of David, Michal the daughter of Saul looked out of the window and saw King David leaping and dancing before the LORD, and she despised him in her heart"

(2 Sam. 6:16). David had brought the ark of the covenant into Jerusalem. In his joy he danced before the Lord. How did Michal, his wife, respond to this public display of ardent devotion? The Scriptures tell us that "she despised him in her heart."

This attitude soon spills over into her words. The writer tells us:

> David returned to bless his household. But Michal the daughter of Saul came out to meet David and said, "How the king of Israel honored himself today, uncovering himself today before the eyes of his servants' female servants, as one of the vulgar fellows shamelessly uncovers himself!" And David said to Michal, "It was before the LORD, who chose me above your father and above all his house, to appoint me as prince over Israel, the people of the LORD—and I will celebrate before the LORD. I will make myself yet more contempt-ible than this, and I will be abased in your eyes. But by the female servants of whom you have spoken, by them I shall be held in honor." (1 Sam. 6:20–22)

We are told that Michal not only thought of David with disrespect but followed through with her thoughts and openly rebuked him. There it was: her lack of respect and reverence for the man God had put over her in love. It flew out of her heart and off her tongue. The consequence of her folly is revealed in verse 23: "Michal the daughter of Saul had no child to the day of her death."

Michal had an unbelieving heart. She neither treasured God's glory nor understood her husband's joyful worship. Ultimately she had no respect for the man God had given her. She saw him as a fool, but what she couldn't see was that his "folly" was for God. Her disrespect came as a result of her lack of trust in the Lord. She might have been jealous of him dancing before the female servants, she might have thought he looked silly, or she might have had her own ideas about how a king should act. Whatever the cause, disrespect overflowed out of her heart, "for out of the abundance of the heart the mouth speaks" (Matt. 12:34).

Michal openly rebuked the king, and the consequences were devastating. While we are not explicitly told that her barrenness was the consequence of her sin, it seems clear that the writer wants us to make this connection. God will not have his faithful servants mocked and demeaned. As he said to Abraham of old, "I will bless those who bless you, and him who dishonors you I will curse" (Gen. 12:3).

I encourage you to take this passage to heart. It stands as a stark warning to us whenever we feel aggravated by the apparent folly of our husbands. God watches how we respond in such moments. In his eyes, disrespect is certainly not a trivial matter. As a fool for Christ, your husband may participate in "dancing" in his zealous expression of love and devotion. It is worth reminding yourself that respect is a fruit of the heart that faithfully trusts in the Lord, in whose presence "are pleasures forevermore" (Ps. 16:11).

AN EXAMPLE TO FOLLOW

In contrast, let us consider the good example of Sarah. Peter describes her respect for Abraham: "This is how the holy women who hoped in God used to adorn themselves, by submitting to their own husbands, as Sarah obeyed Abraham, calling him lord. And you are her children, if you do good and do not fear anything that is frightening" (1 Peter 3:5–6). Regardless of Sarah's many weaknesses, which the Old Testament makes no attempt to hide, the New Testament remembers her for what she did right. She respected her husband, calling him "lord"! Peter calls us to follow her example. This respect flourished through her faith and her hope in God. As such she was not paralyzed by fear, doubt, and worry. Nancy Wilson makes this point well in her book, *The Fruit of Her Hands: Respect and the Christian Woman*. In it, she states, "Trust in God frees us to obey him without regret or worry. Where there is worry, there is no trust. A woman can submit to her husband, even if she thinks he is wrong, because she knows that a sovereign God rules over all to his own purposes."[3]

124

Lest you think wives need only respect their husbands when they behave like Abraham, Peter exhorts Christian wives who are married to unbelieving and disobedient husbands,

> Likewise, wives, be subject to your own husbands, so that even if some do not obey the word, they may be won without a word by the conduct of their wives, when they see your respectful and pure conduct. (1 Peter 3:1–2)

In these verses, wives are explicitly called to respect their husbands as an act of holiness in marriage. Now, my dear sister, your husband does not fall into the category of an unbelieving spouse. However, you are called to live as an example to others in your congregation for whom that might not be the case. You do this by carefully and meekly responding to your husband on those very rare occasions when he is less than sensitive to you before others in the church. At such times, rather than giving our husbands the "look," we should put on a spirit of meekness and gentleness. You must respect his position over you even if it is very hard to respect his momentary lapse of deportment. By such "right behavior"—showing respect for your husband—you encourage other women to lead their husbands to Christ without ever saying a word! How exciting!

In 1 Kings 1, you have another wonderful example of a wife's respect for her husband. You remember the context: although his father David had not yet died, and although David had assured Bathsheba that her son, Solomon, was the appointed heir, Adonijah (one of David's other sons) had just set himself up as king. Nathan the prophet informs Bathsheba of Adonijah's mischief and gives her counsel. What follows is particularly helpful because it exemplifies a wife's respect for her husband in the midst of overwhelming adversity. Bathsheba did not nag her rather decrepit husband. Instead she let David know that he was not being obeyed. In taking this stance, she allowed him to lead. David was the one making the decisions, not her. Look at the way she carried herself before her husband:

125

Bathsheba bowed and paid homage to the king, and the king said, "What do you desire?" She said to him, "My lord, you swore to your servant by the LORD your God, saying, 'Solomon your son shall reign after me, and he shall sit on my throne.' " (1 Kings 1:16–17)

After Nathan affirmed with Bathsheba the right of Solomon and the works of Adonijah, David assured them that Solomon would reign. Bathsheba then "bowed with her face to the ground and paid homage to the king and said, 'May my lord King David live forever!' " (1 Kings 1:31).

Now, of course, your husband is not a king. He does however stand under Christ as prophet, priest, and king over you and your household. Scripture commands that you respect him. As you deal with difficulties and as you feel overwhelmed by the trials of life, you should approach your husband by humbling yourself and informing him of all the relevant aspects of your concerns. This is the posture of faith through which you submit to the Lord, trusting him for all things, and by which you are liberated from fear and worry to respect and submit to your husband in his counsel toward you. This is not only for your good but also for his. If a husband is respected and trusted, he can work out his calling with great freedom. He has no fear of you going against what he has said or telling others what you think he should have said.

> The heart of her husband trusts in her,
>   and he will have no lack of gain.
> She does him good, and not harm,
>   all the days of her life. (Prov. 31:11–12)

RESPECT AS A PASTOR'S WIFE

It is important to realize that even though your husband is active in ministry and you know so much about the virtues of submission and respect, it does not necessarily follow that you will be a submissive and respectful wife. How easy it is for you to think that you respect your husband because you speak highly of him or admire his work, piety, and discipline, yet all the while constantly belittle him in those little telltale actions of everyday life that reveal your true posture toward him.

To be more specific, your husband, the pastor, is in a tough position. True, he has been called to be a pastor, and while this work brings much encouragement and joy, it can also be painful and unbearably heart wrenching. Your husband is preaching nothing less than the very Word of God. He cannot afford to be careless. Souls are at stake. Your husband has no power in himself to save people or do them any spiritual good by himself. Yet God will hold him accountable for the tenor of his ministry.

Think about this for a moment. Your husband will deliberate, study, and find great joy in God's Word. He will preach with the weight of dispensing God's Word and all its delights while people yawn, fuss at their children, and text with their phones. He will pray, weep, and counsel. People will misunderstand him. He will love people and encourage them, and many will love him back, but not all. Some will speak unkindly about him or stir up strife within the church. Some people will say that they want to serve, then be upset when they do not get their way. The church is set up by God, but it is filled with sinners—which includes the pastor, his wife, and their children. Members will sin against you and your husband, and you and your husband will sin against them. Sadly, over the years of his ministry in the church, your husband will be disrespected by many people; be sure you are not one of them. As a pastor's wife, you must respect him, keep his secrets, always speak well of him, hold your tongue, and absolutely, hands down, adore him.

If you have struggled in this area, ask the Lord and your husband to forgive you. Repent and seek the Lord's help. "If we confess our sins, he is faithful and just to forgive us our sins and to cleanse us from all unrighteousness" (1 John 1:9). "Draw near to God and he will draw near to you" (James 4:8). Humble yourselves before God that you may receive more grace (James 4:6). Ask God for more of his Spirit and set your mind on the things of the Spirit (Rom. 8:5), seeking to walk in step with the Spirit (Gal. 5:16). Ask him to help you before disrespect deceives you and slips out of your mouth. Consider the fact that your husband is loved by God and accepted by him in Christ, being sealed to life in him by the Holy Spirit. Consider also that your husband is perfected through Christ's offering of himself and is at the same time being sanctified (Heb. 10:14). Meditate on the things that you love about your husband. Remind yourself why you married him. Feed your heart and mind with his good qualities and know that you too are a sinner who expects to be loved even when you are not loving. Stay in the Word, go to church, and attend prayer meetings. Ask your husband what you can do for him and how you can help him. Pray for the Lord to help you to respect your husband. Trust your Father in heaven who has put you where you are and has planned the path for your life. Trusting the Lord with your life means you have the freedom to respect your husband. Trusting the Lord wholeheartedly makes respecting your husband a joy.

Here are a few more thoughts in closing. If you are a strong leader and like to speak your mind, be careful, especially if you have a quiet husband. As a pastor, your husband is faced with many challenges and situations in which calculated risks must be taken. Be careful you do not speak for him. Discussions are helpful; your input is important. Make sure you do not nip opportunities before they have time to flourish. Before you speak, ask yourself if you are leading your husband and therefore disrespecting his role as head of you. Additionally, if you are a quiet person who is naturally predisposed to letting your husband lead, and you find yourself saying nothing when he is in sin, you are not lovingly respecting your husband. If you believe that your silence is a display of respect, then consider Proverbs 27:5–6:

Better is open rebuke
    than hidden love.
Faithful are the wounds of a friend;
    profuse are the kisses of an enemy.

You can respectfully approach him and even respectfully approach the elders, if necessary. There is nothing respectful about letting your husband persist in deliberate, presumptuous, soul-ensnaring sin (Gal. 6:1). In this situation the opportunity for bitterness is often at your doorstep. Be very careful; this will invariably lead to disrespect.

A WORD OF CAUTION

If you spend considerable time watching television, watching movies, or being on the computer, be warned. Too much time around worldly examples of marriage is never a good idea. What you know is right from Scripture can easily be clouded by the constant bombardment of televised relationships dripping with disrespect. They may seem cute and funny on screen, but these godless women and their godless examples may well do more damage than you might ever care to admit. God and his precepts, not our culture, must always set the course for our lives. Lastly, if you struggle with your appearance and are constantly thinking or actively participating in improving yourself physically, then I would encourage you to look back at 1 Peter. Peter says,

> Do not let your adorning be external—the braiding of hair and the putting on of gold jewelry, or the clothing you wear—but let your adorning be the hidden person of the heart with the imperishable beauty of a gentle and quiet spirit, which in God's sight is very precious. (1 Peter 3:3–4)

I am not saying you should not care about what you eat or how you look. I am not saying you should not exercise, put on makeup, or dye your hair. The danger lies in the amount of time and thought put into your outward adorning. Practically speaking, if your mind is continually on those things, then it is not on the Lord, his Word, or respecting your husband. "Only do not use your freedom as an opportunity for the flesh, but through love serve one another"(Gal. 5:13). "Let each of you look not only to his own interests, but also to the interests of others"(Phil. 2:4).

Let us both press on toward our upward call in heaven, where we will one day live in the perfection of love with God and his redeemed creatures and where respect and reverence for one another will be practiced unhindered by sin.

Love,

NOELLE

STUDY QUESTIONS

1. What are three specific ways you disrespect your husband?

2. How can you combat the thoughts of disrespect in your own heart?

3. In the last section of the letter, where several approaches to respect are mentioned, which of these is most characteristic of you?

4. What is God's purpose for a wife's respect of her husband?

5. List some positive and negative examples of a wife's respect for her husband that are demonstrated in the culture in which you live.

RECOMMENDED RESOURCES

Peace, Martha. *The Excellent Wife: A Biblical Perspective.* Bemidji, MN: Focus Publishing, Inc., 1996.

Wilson, Nancy. *The Fruit of Her Hands: Respect and the Christian Woman.* Moscow, ID: Canon Press, 1997.

CHAPTER NINE

Sharing My Husband: With Whomever and Whenever

Joan Hamilton

It is the easiest thing in the world for me to commend this letter to you. Joan is my other and better half. For thirty-two years she has been the best of wives to me, unfailing in her love, support, patience, and forbearance. She has made my life complete, mothered and loved our four children, made our home a haven, and never complained when our house has resembled a hotel more than a home. I thank the Lord for her every morning in life.

REV. DR. IAN HAMILTON

Dear sister in Christ,

When I was a little girl, I had a notion that I would like to marry a farmer. I imagined living in a pretty farmhouse with roses around the door, a duck pond

131

in the yard, pigs grunting in the sty, giving us home-cured ham for dinner; cows mooing in the field over the back fence, giving us frothy milk to drink; and chickens scratching about, giving us fresh eggs for breakfast. I thought it would be lovely to have a little orphan lamb in the corner of the kitchen by the stove needing to be bottle-fed and to receive some tender loving care.

I actually don't know how well I would have coped with the reality of life on a farm. Later, when our son Jonathan was at nursery school, I shared the run to and from the nursery with a friend who was a dairy farmer's wife. I realized that year how different reality was from my idealistic picture of farm life. There were cows mooing over the back fence certainly, but I had not realized the level of smell that went with them, especially at silage time—nor the level of mud that was involved in farm life!

However, I fell in love with a man who was training for the pastoral ministry, and the farm never materialized—although there are many parallels between a minister's work and that of a farmer. A pastor seeks to sow the seed of God's Word throughout his ministry, both in and out of the pulpit. He prays for God to bless his ministry and looks for fruit in the lives and hearts of his flock. Like a shepherd, he cares for his sheep, seeking to get to know them, their cares and burdens as well as their interests and joys, so that he can preach wisely to all his people and pastor their hearts. How would I cope with the reality of life on this kind of farm?

A SCARY PROSPECT

If I am honest, the thought of marrying a minister scared me to bits. By nature I would far rather be in the background, in the kitchen with a tea towel, and not in any kind of public position or limelight. The whole public side of life was scary—people would be watching me and would probably know who I was, as my husband's first ministry was in a small town where everyone knew everyone else. If we were ever to have children, they would have to live with some public eyes on them. Would I be a hindrance to my husband? Would I be the kind of support and encouragement to him that I began to realize he would need? Would I cope with all the different demands and expectations that I could not even begin to imagine when I first wore my beautiful engagement ring with such joy in my heart? All I knew was that I loved Ian and that with God's help and by his grace, I would be the best "me" that I could be for him. I was delighted and excited at the thought of being Ian's wife but not so thrilled or excited at the thought of being a pastor's wife!

ENCOURAGING PROMISES

In those days, I found many promises in God's Word that encouraged me not to faint, but to trust God's mercy and strength to enable me.

> Blessed is the man who trusts in the LORD,
>   whose trust is the LORD.
> He is like a tree planted by water,
>   that sends out its roots by the stream,
> and does not fear when heat comes,
>   for its leaves remain green,
> and is not anxious in the year of drought,
>   for it does not cease to bear fruit. (Jer. 17:7–8)

Psalm 138:8 was a particular solace to my heart: "The LORD will fulfill his purpose for me; your steadfast love, O LORD, endures forever. Do not forsake the work of your hands." Above my bed, I pinned the words of Paul Gerhardt's great hymn, which John Wesley translated into English. When I went to sleep and when I awoke, it reminded me that God was not about to desert me and that he was more than able to help and strengthen me. We sang this hymn at our wedding. The whole hymn is great theology; here are three of the verses:

> Put thou thy trust in God,
> In duty's path go on;
> Walk in His strength with faith and hope,
> So shall thy work be done.

Leave to His sovereign sway
To choose and to command;
So shalt thou wondering own His way,
How wise, how strong His hand.

Thou seest our weakness, Lord;
Our hearts are known to Thee;
O lift Thou up the sinking hand,
Confirm the feeble knee.

EVERYONE IS DIFFERENT

I have come to realize over time that there is no such thing as a typical pastor's wife. Everyone is different, with unique gifts and qualities that will vary from wife to wife—and your husband needs you to be his own special and unique wife. Don't try to be what you are not. Of course, pray by God's grace to emulate godly examples of any lovely Christians you admire and respect—but do so within your own personality. The Lord made you uniquely to complement your husband, and you are his wife before anything else.

The wife is not subservient or inferior to the husband. Your ideas and opinions will always be needed and should always be valued by your husband; two minds working prayerfully together will hopefully arrive at better and wiser decisions. There needs to be openness, honesty, and awareness of each other's needs and thoughts at all levels. Your husband needs to know if you are struggling in some area or over a particular issue—and he may not realize that without you sharing it with him. It's good to talk!

Home should be a haven for you both and for any children the Lord may bless you with. Creating and maintaining that home will be the first call on your time and energies. There can be a temptation to look at others and feel inadequate, envious, or even bitter. We are all sometimes tempted to think that the grass in someone else's field looks far greener, juicier, and easier to digest than ours. But we cannot see into people's lives and hearts. We may be quite unaware of secret battles or sorrows that go along with that seemingly greener grass. Pray for the Lord to help you to be content wherever he places you—to look for the positives and to be grateful for them. Remember Jeremiah at the potter's house: we pots are all different shapes and sizes, colors, and designs with different functions to perform. The Lord has a unique ministry for you to do alongside your husband, one which no other couple will be able to do. Be the pot he meant you to be! "Behold, like the clay in the potter's hand, so are you in my hand" (Jer. 18:6).

SETTING YOUR HUSBAND FREE

I have always prayed that our home would be so ordered that my husband would feel free to minister and serve whenever and wherever. At some stages in our married life, that has been easier than at others! When our children were small, I found Sundays quite hard. Ian was focused on the services and had a sermon going around in his head, and I would arrive in church wondering if I were completely dressed! I knew the children were, but was I?! I used to think that a sheepdog would be handy to have to round the children up, keep them going in the right direction, and make sure that none of them wandered off task! That was especially true when our youngest child, Sarah, was born.

Develop consistent, manageable, and child-friendly routines to keep a manse calm and relatively organized on a Sunday morning!

Organization is the key. One Sunday I carefully wrapped the chicken in foil for lunch, placed it in the fridge instead of the oven, and hurried the children into the car—lunch was late that day! One other Sunday morning I managed to scratch our car on a low wall. It was a tight maneuver to get our car reversed out of the garage and around to the front, but I had done it hundreds of times. As I reversed this particular Sunday, with all the children safely belted in, I caught sight of our eight-year-old Rebecca in my rearview mirror. "Did you actually brush your hair?" I asked her and then heard the horrible sound of crunching metal against the wall!

Having children does affect your mental processes—especially on Sundays! But children are little for only a while. Believe me, all too soon, they are grown, getting married, and having children of their own. Try not to wish your children were on to the next stage of growing up but to enjoy them at each of the stages; they pass soon enough. I don't know if a mother's mental processes ever return to the pre-maternal state, though!

TOTALLY COMMITTED

In order for your husband to pastor his congregation effectively, he will need your full-hearted and 100-percent support. He is an under-shepherd of God's flock, and he will need your unfailing love, prayers, support, and encouragement. Our husbands need to know that we are behind them, interested, and supportive in all their endeavors for the Lord. You are in this together, and it will help other people to respect and receive your husband's preaching more easily if they see that you are respectful and supportive of him. Eve was Adam's *ezer*, his helper, so that together they would complete each other and be united in their love for one another and in their functions and functioning.

Sometimes there can be days or spells of time that are filled with a great sense of loneliness in the life of a pastor. Part of his job means that the buck will usually stop with him. He may be misunderstood or miscalled over decisions he has made or things he has said. Grave personal tragedies or dark spiritual concerns may be unburdened onto his shoulders, and there may be no one he can share them with—except you. You will be the one to whom he will turn. You may not be able to offer advice in every situation, but you can be a huge help by just listening, by making time to listen, and of course by praying that God will give him all the wisdom he needs for any given situation. We need to share ourselves unreservedly with our husbands.

There is often no set routine to a week, and some wives will find that more difficult than others. We found that having children brought a degree of structure and routine to life, a routine we all needed, so that family life could operate smoothly and give the children security. That will be largely your area of responsibility, for there will be times when your husband's plans will be completely knocked out the window by an unexpected phone call or ring of the doorbell—usually at mealtimes! My husband has always coped with interruptions to his day far more easily than I have.

A friend from my university days in Aberdeen introduced me to Amy Carmichael, and over the years I have been greatly encouraged by many of her books. In *His Thoughts Said . . . His Father Said*, she wrote a short piece on interruptions.

> The son wondered how it could be possible to sit in the heavenly places in Christ Jesus when life was so full of interruptions. Hardly an hour was without something that broke its ordered flow. One day as he sat by a mountain stream he noticed the lovely way of water when interrupted by the boulders that broke its ordered flow. The river turned each into an occasion for beauty. And he understood that it was possible to live the river's way if only he took the interrupting things, not as interruptions, but as opportunities, and indeed as very part of life.[1]

"BOULDER" OPPORTUNITIES

Interrupting "boulder" opportunities are very much a part of life. It has always helped me to consider Romans 8:28: "We know that for those who love God all things work together for good." "All things" allows for no exceptions. The Lord knows all about your boulder-strewn days before you even put your big toe out of your bed in the morning!

Your life will be on view perhaps more than if your husband were in any other line of work, but where God calls he also promises the required grace sufficient for the day's demands. You will have to share your husband with many others and not always at times that seem best for whatever is going on at home. But consider what Christ gave up for us, and that will help to put any little sacrifices into perspective. What if God had decided he could not face the thought of sharing his Son with this poor, sad, sin-stricken world? What if Jesus had counted the cost of leaving his heavenly home and decided not to bother—that the cost was going to be too hard to face? Where would we have been then?

"He who did not spare his own Son but gave him up for us all, how will he not also with him graciously give us all things?" (Rom. 8:32). God the Father has been so unselfish in his dealings with us. He did not hold on to his only Son but generously gave him to us. The Lord Jesus Christ selflessly gave up his intimate fellowship with God the Father and left all heaven's glories to come to this broken world to fulfill the Father's purposes of love for us. Paul's words in Philippians 2 put our selfish inclinations into perspective.

> Have this mind among yourselves, which is yours in Christ Jesus, who, though he was in the form of God, did not count equality with God a thing to be grasped, but emptied himself, taking the form of a servant, being born in the likeness of men. And being found in human form, he humbled himself by becoming obedient to the point of death, even death on a cross. (Phil. 2:5–8)

THE SPIRIT'S REPLICATING MINISTRY

What the Spirit first produced in Christ, he comes to reproduce in us. We are called to follow the Savior's example, to be unselfish with what he has given us, and to be generous-hearted in our sharing of what he has given. We must serve him humbly wherever, whenever, and however we are able by his grace. "What do you have that you did not receive?" (1 Cor. 4:7). God is no man's debtor. "Those who honor me I will honor" (1 Sam. 2:30).

Sharing my husband with whomever, whenever, has been an area in which I have had to pray for grace over the years and ask for a more humble servant heart. I have prayed that I would not be selfish with him so that he would not find it hard to be away from home whenever he had to be. And God is good. He answers prayer, not always quite in the way we think we would like him to or expect him to—but it is often through the briers that he causes blooms to grow in our lives.

Thou hast not that, My Child, but Thou hast Me,

And am not I alone enough for Thee?

I know it all; know how thy heart was set

Upon this joy which is not given yet.

I know it all; but from thy brier shall blow

A rose for others. If it were not so

I would have told thee. Come, then, say to Me,

My Lord, my Love, I am content with Thee.[2]

AN "OPEN PALM"

I remember reading a book by Isobel Kuhn many years ago, *In the Arena*, in which she spoke of learning to hold God's treasures or gifts on an open palm. Since all we have, including our husbands, has come from the Lord's gracious hand, we can trust him completely to give us the daily grace for the doing of his will.

God has given you a dear husband; pray that you will not be selfish with him, that God will give you a sharing heart for those in need around you who may make claims on his time when you too want to stake your claim. Hold him on an open palm so that God will be able to use him to bring blessing to many beyond your home and family.

My husband would usually be out doing pastoral visits four afternoons and possibly three or four evenings a week, depending on other church meetings and the midweek Bible study and prayer meeting. He has always felt that it is very important for him to get to know his congregation by faithfully visiting people in their homes. That takes time. In Scotland, he had over seven hundred funerals in the twenty years he was there, which also made a huge call on his time as he visited many different homes before and after the funerals. So there is a cost inevitably for the wife and family at home.

Yet I have always felt that I have had the benefit of Ian's company at other times when many other husbands are away at work all day or possibly even all week. Ian so orders his day that his mornings are usually spent in the study preparing, and we have coffee together and often lunch too. Once we had children at school, he changed his Saturday routine so that the afternoons were free for family time, and he has always been at home for the evening meal. For me, it has always been a help to know that if there were a choice, my husband would always far rather be at home with me than anywhere else in the world. That knowledge sweetens the time when he must be away!

We are all different—there are no two pastors the same and no two pastoral situations the same. Therefore the balance of time spent together as a family and time spent apart due to pastoral needs or demands will vary from one couple to another.

Life in Cambridge has been very different for us. We are no longer in a parish situation, and our children are now almost all grown up. We still feel as if we are about thirty-five inside our heads, and we want to run as if we still were, but our bodies are telling us different! Energy levels are not what they once were and so the pattern of our days has slowed a little bit. We pray, however, by God's grace, that we will still be producing green leaves:

> They still bear fruit in old age;
>> they are ever full of sap and green,
> to declare that the LORD is upright;
>> he is my rock, and there is no unrighteousness in him. (Ps. 92:14–15)

A GODLY BALANCE

Don't let the balance between ministry and family swing too far in either direction. A husband ought not to neglect his wife or family, and there is no substitute for time spent together. Pastoral duties must not push aside family duties or become an excuse so that the wife feels abandoned and the marriage comes under stress. Consider Ephesians 5:25: "Husbands, love your wives, as Christ loved the church and gave himself up for her."

There needs to be quantity as well as quality time together. There may be times when you have to hang up the "closed" sign and deliberately say, "No more people today; this family needs to leave the world outside its front door." There have been some occasions when I have felt so exhausted that we have done just that, and Ian has stayed home to help to support me.

Running a home and looking after children—especially young ones—is physically, mentally, and emotionally exhausting. It is when we are tired that the normal molehills of a day can become huge black mountains that threaten to crash on top of us. Prioritize and do only what is necessary so that you can have a rest at some point in the day. Jesus himself knew what it was to be tired. And he encouraged the weary and heavy-laden to come to him for rest.

> The LORD is my Shepherd; I shall not want.
>> He makes me to lie down in green pastures.
> He leads me beside still waters.
>> He restores my soul. (Ps. 23 1–3)

I remember William Still, my minister in student days, leaning over the pulpit one evening and saying, "You young folk sometimes want God's guidance to come with bright flashing lights in the sky, while the Lord wants you to use your sanctified common sense!" He wrote a helpful booklet called *Rhythms of Rest and Work*. At times you may have to be the one to point out that life is getting too fast and crazy and things need to slow down so that you can remember what your husband looks like!

GENEROUS HOSPITALITY

The Bible encourages us to have homes like little hospitals where people feel welcome and cared for. Christian hospitality is always seeking to minister the grace of Christ to broken and disordered lives.

> Do good . . . be rich in good works . . . be generous and ready to share.
> (1 Tim. 6:18)

Do not neglect to show hospitality to strangers, for thereby some have entertained angels unawares. (Heb. 13:2)

Show hospitality to one another without grumbling. As each has received a gift, use it to serve one another, as good stewards of God's varied grace. (1 Peter 4:9–10)

I have always prayed that the Lord would help us to create a home where people would feel at home when they came through the door. We need to pray for the mental attitude to see hospitality as a privilege. The joys are often very rewarding and encouraging. It is a wonderful privilege to have a home that you can use for the Lord. Some people are easier to host than others, but Scripture requires us to encourage one another, and in a unique way a pastor's home can be a place of refuge and welcome to needy souls.

Did our four children suffer or feel cheated with all the people we have welcomed into our home? I really don't think so. We have met so many lovely and interesting people over thirty-plus years of our marriage now, and I honestly believe that we all have been richly blessed through the people we have hosted in our home. The children have grown up knowing no different, and we have always encouraged them to be welcoming to whomever we have had in our home. I remember when David was very young and so eager to help that some unsuspecting guest had a whole plate of biscuits tipped into his lap in David's exuberance to be welcoming! I believe it has helped our children to be considerate and sharing in their attitude toward others. We have had the great joy of seeing our two married children often opening their homes to welcome others.

You may never know what lonely, battered, or needy souls you encourage by inviting them home for a cup of coffee. Don't get tied in knots about not being a brilliant cook. Most people are just grateful to be invited into your home and appreciate your care; they are not looking for elaborate meals. I knew how to make only scones when I got married; a sponge cake was beyond me, and my one attempt at broth soup before we were married could have been used to lay the foundations for an interstate. Indeed, Ian reckoned he needed a knife and fork to eat it! But a few recipe books and several trial-and-error disasters gradually helped to remedy my culinary weaknesses.

Often all that people need is a genuinely sympathetic ear and time to share and feel that their story will go no further than the four walls of your home. I remember having a new undergraduate in our home one evening; our living room was bursting for space with students. I apologized that she had to sit on the floor. She smiled sweetly and said "Oh, that's quite okay—it is just so lovely to sit on a carpet again!" It made all the work of having the students come for supper so worthwhile. Often we have had little lambs just needing some love and care!

I am praying for God's enabling power as you and I seek to live for Christ and support our husbands. As I have written this letter to you, I realize that I have often failed the Lord in these things. I have a wonderfully encouraging and thoughtful husband who has made it easy for me to be his wife and to cope with all that goes with being a pastor's wife, but I know I have not always got it right and I am still learning. I have not reached the point where this sharing of myself, my husband, our family, and our home is always easy. Holding these treasures on my open palm is a daily challenge and requires a daily coming to God for his help and grace. Maybe it is just as well that it is not easy, otherwise I might be tempted to think I could do it all on my own. We are called to persevere and keep running the race laid out before us, remembering that we have a great God, who is plenteous in mercy and forgiving to his struggling children. He delights to pick us up and set us on our feet again and again and again.

A SYMPATHETIC HIGH PRIEST

Be real, be yourself, and pray that God will richly bless and use your marriage. Pray that many souls will see your married life as a lived-out example of Christ's sacrificial love for the church and the sweet submissive returning love and service of the church to her Savior. May the Lord richly bless, equip, and guide you through all the days that lie ahead as you enter into the high calling of serving our Lord Jesus Christ and his church together.

> Since then we have a great high priest who has passed through the heavens, Jesus, the Son of God, let us hold fast our confession. For we do not have a high priest who is unable to sympathize with our weaknesses, but one who in every respect has been tempted as we are, yet without sin. Let us then with confidence draw near to the throne of grace, that we may receive mercy and find grace to help in time of need. (Heb. 4:14–16)

Your sister in Christ,

JOAN

STUDY QUESTIONS

1. Is there an area of your life that you sense you are trying to keep back for yourself, and are there nonnegotiable areas that you are telling God not to touch?

2. What we need is a greater view of our God, of his greatness, and of his infinite love. How do you think a bigger view of God would help us to be more selfless? Passages for reflection: Psalm 138:8; Isaiah 40:12–31; John 3:16; 1 John 4:9–10; Jude 1:24–25.

3. What will it mean in practice for you to have a servant heart in the home and in the church? Passages for reflection: "He went about doing good" (Acts 10:38b); 2 Corinthians 8:9; 9:6; Philippians 2:5–9; 3:12–14.

4. Do you think that God may not live up to his promise to give you "grace to help in time of need"? Read the promise in Isaiah 40:10–11 . . . such encouraging verses for mothers with young children! Passages for reflection: 1 Samuel 2:1–10; 2 Corinthians 1:20; Hebrews 4:15–16; 1 Thessalonians 1.

5. Sunday mornings are stressful times for mothers who are trying to shepherd children toward leaving home for church. Make a list of

simple tasks (age appropriate!), with a timetable, for all the members of your family to follow on a Sunday morning. This should help to keep things running smoothly and calmly until the moment you arrive at church. My girls used to like ticking the boxes for things accomplished. Passages for reflection: Proverbs 3:1–7; Ephesians 6:1–4.

RECOMMENDED RESOURCES

Carmichael, Amy. *His Thoughts Said . . . His Father Said*. Fort Washington, PA: CLC Publications, 1958.

———. *Rose from Brier*. Fort Washington, PA: CLC Publications, 1973.

Chantry, Walt. *The High Calling of Motherhood*. Carlisle, PA: Banner of Truth, 1986.

Elliot, Elisabeth. *Keep a Quiet Heart*. Ann Arbor, MI: Vine Books, Servant Publications, 1995.

———. *Let Me Be a Woman*. Carol Stream, IL: Tyndale House Publications, 1976.

Kuhn, Isobel. *In the Arena*. Singapore: OMF Books, 1960.

Leone, Sara. *Her Husband's Crown: A Wife's Ministry and a Minister's Wife*. Carlisle, PA: Banner of Truth, 2007.

CHAPTER TEN

Handling Criticism:
Two Approaches

Mary Beeke

*My dear wife Mary is my better three-quarters—my tenderhearted,
God-fearing, perfect-helper-for-me woman. She packs our days, weeks,
and months with love, kindness, understanding, and pleasure. Next to
Christ himself, she is God's very best gift to me. She is so lovable that
loving her becomes an automatic joy that cannot be restrained rather
than a duty to be done.*

*The whole church knows that she models integrity, godliness, and
kindness. Her simple, childlike humility of which she is not even aware
is a fresh joy all over again every day in the home and among the
church family. I thank her often for a peaceful, open relationship that
houses no secrets. I thank her for a twenty-plus-year, argument-free
marriage, even in times of great stress in the ministry when others
desired our ruin. She takes my ministry as seriously as I do, and often
is much wiser than I am.*

Her unflagging support and undying loyalty are beyond words. She is the sunshine of my life in winter's cold blasts. In her tongue is the law of kindness (Prov. 31:26). She is far and away my best friend and confidante. I love her more than yesterday and less than tomorrow. My ministry would be far less effective without her.

REV. DR. JOEL BEEKE

Dear sister in Christ,

You and your husband are on the verge of an exciting venture. You are both zealous for the Lord. You are eager to follow his call, though you may have some misgivings about the unknown future. Your husband is anxious to bring the gospel to lost souls with you by his side. You are dreaming of sinners being saved and saints growing in grace. I hope that you will always retain this energy and excitement for the things of God and for the promotion of his kingdom, because there is no greater cause than the cause of Jesus Christ. You are entering a vocation of utmost worth: your husband as the preacher and pastor and you as his close helpmeet.

I don't want to pop your optimistic bubble, but I need to warn you that there will be times when thoughts of the beauty and glory of God and his Word will be abruptly interrupted by the harsh words of the people you serve. Maybe you have experienced this already. Whether you have or haven't, I would like to share what I have learned from difficult experience, from my loving husband, and most of all, from rock-solid Scripture about criticism of a minister.

We all have tender feelings, especially about ourselves. Therefore dealing with criticism is a process that you will have to work through every time you are criticized. If you know what to expect and how to handle it, you will get through it more smoothly. So I would like to give you some advice: first, on how to be prepared before it comes; second, on how to receive it when it comes; and third, on how to deal with it and grow from it afterward. Finally I would like to share some thoughts with you, my sister, about how to lovingly criticize your husband.

BEING PREPARED

My dear friend, you may react to criticism of your husband in a variety of ways. Some pastors' wives see the discouragement of their beloved husbands and become defensive and angry at their critics. Some get depressed and overwhelmed. Some can let criticism roll off them. Some husbands internalize all negative circumstances of the ministry, so their wives feel hopeless to help. Some women remove themselves from the situation and don't care. And some wise women know when to listen, when to give space, when to encourage and comfort, and when to help. This is the type of woman I encourage you to be.

Criticism may not come today or even this year. Most ministers receive a "honeymoon period" that can last up to three years. But it will come, sooner or later. Knowing this is an important first step in dealing with it. How do we know it will come? God promised it would. When Jesus called his twelve disciples to follow him, he gathered them for a brief "seminary training." He told them to go out in faith, but he was very realistic: "I send you forth as sheep in the midst of wolves. . . . Ye shall be hated of all men for my name's sake" (Matt. 10:16, 22). He again reminded them of these matters just before his death on the cross. After serving his apostles the Last Supper, he encouraged them, "Ye are my friends. . . . I have chosen you . . . whatsoever ye shall ask of the Father in my name, he may give to you. . . . Love one another" (John 15:14–17). It seems that he was bracing them for his next words: "The servant is not greater than his lord. If they have persecuted me, they will also persecute you" (v. 20).

Servants who walk with the Lord will receive criticism. It will be painful, but it will also be profitable.

The underlying reason for this promise is the nature of our constituency. We deal with sinners. Some are saved; some are not. All are capable of criticizing us. But then we are sinners too, and some of the criticism will be founded, some unfounded. When the criticism is unfounded, persistent, and cruel, it becomes persecution. If we look into the shadows, we see Satan behind the scenes. He wrote the recipe for sin and confusion, and he loves to continue to stir the pot, especially in the church of God.

Another way to be prepared when criticism comes is for you and your husband to have a pulse on the congregation. Know when storms are brewing under the surface. Be proactive. Small problems are easier to deal with before they explode, sending shrapnel into the congregation. Private sins should be kept private; if they can be dealt with according to Matthew 18, and the member repents, then no further steps are necessary. Pray for balance. You don't want to ignore problems, sticking your head in the sand, but you also don't want to be a sleuth, examining the lives of your people with a magnifying glass.

A healthy dose of "people sense" goes a long way in the ministry. Loving all your people is the foundation, and I mean really loving them, whether they deserve it or not. But you can love them and still be fully cognizant that they are sinners of different sorts. You can be a big help to your husband in this way. Some men can read people well, but sometimes their wives have that sixth sense that goes a bit beyond their perceptions. I guess it's called women's intuition. Your husband will do well to listen to you if you have this.

That said, use your intuition cautiously, not judgmentally. Know what to expect from certain types of people. Beware of flatterers who fawn over you when you arrive; they may be the first ones to turn against you, and with that same energy. Closely related are those who crave special attention; if you treat everyone equally, they are hurt and can reject you. Similarly, the power-hungry work with you as long as they have some control and things go their way. But if you cross them, they see you as a threat and can turn church life into a battleground. Gossipers are like moles, working underground, disturbing the beautiful sod in the church and making a mess by dumping their piles of dirt. Those with a critical spirit can be a wet blanket on the joyful atmosphere of the church. In our experience and observation, the most severe persecution seems to come from certain individuals who are mentally ill. I say this with extreme caution, because we must have great compassion on these people. But you may encounter someone who is obsessed with destroying you. This person will not behave in a reasonable way, and it may be frightening. All these personality types are part of the motley crew that comprises the church of God on earth. But take heart: it's a beautiful variety, God will generously give wisdom to those who ask, and you will be the better for it.

Certain types of criticism can be prevented by your own behavior. In Micah 6:8, we read what the Lord requires of us, that is, "to do justly, and to love mercy, and to walk humbly with thy God."

These character traits will lay a good foundation for our relationships with our people. When we do justly, we simply do what is right. Our members will observe over time that we walk a straight path, and they will respect us and entrust themselves to the ministry of you and your husband. If we follow God's Word, then we have that same Word to fall back on if we receive criticism. If we are living outside the Word, then we are on our own and we need to be criticized.

Next, love mercy. Since our Lord and Savior Jesus Christ loved mercy, we ought to as well—not only mercy extended to us, but especially mercy shown to fellow sinners. Being recipients of God's mercy, we ought to have a burning desire for other souls to experience that same joyful relief from the wrath of God. Mercy was and remains the central plank of Christian ministry, and if our people sense mercy in our treatment of them, they will, with rare exception, treat us with mercy.

Naturally flowing from a heart that loves mercy are feet that walk humbly with God. Being aware of God's awesome holiness in contrast with your utter sinfulness will make you walk humbly before God and with the members of your congregation. This will create a bond with them

151

because they know you are not standing above them but leading alongside them with love.

These characteristics of justice, mercy, and humility can and must coexist with your husband's bold preaching against sin, because God himself is strong in his law and in his love. Thus, together you must be unapologetic in standing for the Lord. Don't be rough or harsh, for this will stir up matching abrasiveness in your people, but be loving and forthright. We cannot fake godliness in order to keep criticism at bay, lest our people detect our insincerity and despise us for it. Sincere godliness, wrapped in love, will allow our people to criticize us calmly and with love. The Lord knows our hearts and will bless sincere motives that honor him.

How can we obtain these Micah 6:8 traits? They come only from the Holy Spirit when we use the means of grace. Walking closely with the Lord, meeting with him daily in prayer and meditation, letting our hearts be instructed in the Word—these are the best ways to be equipped to receive criticism.

RECEIVING CRITICISM

Criticism will come to you in different forms. Someone may not like your husband's preaching. Another may find fault with his pastoring. Others may criticize your family or you in particular. There may be different opinions on how the church should be lead or in what manner women should be involved. The criticism may arrive by e-mail or straight from the mouth of the critic, sometimes calmly, other times with intensity. Or you may hear it through the back door. Often it will be unexpected.

In the course of preaching and teaching in the church, my dear husband, Joel, instructs our people to present criticism verbally, face to face. This tends to result in a more levelheaded interaction, and it gives both parties an opportunity to explain their positions and understand each other. Some follow this advice, but others choose to convey their feelings in another manner, and you have to accept that.

I do hope your husband shares these burdens with you, because you can give him love and support. You love your husband very much, and you are one flesh, but you are not often the direct recipient of the criticism, and thus you may be able to offer some helpful wisdom. Even as he explains the situation to you and opens his heart, he may come to some resolution himself. Often two minds are better than one, and if you have a strong, healthy relationship, you can make good things happen by the grace of God. Of course, you know that confidentiality is extremely important.

I believe your first response toward criticism should be to accept it with an open mind and heart. Stay calm, even if you are not calm inside. You can take time to analyze it later, but listen first. Why? Because we are servants—servants of the almighty God and of the people of our flock. We are sinners, though we are saved from those sins. Humility demands we listen thoroughly and consider any criticism that is leveled against us.

As we are listening, we will be formulating an answer. If we are in a face-to-face conversation, and we can convey a reply that we won't regret in a manner we won't regret, then we should answer right away. If steam is escaping from our ears, we should calmly say, "I need to digest what you are saying and pray about it. I will get back with you in two days." Written or backdoor criticisms spare us from needing to give an immediate response, and this is an advantage. However, the criticism is often harsher, because the critic didn't have to face us and may be bolder.

Everyone processes criticism in different ways and at different speeds. You and your husband have to know yourselves and respond after you have thought things through and come to a wise, God-honoring response. Even if the criticism was delivered by mail or e-mail or voice mail, do attempt to meet face to face to discuss it, or second best, speak over the phone.

As you or your husband receives criticism, there are several things to consider. (I recommend further reading of chapter 18 of my husband's book, *Overcoming the World*, where he goes into detail on these factors to consider.) First, try to decipher a motive. Does my critic genuinely want improvement in the church? Is love in his heart? Or is there an underlying factor, such as jealousy, revenge, unresolved anger, or low self-esteem? Give the benefit of the doubt, but do explore these possibilities. In the same vein, consider the source. While we must value everyone, we will receive a criticism differently from a mature believer who is involved in helping the church, compared to someone who chronically complains and does nothing to help at church. Listen to both, but you might respond differently.

Next, consider yourself. Critics are a gift of God. If we never had them, we would be very puffed up in ourselves, we wouldn't need God so much, and we would not grow. Don't ask yourself, "How can I get this over with?" but ask, "How can I benefit from this?" Remember, "iron sharpeneth iron; so a man sharpeneth the countenance of his friend" (Prov. 27:17).

Granted, criticism may come from individuals whom you might not call friends, but it's okay. It is still useful. Beware of your own weaknesses as you absorb their words. Do you get defensive? Angry? Hurt? Or do you calmly take it in and analyze the situation? It is helpful to have a method with which to work through criticism. For example: talk about it, write down possible responses, pray, sleep, pray, respond.

Consider the content. "Faithful are the wounds of a friend; but the kisses of an enemy are deceitful" (Prov. 27:6).

Others can open our eyes to different ways of looking at situations. Maybe our walk isn't matching our talk, or we may be overlooking some duty. We should be thankful for constructive criticism. When receiving criticism, we have to be like chickens: peck away at the food, eating the kernel, and leave the shell. We must take what is valid, apologize when necessary, resolve to change, and leave behind the rest. "Be ye therefore wise as a serpents, and harmless as doves" (Matt. 10:16).

Most importantly, consider Scripture and God's honor. Every action we do and every word we speak must be measured by Scripture. The Bible is our strength and our foundation, and in its pages are answers to every dilemma. The more we have it written on our minds and hearts, the better equipped we are for the joys and challenges of ministry. When we are criticized, we need to set aside our tender feelings about ourselves and bring to the forefront our tender feelings for God. Ask, "What is the priority in this situation? How can the honor of God be best promoted? How would the God whom I adore want me to react?"

Finally, consider Christ and love. Our ultimate example for enduring persecution and criticism is our Savior.

> Christ also suffered for us, leaving us an example, that ye should follow his steps: who did no sin, neither was guile found in his mouth: who, when he was reviled, reviled not again; when he suffered, he threatened not; but committed himself to him that judgeth righteously. (1 Peter 2:21–23)

He turned his back to the smiters. He willingly wore a crown of thorns. As he hung on the cross, he asked his Father to "forgive them; for they know not what they do" (Luke 23:34).

What love! It should be a small thing for us sinners to be loving and forgiving to anyone who comes against us. In our self-pity we may need to be reminded of his great sacrifice. Then we simply need to return to the cross and cry out to our Savior to help us forget about ourselves and instead to love and glorify him.

AFTERWARD

You and your husband have put careful thought and prayer into your response to your critic. You may or may not have agreed on a solution with him, but you have clearly conveyed your answer. Now the most important thing is to carry through with what you have resolved to do. Make sure your actions back up your words. Integrity is vital to the strength and validity of your ministry.

There are several things you should not do after a bout of criticism. Do not seek revenge; that department belongs totally to the Lord. Do not wallow in self-pity. Sometimes we deserve criticism, sometimes we don't, but life isn't always fair. "Count it all joy when ye fall into divers temptations [various trials]" (James 1:2).

Don't allow yourself to enter into a victim mentality. A husband and wife can feed pity to each other and drag each other down; don't travel that path. Don't get depressed. A bit of sadness is normal, but with prayer and Scripture, discipline yourself to count your blessings. Don't develop a negative attitude toward your people or the ministry. You knew you weren't entering a glamorous occupation. You are, however, in the most blessed of occupations. Don't get into the habit of blaming other people or circumstances for your problems; you are leaders and you need to take responsibility for yourself and for the ministry.

Remember, every experience of criticism or persecution is useful. I recommend that you do several things to gain the most from it. First, move on! Don't dwell on the problem. My dear husband buries himself in other work. It is good to have different projects going for this reason. If a problem arises in the church, you can deal with it, then get your mind involved in a project. Second, for your sake and for the sake of your critic, demonstrate that you have moved on by showing kindness to him. Be polite and friendly, not in an exaggerated way, but in the same manner you would treat any other friend. If he rebuffs you, just keep being friendly. My dear husband is an expert at this. He can't live with disharmony, so he goes out of his way to show love, sometimes meeting people in their trials in the hospital or the funeral home. Eventually hearts soften, though it may take years. Along the same line, demonstrate the Golden Rule. Be empathetic to your critic; he is a human being just like you. Fourth, remember that you are an example to your flock; make sure your leadership is humble and loving. Finally, walk closely to Jesus, in prayer and in Scripture and in behavior. Wear the whole armor of God (Eph. 6), wash one another's feet, pursue humility, and be joyful and thankful.

HOW TO LOVINGLY CRITICIZE YOUR HUSBAND

There will also be times, dear sister, when you, as your husband's best friend, will need to criticize him. Your husband is the face of the ministry, but you fill a very important, behind-the-scenes role. You have insights into the dynamics of the church. You might see something that can be improved on that your husband doesn't see, so you can influence him in a way that benefits the church. There is a power that comes with your position as pastor's wife. You have the power to drag him down and defeat him, or you have the power to build him up to fulfill all the potential God has given him. Always use that power positively and properly.

People vary in how sensitive they are in delivering and receiving criticism. You must know yourself and your husband in this way. My husband feels vulnerable and exhausted after preaching, so if I have constructive criticism, he asks that I wait until Tuesday to approach him about it. We have ministerial friends who are brutally honest with each other and just say it like it is, whenever it comes to mind. This seems unkind to Joe and me, but it works for them. Everybody's sensitivities are different.

A canvas must have a foundation of primer before the oil paint can adhere properly. Your regular encouragement, respect, and appreciation of your husband are like the primer, and your corrective advice is the oil paint. Don't let Proverbs 27:15 describe you: "a continual dropping in a very rainy day and a contentious woman are alike."

Rather, let your everyday conversations about church life be the setting in which you discuss your thoughts with your husband. As best friends, you can bounce ideas off each other and help each other. Be positive and pleasant. Give him space to make decisions. Respect his judgment. Respect his calling; it's a sacred thing between him and the Lord. Pray for him. Sometimes you will need to criticize something he is doing. If it is inconsequential and just a matter of personal preference, let it be. If it is more important, be wise as you criticize. Weigh it carefully. Measure it by the principles of Scripture. Aim for the honor of God and the well-being of the church. And do it with kindness and love.

Love is the rule. Your relationship is built on love. The gospel is built on love. Love is the first commandment. So whether you are gentle or forthright, love rules when you need to criticize. Keeping love in view will keep you aware that the problem you are addressing has a context. Don't let the problem become so big that it is the only thing you see.

Using the "sandwich principle" that my husband advocates will ensure that you keep things in perspective. Let me give an example. First comes the bread: "I love you, dear. You are very skilled at dealing with people at church, such as when you interact at coffee time." Next, the meat: "But I noticed that when teens who have piercings and tattoos approach you with a complaint, you brush them off." Finally, the second slice of bread: "I know you want to help them; you are very good at communicating with youth. Maybe we could talk about some different approaches to help them." Because you stated the positive with the negative, your husband will eat the sandwich.

Approaching your husband in private about your complaint is very important to protect his dignity. Hopefully you can reach a resolution; if not immediately, then over a space of time. I hope you never need to deal with a serious infraction of which your husband does not repent. But if so, you would need to follow the Matthew 18 principle that instructs you to confront him with a witness present, then go the church leaders if there is still no solution. Pray God this never happens.

Because the ministry deals with personal lives, you are in the public eye. Your husband teaches about family life, so your family is being watched to see if you practice what he preaches. To be honest, people are looking for cracks in the structure. I believe you need to find a balance between being transparent and not airing your dirty laundry. It is fine for you to share some struggles you have, but be careful about exposing your husband and your family beyond their comfort level. Inner family struggles should remain private, unless you make a well-thought-out decision to share it. It is fine to reveal human foibles of your husband (be sure to deprecate yourself too) but not something that he is sensitive about or that would make your people respect him less. It is fine to light-heartedly and lovingly jest about a quirk he has (if he's okay with it). I can do this with my husband's (lack of) singing abilities. But never, ever use a spiteful, biting tone to mock him in his presence or behind his back. You must always respect him so that your people will respect him too.

In fact, why not do the opposite and tell others about your spouse's positive traits? My husband is an expert at this, way beyond what I deserve. Why not go contrary to society and praise him to other people? Tell them how wonderful he is. You will set the pattern for others to do the same. You will demonstrate that a Christian marriage is full of joy. You will make your children and others feel secure. And you will give a shot of encouragement and joy.

CONCLUSION

My dear friend, God has chosen you for a most blessed life as the wife of a pastor. You are privileged to have a front-row seat to watch the workings of the Holy Spirit among your people. You also have the opportunity to lovingly support your husband in his position as a frontline soldier in the army of King Jesus. You will experience incredible joys, but you will have trials as well. But don't worry; our Lord is in control. He will be there with his grace to guide you through every stormy day and every sunny day. Trust him and follow him together with your beloved husband.

Your sister in Christ,
MARY

STUDY QUESTIONS

1. As you look forward to being at your husband's side as he enters the ministry, what are your expectations in the area of a relationship with your congregation? What are your hopes and dreams? What challenges do you expect?

2. What are some ways that you can prevent discordant relationships with members of your congregation? What are some potential situations in which you could not and would not want to avoid conflict?

3. What two portions of Scripture will help you when criticism comes? What are two practical principles that will help?

4. How do you normally react to criticism? How does your husband react? In what ways could you improve on your reaction? In what ways could your husband improve on his reaction? What are some specific ways you and your husband can work together to deal with criticism?

5. Read 1 Peter 2:17–25. How might this apply to a difficult, personal situation in the church?

RECOMMENDED RESOURCES

Beeke, Joel. *Overcoming the World: Grace to Win the Daily Battle.* Phillipsburg, NJ: P&R, 2005. See especially 142–157.

Somerville, Mary. *One with a Shepherd: The Tears and Triumphs of a Ministry Marriage.* The Woodlands, TX: Kress Christian Publications, 2005.

Strauch, Alexander. *If You Bite and Devour One Another.* Littleton, Colorado: Lewis and Roth Publishers, 2011.

Taylor, James. *Pastors under Pressure: Conflict on the Outside, Fears Within.* Surrey, UK: Day One Publications, 2001.

Wragg, Jerry. *Exemplary Spiritual Leadership: Facing the Challenges, Escaping the Dangers.* Leominster, UK: Day One Publications, 2010. See especially pp. 90–102.

CHAPTER ELEVEN

Conflict within the Church: Keeping Your Heart Pure

Sue Rowe

As a pastor of thirty-five-plus years, I sadly have some experience with church conflict, and as a result, so has my wife. It is hard to express what it has meant to me to be always confident that Sue was beside me. I have been tremendously blessed to know that she felt as called to be a pastor's wife as I did to be a pastor, to know that when I got home I wasn't going to have to convince her that we should stay in a particular church or even in the ministry, and to be able to minister to the congregation without worrying about whether she was going to say something inappropriate or end up in the middle of a situation I was having to address. Sue is well qualified by both her experience and her maturity in the faith to write this chapter. May you feast abundantly on the fruits of the

Spirit grown in the garden of pastoral life and pruned with the shears of conflict.

REV. DR. CRAIG ROWE

Dear sister in Christ,

Well do I recall many joyful "firsts" in my new role as pastor's wife, but in time I was faced with our first church conflict, and with it came great sorrow and bewilderment. I see now that I was very naive and ignorant of the depth of the sinful depravity of the Lord's beautiful bride, his church. I thought the church would be a loving and glorious place to serve the Lord. I thought that every member of the church loved Jesus, loved his Word and wanted to believe and obey it, loved each other, and loved my husband and me. I especially thought this would be true of the ordained church officers. Sadly, I was caught off guard when I got wind that slander, gossip, and criticism against my husband were circulating among the members of the congregation. I became troubled, confused, and disillusioned; my heart vacillated between anger and fear, and I mourned as I saw the depth of the depravity of my own sinful heart. I cried many tears, meditated on comforting psalms, and poured out my heart to God with fervent prayers.

Sadly, I am not alone in my church conflict sorrows. When asked to pen their thoughts about the role of pastor's wife, some women commented that they felt hated most of the time by most of the people in their church. They were given hateful looks and shunned and ignored in public. They grieved that some who had the most orthodox theology could be the most hateful, selfish, mean, conniving gossips bent on hurting their pastor and his family. They wished that they had been prepared to deal with "deeply evil people" who looked wonderful to everyone in public but who seemed to do all they could to destroy their pastor and his ministry. Conflict in the church is known to be the most common underlying cause for pastors to leave their churches,[1] and conflict management was the area of instruction they felt was most lacking in their ministry training.[2]

As wives, we deeply feel the hurts and rejection that can come when our husbands are ousted from the churches they were called to shepherd. Resolving the conflicts that led to the rejection, however, is not usually our responsibility. As wives of pastors, our involvement can often be compared to that of spectators who stand on the sidelines watching their husbands coach the game. If either the plays that are called or the style of the coaching frustrates the expectations of the players and spectators, conflict can result.

The Scriptures have much to say about the cause and resolution of conflicts. My purpose, however, is to share with you some of the things I have learned about keeping my heart pure and glorifying God both as a pastor's wife and as a spectator to grievous conflicts in the church. Such times have been filled with perplexity, much sorrow, and many tears for me, but God has used them to grow my faith in his steadfast love and to teach me more about loving him with all my heart, soul, mind, and strength and about loving my neighbor as myself.

Conflict can be simply a difference in opinion or purpose, or it can result when two people are in open opposition and sin against each other in word or deed. Not all conflict is bad; however, not all conflict is neutral or beneficial. James addressed the sinful heart causes of conflict when he stated that quarrels and fights are caused by warring passions and covetous desires (James 4:1–2). The apostle Paul provided a glimpse of the spiritual forces that are at work against the peaceful unity of Christ's church when he wrote, "We do not wrestle against flesh and blood, but against the rulers, against the authorities, against the cosmic powers over this present darkness, against the spiritual forces of evil in the heavenly places" (Eph. 6:12).

Actually, we should not be surprised and think that something strange is happening to us when we face a fiery trial arising from conflict in our churches. The apostle Peter said these trials "[come] upon you to test you" (1 Peter 4:12). Peter did not see the suffering as much as he saw the joy and blessing it would bring to God's people, and neither should we. Peter continues to tell us how to view the troubles that we do not bring on ourselves: "But rejoice insofar as you share Christ's sufferings, that you may also rejoice and be glad when his glory is revealed" (1 Peter 4:13).

As Peter sees it, the problem is not the real trouble; what is important is the view that we take of the problem and how we handle it. Trouble is common, and in whatever form it appears, we should realize that it is inevitable in this world of sin for all who live godly lives to suffer tribulation. Peter gives us another view of fiery trials when he says that they are nothing less than sharing in the sufferings of Christ. This does not mean that Christians enter into Christ's redemptive work: what Jesus did on the cross was full and final—nothing ever needs to be added to it! Rather, because Christians bear Christ's name, are united to him, and are brought into close identification to him, they share Christ's suffering by experiencing similar mistreatment because the world hates Christ (John 15:18, 19; 17:14). Christians (pastors and their wives) who stand on God's truth by faithfully teaching and living it through life and lip are to rejoice when they suffer for their faithfulness to Christ. We who serve Christ are surrounded by a great cloud of witnesses who have gone before us, persevering in faith, trusting God's promises, and obeying his Word. The writer of Hebrews 11 gives us a glimpse of the sufferings endured by some of God's faithful saints.

> They were stoned, they were sawn in two, they were tempted, they were killed with the sword. They went about in skins of sheep and goats, destitute, afflicted, mistreated—of whom the world was not worthy—wandering about in deserts and mountains, in dens and caves of the earth. (Heb. 11:37–38)

CLARIFYING CONCERNS AND RESPONSIBILITIES

Conflict can be one of the most painful aspects of church ministry. When it is the result of others' sinful desires or actions that are too serious to be overlooked, you and I may find ourselves tempted to escape or to attack. Whether we are spectators observing the conflict or one of the players offending or being offended, we have certain responsibilities related to our response to the conflict. We must first clarify the difference between our concerns and our God-given responsibilities in the conflict. As spectators, resolving the conflict in the church is usually not our responsibility. However, there may be issues surrounding the conflict and results from the conflict that affect us to the point of deep personal concern. These concerns may tempt us to worry, to be anxious, or to become angry and bitter. What does God want us to do with our concerns? Jesus taught that we "ought always to pray and not lose heart" (Luke 18:1), and the apostle Paul told us not to be anxious or worried about anything. To do so is to sin. Instead we are always to pray.

Paul wrote, "Do not be anxious about anything, but in everything by prayer and supplication with thanksgiving let your requests be made known to God" (Phil. 4:6). Notice the two requirements for prayer. First, prayer must always replace worry; second, prayer must be fervent, specific, and accompanied by thanksgiving. To thank God for the problem doesn't mean that we thank him for the ensuing pain and sorrow but that we thank him for the good he is accomplishing through it all. Our prayers are not just pleading that God remove the difficulties but rather that God's will be done in the circumstances to his glory and to the ultimate benefit of the church and to all who are involved.

Once we have clarified in our own minds each concern we have regarding a disturbing conflict and we have prayed specifically, fervently, and with thanksgiving about each concern, we need to list our responsibilities as they relate to our role in the conflict. Responsibilities are those things given by God for us to obey, and we cannot pass them on to anyone else to obey for us.

For example, consider that I am an offending party in a conflict and have offended a sister in Christ by sinning against her in some way. My responsibility is to confess and repent of my sin to God and then go to her, confess my sin, and ask her to forgive me for my offense against her. I must then do all I can to rectify the loss my sin has caused her and by this bring loving, peaceful reconciliation to our relationship. My concern is that she will forgive me, be willing to reconcile our differences, and be kind and tenderhearted toward me (Eph. 4:32). Responding to me in this way is her responsibility. I will pray for her to this end.

Let's assume that the responsibility for bringing a peaceful solution to the conflict is not mine but belongs to others. I still need to come to grips with the reality that I have the responsibility to keep my heart pure before God as I respond to conflict and the effect it has on me and on those I love. I do this when I resist the temptation to respond in sinful ways that are motivated by the feelings of my flesh (Gal. 5:16–21). I will be instructed by God's Word and motivated and empowered by his Spirit to respond with faith and obedience (Gal. 5:22–24). Jesus said it in a nutshell: to keep our hearts pure during church conflicts and in every other challenging situation in life, we must love God and love our neighbors. Both of these commands are other-focused. We are born into this world self-focused and loving ourselves. When we yield to life's temptations (which often ride on the coattails of conflict within our churches), either we are not loving God with all our hearts, souls, and minds, or we are not loving our neighbor, or both. Thus we should respond not with anger and bitterness, but with forgiveness; not with hate, scorn, and withdrawal, but with love; not with gossip and slander, but with kindness; not with worry and anxiety, but with thankfulness and patience; not with malice and evildoing, but with self-control; not with despair, but with hope; not with fear, but with faith.

Philippians 4 is a key passage that has helped me to know how to keep my heart pure during church conflict. Paul was a prisoner in Rome while he penned the letter to the church in Philippi, and I imagine the Lord was perfecting Paul's faith and teaching him to keep his own heart pure in that dark, lonely, and life-threatening place. Paul was suffering as a prisoner because he was not a people pleaser but lived for the Audience of One and made it his aim to please God.

On another occasion, Paul wrote, "For am I now seeking the approval of man, or of God? Or am I trying to please man? If I were still trying to please man, I would not be a servant of Christ" (Gal. 1:10). One way I keep my heart pure is by pleasing God alone and making this my life goal.

I find it interesting that Paul began the fourth chapter of Philippians by addressing two women, Euodia and Syntyche, and by entreating them to "agree in the Lord" (v. 2). Paul knew these women; they had labored side by side with him in the gospel ministry, and their names were in the book of life. There were evidently differences between them that were sharp and heated enough that even in Rome Paul was aware of them. Some commentators suggest that these women were the heads of two factions in the church. Yes, there was a conflict in this ancient church, and Paul asked a "true companion" (v. 3) in that congregation to help them to work out their differences. Paul entreated these women, these workers in the church, to "agree in the Lord," not to agree with each other. They were to have the attitude of humility before God and toward each other that Paul discussed earlier in Philippians 2:1–6.

When there are warring factions, disunity, and grievous conflict in my church, what can I learn from Paul's next exhortations: "Rejoice in the Lord always; again I will say, rejoice" (Phil. 4:4)? I must always praise the Lord instead of focusing on my own desires or worrying about what others may do. There is no situation in which I cannot rejoice, because no matter how bleak it may appear, I know that all things work together for good to those who love Christ (Rom. 8:28). God is surely at work, and he will bring good out of evil. Rejoicing in the Lord means I must glorify God by depending on his forgiveness, wisdom, power, and love as I press on faithfully to obey his commands and pursue a loving, merciful, and forgiving attitude toward all people, even toward those I may view as my enemies. I can rejoice in the Lord always in the midst of conflict, adversity, and deprivation because joy does not rest on favorable circumstances but "in the Lord."

"Let your reasonableness be known to everyone. The Lord is at hand" (Phil. 4:5). Paul tells us to be reasonable and lenient rather than severe, to be gentle, to display a meek, generous, and forbearing spirit that rises above offenses by not insisting on our own rights. I must admit to myself and to God the supposed rights I am claiming and yield these over to him. A right is something I have earned, and before God I have earned only one thing—death. "For the wages of sin is death" (Rom. 6:23). I must take the log out of my own eye so that I can see clearly enough to take the splinter out of my brother's eye (Matt. 7:1–5). I must trust God's mercy and take responsibility for my own contribution to conflicts instead of blaming and judging others or resisting correction when I am wrong. I must confess my sins to those I have wronged. As a spectator to the conflict, I may have slandered or gossiped or complained to others. These are my sins, and I must not excuse or ignore them. I will reap joy when I remember that "the Lord is near" to help me. He is near to me, the sinner, to me, the broken-hearted (Pss. 34:18; 51:17). I will reap joy when I ask him to help me to change sinful attitudes and habits that led to conflict or resulted from my response to conflict. I will rejoice in the Lord when God wonderfully turns my hard heart around and "renew[s] a right spirit within me" (Ps. 51:10).

Scripture often uses the words *heart* and *mind* interchangeably. Keeping my heart pure means that I must guard my thoughts by disciplining what I will and will not think about. Paul gives further steps for finding peace in Philippians 4:8–9.

> Finally, brothers, whatever is true, whatever is honorable, whatever is just, whatever is pure, whatever is lovely, whatever is commendable, if there is any excellence, if there is anything worthy of praise, think about these things. What you have learned and received and heard and seen in me—practice these things, and the God of peace will be with you.

Praying about my concerns is good, but it is not enough. I must also address my mind and my thoughts. I ought to replace anxious thoughts with thoughts that follow the eight criteria Paul lists. I can evaluate my thoughts by asking myself the following "mind filter" questions:

- Are these thoughts trustworthy according to truth?
- Are these thoughts worthy of lasting respect?

- Are these thoughts consistent with God's standards?
- Will these thoughts contaminate godly morals?
- Will these thoughts encourage genuine love and peace?
- Would I want these thoughts quoted in my name?
- Do these thoughts encourage eternal values?
- Does God look on these thoughts with approval?

Training my mind to think in disciplined ways will happen only when I practice these things. Peace will not arrive after the first attempt, but I will begin to see God's peace replace my anxiety and concern as I consistently practice persistent, fervent prayer with thanksgiving and with disciplined, God-honoring thinking. The peace of God, which surpasses all understanding, will guard my heart and mind in Christ Jesus (Phil. 4:7).

RESPONDING WITH FAITH

Whether we find ourselves as spectators or players, we keep a pure heart when we respond to conflict with faith. How do we do this? Faith has been defined as "believing the word of God and acting upon it, no matter how I feel, knowing that God promises a good result."[3] The "Hall of Faith" in Hebrews 11 records the names of many Old Testament saints who believed God's Word and were motivated to obey him—not by their feelings, but by their faith in God and in his promises.

> Now faith is the assurance of things hoped for, the conviction of things not seen. (Heb. 11:1)

> And without faith it is impossible to please him, for whoever would draw near to God must believe that he exists and that he rewards those who seek him. (Heb. 11:6)

The good rewards on which these early saints focused were eternal in nature. If we are motivated by our feelings, we will do only those things we feel like doing. These will be things that make us feel good, and the rewards we experience will be fleeting. The promises of God motivated the saints of Hebrews 11 to persevere in obedience to God even when God did not grant the rewards in their lifetime.

The goal of a faith-motivated response is to glorify God by trusting his promises and obeying his Word, no matter how I feel. Let me suggest three promises of God that can encourage a faith- and obedience-motivated response to conflict in your church. First, God promises a good purpose for conflicts within the church and the trials that come with them. He uses trials to increase our awareness of his sustaining power and his steadfast love (Pss. 55:22; 68:19). He uses trials to refine us, perfect us, strengthen us, and keep us from falling (Rom. 5:3–4; James 1:2–4). He uses trials to teach us that the Christian's greatest good is Christlikeness (Rom. 8:28–29; 2 Cor. 4:8–10). Second, God promises to give us wisdom to deal with the conflict (James 1:5–6). Third, God promises to comfort us by giving us grace to persevere through all the trials of life (1 Cor. 10:13).

God has promised to be with us in each of our trials. We may wonder where he is and what he is up to in it all, but 1 Corinthians 10:13 promises that God is faithful and that he will not let us be tempted beyond our ability to endure. He has promised never to leave us or forsake us and never to place something on our shoulders that his grace will not enable us to bear. This promise does not mean that our burdens will always be easy and make sense to us, but it means that God is in sovereign control of them from start to finish and that we can trust his faithfulness to fulfill all his good promises to us.

Meditating on God's promises is one way that the Lord instructs us, comforts us, and encourages us to respond to trials and conflicts with faith and not according to how we feel. Believing and obeying his Word, no matter how we feel, will help us to keep our hearts pure. Memorizing those promises will enable us to carry them with us all day long.

During one conflict I began to memorize large passages of Scripture, even whole psalms. When my thoughts became a maze of confusion with many unanswered questions, I was tempted to anger, despair, and fear. I desperately needed to have God's truth continually present in my thinking so that I could "take every thought captive to obey Christ" (2 Cor. 10:5). I needed to replace my thoughts with his truth, and memorizing his truth helped me to do just that. The moment I caught myself thinking despairing thoughts, I began to quote the truth-filled Scriptures I had been memorizing. Soon my faith was renewed, I was able to view my trial from God's perspective, and I trusted that he was sovereignly in total control of my seemingly hopeless situation.

IMPORTANCE OF PRAYER

The importance of prayer cannot be overemphasized. There have been times when I have prayed about a church conflict for so many months that I became weary and felt prayed out. At times I didn't even know how to pray anymore; I felt as though my prayers had become a broken record. Three things have proven to help me when I have been in such a sad state. First, my husband and I set aside special time each day to pray for each other and for the problem confronting us. Second, *Valley of Vision: A Collection of Puritan Prayers and Devotions* has given me rich, appropriately meaningful words for my prayers to God when I do not have many words of my own. Third, in one of our pastorates, the Lord provided me with the opportunity to be part of a pastors' wives prayer group that met every other week. Over a period of nine years, every one of the women in that group moved away to other ministries because their husbands were asked to leave their churches. We shed many tears and prayed many prayers, but God gave us each other as prayer warriors during our individual battles and heartaches. I encourage you to consider inviting other pastors' wives to get together for prayer on a regular basis.

The faithful saints mentioned in Hebrews 11 make up the cloud of witnesses that now surrounds us and testifies that God is indeed faithful to his promises. These saints of old believed the Word of God and acted

171

on it in spite of how they might have felt because they believed God promised a good reward. Even now the writer of Hebrews challenges us to "lay aside every weight, and sin which clings so closely, and let us run with endurance the race that is set before us, looking to Jesus, the founder and perfecter of our faith, who for the joy that was set before him endured the cross, despising the shame, and is seated at the right hand of the throne of God" (Heb. 12:1-2).

Growing strong in faith and obeying God's Word in spite of how we feel is hard work. If we are to grow strong in faith, endurance and perseverance are required. Just as athletes train themselves by disciplining their minds and bodies for skill and enduring strength, even so the Lord "disciplines us for our good, that we may share his holiness. For the moment all discipline seems painful rather than pleasant, but later it yields the peaceful fruit of righteousness to those who have been trained by it" (Heb. 12:10–11).

Dear sister in the Lord, we are in God's gymnasium together, and the beautiful reward of faith and obedience is that we will someday share his holiness.

HELPING YOUR HUSBAND

When a pastor becomes heavily involved with trying to bring peace to a conflict within the church, it is very important that his wife does not become offended by the poor treatment her husband receives and also become embroiled in her own conflict, thus causing her husband to have yet another conflict to address. She needs to be on guard not to think that the privacy of her own home gives her license to speak words of gossip and slander against those whom she considers to be offending parties. She needs to remember Paul's exhortation to "let no corrupting talk come out of your mouths, but only such as is good for building up, as fits the occasion, that it may give grace to those who hear" (Eph. 4:29).

Instead of tearing people down with our words to our husbands, we need to encourage our husbands to persevere in righteousness and faith as they do the work of the Lord in the church. We can share with our husbands how the Lord is encouraging us through his Word. We must continue to do good and to reach out with love, forgiveness, and patience toward those who appear to be working against our husbands and the Lord's work. We will not be able to do this in our own strength, but the Lord is always a very present help.

LOVING GOD AND LOVING MY NEIGHBOR

How do I express my love to God during conflicts within the church? I do this by keeping my heart pure when I trust God's steadfast love for me and when I respond with faith-motivated obedience to God rather than with feeling-motivated, selfish thoughts and actions. How do I love my neighbor with the same passion with which I already love myself? I do this by becoming a peacemaker. Ken Sande describes peacemakers as "people who breathe grace" and draw continually on the goodness and power of Jesus Christ so that they can bring his love, mercy, forgiveness, strength, and wisdom to the conflicts of daily life.[4]

What we experience during such trails is the precious process that James spoke of to suffering readers:

> Count it all joy, my brothers, when you meet trials of various kinds, for you know that the testing of your faith produces steadfastness. And let steadfastness have its full effect, that you may be perfect and complete, lacking in nothing. (James 1:2–4)

Our Lord is both the Author and the Perfecter of our faith. He desires to cultivate in us mature and complete faith, faith that brings glory to our Father, faith that stands strong in the storms of life, and faith that speaks about the great joy and riches of knowing and loving him. This kind of faith grows and is perfected in the environment of trials. Trials and conflicts are not joyous, but they are effective in producing steadfastness, and they will cause our faith to grow and mature and to be complete and whole. See your conflict not as an accident but as an opportunity!

> With love,
> Your sister in Christ,
> SUE

STUDY QUESTIONS

1. Where do conflicts come from?

2. Consider your role in a current conflict that affects your life. Are you a player or a spectator? What is your primary responsibility as a spectator? As a player?

3. Make lists of your concerns and responsibilities as they relate to a conflict and to your role in it. How should you handle your concerns? How should you handle your responsibilities? What changes do you need to make to glorify God in these areas?

4. How can you be a suitable helper to your husband when he is under attack?

5. How can you express your love for God during conflicts within the church?

RECOMMENDED RESOURCES

Bennett, Arthur G. *Valley of Vision: A Collection of Puritan Prayers and Devotions*. Carlisle, PA: The Banner of Truth Trust, 2001.

Fitzpatrick, Elyse. *A Steadfast Heart: Experiencing God's Comfort in Life's Storms*. Phillipsburg, NJ: P&R Publishing, 2006.

Sande, Ken. *The Peacemaker: A Biblical Guide to Resolving Personal Conflict*. Grand Rapids, MI: Baker Books, 2004.

Scott, Stuart. *Communication and Conflict Resolution: A Biblical Perspective*. Bemidji, MN: Focus Publishing, Inc., 2005.

CHAPTER TWELVE

Ministry Moms:
Perspectives from a PK

Sarah Ascol

Sarah is the first of six siblings born into a pastor's home. She grew up not only as a child of the manse but also as a child of the church. By God's grace she came to trust and love the Lord Jesus early and followed his call to serve in one of the hardest places in the world for two years. Today she joyfully uses her gifts to serve her church family as a preschool and children's coordinator while also working as a homeschool consultant, teacher, and tutor.

Sarah fully understands the challenges of growing up with a pastor dad. The Lord has enabled her to negotiate those challenges with grace, humility, and wisdom. I am grateful that she is sharing some of the insights that the Lord has given her along the way.

REV. DR. TOM ASCOL

My dear sister in Christ,

Throughout my twenty-eight years of being a pastor's daughter, I have done a lot of thinking about life as a pastor's child. I have watched my five younger siblings grow up in our ministry household, seen my parents wrestle with the balance of home and church, and listened to other pastors' children talk about their own experiences with this unique life. I have picked up a few things along the way, and I hope they will be helpful to you as you consider raising your own children.

YOUR PRIORITIES: GOD, HUSBAND, CHILDREN

First, I would encourage you to keep an eye on your priorities. We all need to be aware of what ranks first in our lives.

I love what Jesus says in Matthew 6:33: "But seek first the kingdom of God and his righteousness, and all these things will be added to you." In the preceding verses, he mentions several things that sometimes get in the way of our trust in God, and I think we can safely add, "do not be anxious about your husband, or your children, or your role in the church, or anything else that is looming large in your life" to the list.

Your God

Jesus shows us a better way, lining up our top priority while freeing us from the anxiety that so often plagues the daughters of Eve: "Seek *first* the kingdom of God and his righteousness" (Matt. 6:33).

This is step number one for any woman, and certainly for you as the mother of the pastor's kids. Let your first priority be your relationship with your Savior. "Work out your own salvation," as Paul encourages the Philippians (Phil. 2:12–13). Take the advice of the psalmist and meditate on the wondrous works and promises of God in the Scriptures (Ps. 119). In the midst of the craziness of life in a ministry household, hear the Father calling you to "be still, and know that I am God" (Ps. 46:10). Making Jesus your first priority and highest calling is the best thing you can do for your children.

Your Husband

Second, prioritize your husband. Don't give in to the temptation to put your children and their needs before him. Love their dad and work hard to preserve and prosper your marriage.

I have been blessed to watch my mom model commitment to marriage over many years. I have often heard her talk about her life's priorities, and the pattern is always the same: God first, then Daddy, then her children. As a child, that made me feel a little put out, but as I've grown up I have come to appreciate the comfort of having parents who place great importance on their marriage.

Ministry children have a front-row seat to the difficulties and stresses that come with different seasons of church life. Having the confidence that, no matter what, Mom and Dad are on the same team and committed to their marriage provides an anchor for them in the midst of ministry storms.

Your Children

Finally, put your children before the church. There are ministry families who would disagree with me on this point or agree in theory but in practice unwittingly sacrifice their children on the altar of ministry. I would strongly urge you, my sister, not to make your children casualties of your good desire to serve God in the church.

Consider Paul's admonition to Titus as to what he should teach different people in different times of life in the church. Paul writes, "But as for you, teach what accords with sound doctrine. . . . Older women likewise are to. . . . teach what is good, and so train the young women to love their husbands and children" (Titus 2:1–5).

Look at the qualities Paul lists in verses 4 and 5. It is no mistake that the first thing mentioned is love of husbands and children. After Jesus' command to seek him first, these two should be the greatest priorities in a ministry mom's life. Paul calls this "sound doctrine" or, as one commentator put it, "the type of living that corresponds with the gospel."[1]

177

My friend, your children are your ministry. They need you to help them to deal with their sin, demonstrate repentance and forgiveness, model Christ for them, and point them to the Savior.

GETTING TO THE HEART OF THE MATTER

Being the pastor's children does not keep your children from being what all children are—sinners. Neither does being the pastor's children give them a pass on their sin.

Knowing that your children will be sinful should cause you to remember that their greatest need is not to behave well on Sunday morning, learn all the verses in Sunday school, or greet church members politely. The greatest need your children have is to be reconciled to God.

It is common for children who grow up in a Christian environment to become so familiar with the story of salvation that it ceases to amaze them. This is doubly true for the pastor's children! Sister, you will serve your children well if you keep the gospel and their need of a Savior foremost in your mind and repeatedly present the truth of their sin and Jesus' sacrifice on their behalf.

One way to do this is to be serious about sin when they are young. Yes, it might be embarrassing for you as the pastor's wife to have to take your son out of worship to discipline him during your husband's sermon, but your child's eternal soul is worth much more than your own pride.

Additionally, be serious with your own. You too are a sinner, and consequently you won't be a perfect mom. When you sin against your children, be quick to repent. When your children sin against you, be a quick forgiver. It's hard to measure the impact that this kind of biblical repentance and forgiveness will have on your children.

Geoffrey,[2] a pastor's kid (PK) who is now active in lay ministry at his local church, remembers learning about repentance and forgiveness during his childhood years. He writes,

> One of the biggest and most life-changing lessons my parents taught
> me was the art and practice of repentance, real repentance, not on the

surface. We need an understanding that sin is mixed in all we do, and therefore we can always genuinely repent even when we do not think we have sinned against someone.

On the flip side, we were taught to truly and completely forgive, the definition of which is to choose not to bring to remembrance. When we forgive, it's over and buried and not able to be dug up again.

I have found these two lessons to be completely life altering. Rare is the man or woman who practices true repentance and forgiveness. I don't think we ever master it. But we should practice it often. "Never waste an opportunity to repent," is what Dad would say.[3]

Don't let your children's sin undo you, and don't brush it aside either. Instead, deal straightforwardly with their sins and your own. Model the biblical pattern of repentance and forgiveness, knowing the eternal forgiveness that Jesus offers is truly your children's deepest need.

THE CHURCH

Your labors in the mission field of your children's souls do not exclude you from service in your local church. To the contrary, a mother's work is an essential part of the church's ministry. There will certainly be various seasons in your life when God will open or close doors to other ministries, and you may find yourself serving as a Sunday school teacher, leading in women's Bible studies, or serving as a musician or church hostess. However, one of the greatest ways you serve your church is by your wholehearted devotion to the ministry of motherhood.

Several years ago, Pastor Walt Chantry wrote an excellent article entitled "The High Calling of Motherhood." Here is what he has to say about the importance to the church of the mother in the home:

It is a mother's task and privilege to oversee the forging of a personality in her sons and daughters. For this she must set a tone in the home which builds strong character. Hers it is to take great Christian principles and practically apply them in every-day affairs—doing it simply and naturally. . . . Woman's hope, the church's hope, the world's hope is joined to childbearing with continuance in faith, love and holiness. Young women, here is a life-long calling! It is the highest any woman can enter.[4]

As Chantry points out, by being a faithful shepherd of your children's souls, you serve not only them but the church as well. I have witnessed the reality of his words over and over again in my home church. The faithful work of a mother to raise her children in the nurture and admonition of the Lord serves as an encouragement to the greater body of Christ. As she applies the "great Christian principles" to her children's lives, she provides not only an example to others of godliness in the trenches of life but gives hope to her church and to her world of the continuation of the genealogy of faith. No matter where else you may serve, my dear sister, the enduring ministry to your children is a necessary ministry to your church.

PRIORITIES IN REAL LIFE

The Peterson family lives in Asia, where they minister among an unreached Muslim people group. They have one son, Andrew. While Dad and Mom are busy with their missionary work, Andrew is at boarding school a couple of hours away. He rarely goes home, and his parents don't often visit. During the summer, he stays with grandparents in his native land. The Petersons' ministry is flourishing, but what is going to happen to Andrew?

Hopefully he won't end up like a commenter on a popular PK blog, who wrote the following: "For my parents church always comes first, my brother and I have always had to sacrifice family time so my parents could do what they needed to at church. . . . Today I remarked that the church has stolen my family . . . and I honestly do feel that way."[5]

In contrast, here's what April had to say about growing up in a ministry home: "I think the biggest thing for me . . . is that we were never made to feel that the church was more of a priority than our family. That was huge for us. I've seen the effects of putting the church before the kids, and the family is not really close to this day (though I'm not sure the parents even realize it)."[6]

John, now a pastor himself, had this advice for ministry moms: "SPEND TIME WITH THEM!! Don't let 'The Ministry' become an altar on which you sacrifice your children and your family. You take care of the flock close to home, and God will take care of His Church."[7]

When you bring your priorities under the authority of Scripture, you serve your children in the best way. First is Jesus, then your husband, then your children.

DON'T FIGHT THE FISHBOWL

"[They] live in a fishbowl, or at least it feels that way. Everyone in the church knows [their] names and faces. . . . There is never the safety of anonymity. Details of [their] lives are known by people [they] recognize only from the church directory."[8] No, this is not the opening of some strange Christian spy novel describing the lives of covert operatives who have infiltrated the church scene. It's from a recent blog post written by a pastor's kid, describing growing up in a ministry family. Barnabas Piper, son of pastor John Piper, wrote the article he titled, "Sinners in a Fishbowl," to highlight one of the often downplayed realities of life as the pastor's child.

Piper continues, "With people watching every move, what room is there for a mistake? There can be no missteps, no dalliances, no failings. In short there can be no humanity. You see, PKs are no different than anyone else. We sin. We fail. But there is no being normal when everyone is watching."[9]

Although what some have called the "fishbowl" phenomenon has often been dismissed as a result of hypersensitivity on the part of ministry families, those who have grown up in this environment echo a hearty "Amen!" to Piper's words. Let me share just a few examples of what other pastors' children have had to say on the topic.

181

The Fishbowl in Real Life

Christina wrote,

PRESSURE—I'm sure any PK will tell you . . . that at some point they experienced pressure to behave a certain way or be involved when they really didn't want to be. FITTING IN and STANDING OUT—There's some kind of desire to be just like the other kids at church while still wanting to hold on to the title and privileges of being a PK.[10]

John recognized the reality of being on display too.

I realized very early on that people were looking to me to do things right, to have the answer, to be an example. For me, this wasn't something to resist or resent, just something to accept, and in that sense, it was both a challenge and an encouragement. It's a hard thing sometimes to think that everyone is watching you, but at the same time, what a privilege!

I sometimes wish I had been able to be a little more "anonymous" in my growing-up years. True, it was and is a privilege to be an example for others, but it certainly takes its toll sometimes.[11]

Beth adds,

There is also a tremendous amount of pressure on pastors and their families. They receive a lot of criticism. My parents emphasized how we needed to set an example for others; we always had to be on our best behavior. When we did misbehave, the consequences were big, because there were always people watching.[12]

Redeeming the Fishbowl

Yes, the fishbowl is real. Your home life will be "on display," and your children will grow up in an unusual environment. Everyone will know them, and everyone will be watching. That may sound threatening and even depressing to hear, but, as my sister Grace put it, "It's not bad, just real." And that reality doesn't negate the fact that life in the fishbowl is a wonderful opportunity to put the gospel on display.

Every aspect of the Christian life should be filtered through gospel reality. With that in mind, the question changes from "How can I protect my children from the pressure of the fishbowl?" to "How can I lead my children to demonstrate the glory and goodness of God within the fishbowl?"

Here are a few practical ideas.

Don't Ignore the Reality. Your children are going to realize very quickly how much people are watching them and expecting from them. Ensure that you initiate conversations directing their thoughts away from the temptation of a bitter spirit. If you pretend that they are just like every other child in the church, you not only miss a fantastic opportunity to disciple your children, but also run the risk of making them think you don't "get it" so that they refuse to talk to you when the pressure hits.

Start and End with Jesus. Help your children to stop and consider our Savior. Was there ever a man more "on display" than he was? From the moment of his birth, when angels announced to the shepherds that a Savior had been born, he was an object of people's wonder, scorn, and close scrutiny.

I encourage you to lead your children in studying and seeking to emulate the life of Jesus. Read the gospel accounts, which demonstrate how Jesus related to people. When the expectations placed on your children cross the line from slightly annoying to hurtful, direct their thoughts to what Peter says of Jesus, "When he was reviled, he did not revile in return . . . but continued entrusting himself to him who judges justly" (1 Peter 2:23).

Model Grace under Pressure. It's not just the pastor's children who live under the constant eye of others. You do too. As you seek to follow Christ, set the example in dealing with pressure. Through the many expectations placed on the pastor's family, demonstrate to your children a life resolved to seek out what God would have you do, not what others might think you should do.

Determine, by God's grace, to help your children to learn what Beth did.

> I truly believe that God blesses His children. He always equips them with everything that they need to face every challenge. 1 Corinthians 10:13 has always been such an encouragement and help to me. God never places us in situations that we cannot handle. As hard as it is to be in a pastor's family, you can trust that God will see you through all the challenges.[13]

Be Your Children's Champion. Cultivate a gracious response and seek to put the gospel on display, but don't leave your kids to just "deal with it." As Piper says, "Fishbowls are for fish, not people."[14] Your kids need to know that you understand Piper's statement and that you will help others to understand it too.

That's what I mean by championing your children. Make your home a safe place where your children don't have to think of themselves as "the pastor's kids" but can be *your* children. Resist the temptation to place unwarranted burdens on their shoulders. It is all too easy for parents to require standards from children in order to please people. There really are only two eyes that matter: those of our heavenly Father. Be willing to speak for your children, especially with other adults in the church who may be inadvertently singling them out and holding the bar too high.

John, another pastor's child, commends his parents for not adding to the pressure of growing up in a ministry home: "Even though I knew many people were looking to me to set an example, and my parents certainly encouraged that, I don't remember them ever pushing it on us. They never made a big deal about 'We're the PASTOR'S family . . . ,' they just expected us to live as Jesus would call us to and let the rest play out."[15] Leslie's parents did the same: "My parents made sure that we were treated no differently. We were to try our best to please Christ like every other Christian, it didn't matter that our dad happened to preach. No extra pressure."[16]

SHELTER IN THE STORM

I would also counsel you to shelter your children from church conflict and crisis. I wish I could assure you that your church will never experience the heartache that sin and spiritual attack bring, but it is highly likely that it will. We have an Enemy who loves to attack the people of God, and pastors (and their families) seem to garner his special attention.

The Reality of Conflict

When a church is in crisis, the children of the congregation are not immune to the stress, pain, and confusion that it brings. The pastor's children are particularly at risk in this area. In an article for *Baptist Press* titled "Be Kind to PKs," Gene C. Fant Jr., grown-up PK and professor at Union University, writes, "Too many times, pastors' families bear the painful brunt of church conflict."[17] Another pastor referred to the hurt experienced by pastors' children as the "much too common collateral damage" of conflict in the church.[18]

As a pastor's child, I have had many opportunities to witness the local church under attack. I have had Sunday school teachers who just stopped showing up, have seen biblical church discipline in action, and have heard church members yell, "You're a liar!" at my father during a business meeting. Friends have left the church over doctrinal issues, personality clashes, and for reasons I'll never know.

That's one reason I think it is naive to assume you can completely shield your children from church difficulties. The older they become, the more they will pick up on the undercurrents of conflict, and your refusal to broach the subject will serve only to fuel their questions.

April recalls the impact of her parents' willingness to talk about church difficulties. "Another thing that added to our family's tight bond is that [my parents] didn't hide things from us, like when people were basically trying to 'starve' us out when they didn't like what Daddy preached."[19]

On the other hand, consider Psalm 127:4. In this passage children are compared to arrows. Arrows are meant to be launched out into the world, but not before they have been carefully crafted and prepared. Giving your children all the details, using them as a "sounding board," or asking their advice about church conflict would be akin to shooting an unfinished arrow through a fire. Not only will it miss the target, but it will get burned. When you take no measures to shelter your children in times of church difficulty, you set them up for disillusionment and bitterness.

I am convinced that the best way to shepherd your children through church conflict is to strike a balance between helping them to understand what is happening and protecting them from the details they do not need to know. This will be a learning experience for you in every circumstance and with each child. There are a couple of things you can do to prepare before a crisis hits.

A Firm Foundation. First and foremost, don't wait for a crisis to teach your children good theology. Of course, you do not need to pull out a thick tome to read to your three-year-old. But you need to start early in your children's lives, exposing them to what God says about himself, humanity, sin, the world, and the church. This builds a foundation that will give your children firm footing when life's storms hit.

Underscore to your children how great God is. Talk about Jesus' life, his power over sickness, evil, and even death. Read what he says in Matthew 16:18: "I will build my church, and the gates of hell shall not prevail against it." Knowing and believing that promise will anchor your children in the midst of conflict.

Faithful Friends. Additionally, introduce your children to believing adults outside your church who will give them godly counsel. My siblings and I have a group of "uncles"—other pastors whom we have known for a long time, men who have been in our home and have invested in our lives in various ways. They are men whom we can trust and call on at any time. In a time of church conflict, friends like these are invaluable. As you deal with your own emotions and seek to support your husband during difficult times, such men and their wives can minister to your family by praying for your children and making themselves available.

Peace in the Midst of the Storm

I sometimes jokingly refer to Psalm 55 as the "pastor's family" psalm. Verses 6–8 seem very applicable when the church is in the midst of conflict.

> And I say, "Oh, that I had wings like a dove!
>   I would fly away and be at rest;
> yes, I would wander far away;
>   I would lodge in the wilderness;
> I would hurry to find a shelter
>   from the raging wind and tempest."

By the time I was a young teen, verses 12–14 of this psalm had been highlighted, underlined, and starred in my Bible.

> For it is not an enemy who taunts me—
>   then I could bear it;
> it is not an adversary who deals insolently with me—
>   then I could hide from him.
> But it is you, a man, my equal,
>   my companion, my familiar friend.
> We used to take sweet counsel together;
>   within God's house we walked in the throng.

What betrayal is evident in these heart-wrenching verses! A feeling of betrayal can often be the most confusing and lingering emotion for a pastor's child, especially when friends and trusted adults are caught up in conflict against your husband.

Beth put it very simply, "It's hard to hear or see people criticizing someone that you love."[20]

How can you help your children to process what is going on?

First, speak simply and plainly to your children, giving whatever details you feel are pertinent and age appropriate. Try not to leave any unpleasant surprises for your children to discover accidentally on their own.

Second, invite their questions. Don't be afraid to admit that you don't know an answer or have no idea how God will work this trial for good. Just keep the conversation open and let your children know you are willing to talk to them.

Third, remove them, or give them the option to excuse themselves, from certain church gatherings. This is particularly important for younger children. If their presence is not required in a meeting where sensitive or difficult topics will be addressed, make other arrangements for them if at all possible.

Fourth, remind them of those trusted godly friends who are willing to talk to them.

Fifth, encourage them to be honest with God. I remember my parents telling me, "Sarah, God already knows what you are thinking, so go ahead and tell him. He is big enough to handle all your questions."

Sixth, point your children back to Christ. Despite your best efforts at shepherding them through difficult times, only Christ can heal the hurts and calm the storms in the heart of a pastor's child.

Psalm 55 doesn't end with lamenting and the desire to "fly away and be at rest." Instead, King David pens these words: "Cast your burden on the LORD, and he will sustain you; he will never permit the righteous to be moved" (Ps. 55:22). What a wonderful comfort in times of conflict! This promise is for the pastor, the ministry mom, and certainly the pastor's children.

PASTORS' CHILDREN BELONG TO GOD

My final encouragement for you is to view your children through the lens of gospel realities. While God has given you these children to nurture, and while they are children of the church, ultimately your children belong to God. He made them, he owns them, and he will fulfill his purpose to bring glory to himself through their lives.

Jesus, the Hope for Pastors' Children

One of the greatest fears for a ministry mom is that her children will grow up hearing the truth of their need of salvation but choose to reject it and go their own way. There are many heartbreaking stories of pastors' children who do just that.

Should this happen in your home, I urge you to fight hard to remember the gospel. The same Jesus who rescued you from your sins is the one who can rescue your prodigal daughter or son. The redemption he offers is the only hope for the pastor's children too.

Pray for your prodigals and let them know you are praying. Love them unconditionally and make sure they know it. Repent of your sins against them and forgive their sins against you. Don't condone their sin, but rather speak gently and honestly about it with them. Do what you must to shelter and shepherd any other children in your home from serious issues like drugs and alcohol abuse or physical danger, but do what you can to work for reconciliation with the children wandering far from what you have taught them.

Finally, leave them to God. Let the great Changer of Hearts do his work in his time. His sovereign purposes are not thwarted by your child's sin. Trust that he is working out his plans for his glory and rest in the knowledge of his love for you, his own child.

All the Days Ordained

A framed cross-stitch of Psalm 139 hangs on my bedroom wall. My mom made it for me before I was born, and she has reminded me of these verses again and again. It is liberating to remember God's sovereign knowledge of our lives, how he wrote out all our days before even one of them came to be.

Sister, any children you may have are ultimately not yours, nor do they belong to the church—they are God's. He is the one who has knit them together in the womb. He is the one who has written out the story of their lives. He is the one who fashions them in his image, creating them to bring glory to himself.

At the end of the day, when you have tucked the last little one into bed and fallen exhausted into your own, wondering if you really have what it takes to be a mother to these precious children, remember that all your days (and all theirs) are already written by our heavenly Father.

May you say with the psalmist, "This is the LORD's doing; it is marvelous in our eyes" (Ps. 118:23), and trust your life, your home, and your children to the care of him who does all things well.

Press on, sister!

SARAH

STUDY QUESTIONS

1. Think through a typical day. Does the way you spend your time reflect biblical life priorities?

2. Walt Chantry, author of *The High Calling of Motherhood*, wrote, "Woman's hope, the church's hope, the world's hope is joined to childbearing with continuance in faith, love and holiness. Young women, here is a life-long calling! It is the highest any woman can enter." Do you agree with that statement?

3. What practical steps can you take to help your children thrive in the ministry fishbowl?

4. Read through Psalm 55 again. Can you identify with the psalmist as he cries out to God? How do Jesus' words in Matthew 11:28–30 complement the promise of Psalm 55:22?

5. In John 14:6, Jesus says, "I am the way, and the truth, and the life. No one comes to the Father except through me." How can this reality encourage you as you mother the pastor's children?

RECOMMENDED RESOURCES

Graustein, Karl, and Mark Jacobsen. *Growing Up Christian: Have You Taken Ownership of Your Relationship with God?* Phillipsburg, NJ: P&R Publishing, 2005.

Lloyd-Jones, Sally. *The Jesus Storybook Bible: Every Story Whispers His Name.* Illustrated by Jago. Grand Rapids, MI: Zondervan, 2007.

Plowman, Ginger. *Don't Make Me Count to Three.* Wapwallopen, PA, Shepherd Press, 2004.

Tripp, Tedd, and Margy Tripp. *Instructing a Child's Heart.* Wapwallopen, PA: Shepherd Press, 2008.

Tripp, Tedd. *Shepherding a Child's Heart.* Wapwallopen, PA: Shepherd Press, 1995.

Ware, Bruce A. *Big Truths for Young Hearts: Teaching and Learning the Greatness of God.* Wheaton, IL: Crossway Books, 2009.

Chapter Thirteen

Depression: A Dark Valley

Mary Somerville

My beloved wife is writing out of the crucible of her experience with helping me through the stubborn darkness of depression. As Mary's husband I want to bless her for her patience and the steadfast love that she has demonstrated all through our marriage and especially when I needed it the most. I know you will be encouraged as she shares our journey and how she was used of our Savior to minister to my soul from her reservoir of having walked with God and knowing his faithfulness over a lifetime. I can testify that God will make his strength known in your weakness and will guide you in using the comfort he gives to you to comfort others.

DR. ROBERT B. SOMERVILLE

Dear sister in Christ,

If you or your husband are going through the dark valley of depression, I want to give you the hope that we experienced. Just a few years ago, we were stripped of everything that we thought we needed—our health, ministries, work, beautiful home, and Bob's ability to think and feel normally. My heart goes out to you, knowing that a time of depression can be the most excruciating time of your life. I have seen the horrors up close. The pain of major depression may be greater than any other malady you are called to go through. It impacts your relationships with your spouse, children, friends, and extended family.

I write from experience. My husband—the strong man who was always cheerful, athletic, resilient, and hopeful no matter what, full of faith in God, taking his Word at face value, comforting anyone in the midst of his or her adversity—was himself in severe depression! *How could it be?* The man who had been my pastor for thirty-five years and then a favorite professor had become like a child needing my constant care.

The purpose of this letter is to give you not merely the reasons for suffering but my testimony of how God ministered to me. I want to share with you some of the verses that became my meat, drink, comfort, and encouragement. I want to tell you about the practical ways God ministered to me through the realizations that dawned on me and the wonderful nuggets of truth that I gleaned in a difficult place.

What were some of the issues that precipitated this depression? Bob had suffered from prolonged back pain due to a herniated disc. For more than a year, his pain was so immense that he could hardly walk. The result? An unsuccessful surgery and strong pain medication, culminating in two months of total debilitation. This had been preceded by two years of overwork and emotionally draining counseling.

Depression has many causes, both physical and spiritual. Many pastors and their wives experience depression as the result of similar circumstances: physical problems compounded by the weight of ministry, spiritual, and emotional burdens. You have particular stressors associated with ministry in your life. Since our bodies and souls are so interrelated, it is hard to separate out the direct cause.

Depression can be brought on by overwhelming grief or difficult circumstances, such as relationship problems, church conflict, a rebellious child, or severe financial problems. If you are a missionary wife, add to that list language barriers and cultural differences, feelings of inadequacy, and loneliness. Other causes can be unconfessed sin, failures, and other disappointments.

In Christian ministry, the physical factors are often overlooked but include exhaustion from years of overwork. One pastor called my husband to tell him that when he went into severe depression, a fellow pastor had counseled him to cut back because he was doing the work of five pastors. He was out of the ministry for five months and learned that he had to evaluate physical factors more carefully.

Chronic pain, injury, a thyroid problem, sickness, or lack of sleep can be contributing factors. Postpartum depression (not to be confused with a case of "the baby blues") can be caused by a severe hormonal problem. Medications taken for different conditions produce depression as a side effect. Eating disorders or a diet of fast foods and junk foods can also bring on depression.

What are the symptoms? Everything is black and hopeless! While there are different degrees of depression ranging from mild to severe, certain characteristics identify it. They are a depressed mood, markedly diminished pleasure in activities, weight gain or significant weight loss when not dieting, insomnia, psychomotor agitation, loss of energy, feelings of worthlessness or excessive guilt, diminished ability to think, indecisiveness, and recurrent thoughts of death or suicide.[1] My husband experienced all of these.

Your brain feels as if it is working in slow motion, and you are constantly fatigued. You have trouble concentrating and find it hard or impossible to make decisions. Sleep escapes you. You are restless and irritable. You have unaccounted-for pain. You feel like a child. You don't want to be alone, but you don't want to be around people or have to make conversation. All of this produces thoughts of death or suicide.

The mental pain is excruciating, and there seems to be no way of escape. You can't even escape in sleep. When combined with physical pain and exhaustion, depression is an incomprehensible horror. You truly wish to die. It is a living hell—the dark night of the soul!

I would like to help you to see some meaning in your suffering and show you how you can bring glory to God in the midst of it. God doesn't promise immediate relief, but he does promise to eventually wipe every tear from our eyes and make every crooked thing straight. As you deal with the physical and spiritual causes of your or your husband's depression, you may find complete deliverance. You will certainly find that God's grace is sufficient for each day as his power is made perfect in weakness. There is hope for you.

EXAMINE THE PHYSICAL FACTORS

First you must examine the physical factors. Sometimes they need urgent attention before the spiritual causes of depression can be addressed. God ministered to the physical needs of the prophet Elijah before he delved into the deeper cause of his depression (1 Kings 19). God sent an angel to give him food and drink and let him sleep before answering his questions. God has compassion on us. He knows our frame, and he is mindful that we are but dust (Ps. 103:14).

It is good to start with a thorough physical exam, including a thyroid test. If you are the one struggling with depression, as opposed to your spouse, ask yourself if you are in a hormonally transitional time of life. Then examine your eating and sleeping habits. Maybe you need to change your diet. Maybe you need to fix your sleep patterns. Sleep loss can impact your health and mood. Getting proper exercise is important. Are you taking one day in seven to rest? This is very important for both you and your husband. That is a creation ordinance and there are consequences if it is neglected (Ex. 20:8–11).

We are fearfully and wonderfully made, both physically and spiritually. There is a definite connection between the mind and body. John Piper points this out when he says, "What we should be clear about . . . is that the condition of our bodies makes a difference in the capacity of our minds to think clearly and of our souls to see the beauty of hope-giving truth."[2]

Our bodies are temples of the Holy Spirit. Taking care of that temple through good rest, nutritious meals, exercise, and proper supplements is a wise course of action and can even help with the affliction of depression. Then you can rest in the knowledge that you are doing all you can physically do for healing to take place.

What about psychotropic medicines? Aren't they also necessary to bring healing? We must consider that these drugs deal with the physical symptoms of depression, not the underlying cause. Dr. Ed Welch in his book *Blame It on the Brain* counsels us to use them carefully and sparingly:

> If the person is not taking medication but is considering it, I typically suggest that he or she postpone that decision for a period of time. During that time, I consider possible causes, and together we ask God to teach us about both ourselves and him so that we can grow in faith in the midst of hardship. If the depression persists, I might let the person know that medication is an option to deal with some of the physical symptoms.[3]

My husband found that medication was necessary for a period of six months to bring about the balance that was needed for him to return to normal functioning. He took it with the direction of those who were counseling him biblically as well as those treating him medically.

While the medical psychiatric community focuses on the physical factors primarily, we must focus on the whole person while not ignoring the physical. We know that the answer to our deepest needs is not found in a pill. Medication should never be our first and only plan of attack. Our inner person needs to be addressed. Welch further clarifies: "The bottom line is this: don't put your hope in medication. Be thankful if it helps, but if it becomes just another place to put your hope instead of Jesus, you are just perpetuating the cycle of hopelessness."[4]

While the body is being cared for, how do we care for the soul? We need to look to Jesus, the Author and Finisher of our faith, and tap into the resources in God's authoritative and all-sufficient Word to find the best way to handle depression from a spiritual perspective.

Dear sister, God desires to bring glory to himself through this circumstance as he displays his love and grace in your life. He is the Blessed Controller of all things. This hasn't come on you without his superintending over the events of your life. He designs to use your suffering to make you more like his Son, which will bring him glory. Remind yourself that he is working all things together for your good (Rom. 8:28–29). He is up to something good that can be grasped only by faith. He is pressing you closer to himself. He wants to become all your hope. Petition God to give you the perspective of eternity.

Because he loves you and has a goal in your suffering, your response to his immeasurable love will include some of the following things that you can do for his glory.

EXAMINE YOUR GUILT

Depression and guilt go together. Unlike the secular approach to depression, we as believers can face our sins because the price has been paid for them and God's great love motivates us to deal with them. We all stand guilty before the holiness of God, and we are drawn to examine our lives in light of the cross and repent of any known sin.

Scripture tells us that if we confess and forsake our sins we will obtain mercy (Prov. 28:13). As you come to God and confess your sin, you can know that it is covered by the blood of Christ (1 John 1:9). Perhaps sin has precipitated this depression. The Scriptures give us an example of this in the life of David. He wrote,

> For when I kept silent, my bones wasted away
> through my groaning all day long.

198

For day and night your hand was heavy upon me;
    my strength was dried up as by the heat of summer.
I acknowledged my sin to you,
    and I did not cover my iniquity;
I said, "I will confess my transgressions to the LORD,"
    and you forgave the iniquity of my sin. (Ps. 32:3–5)

The Holy Spirit's work is to let us know what grieves the heart of God in our lives. When we put other things in the place of Christ, they become idols. Though it's often hard for us to see our own idols, we can ask God to reveal them to us. Are we treasuring anything more than we treasure Christ? There are many things that can easily gain higher priority in our lives than Christ—whether we intend them to or not.

If so, you need to come to the Lord—the one who loves you—with a heart broken over your sin. Jesus died to set us free from such enslavement. His death made full atonement for it. You don't have to do penance for it or cower before him. Your sin is covered by the blood of the spotless Lamb of God. He wants to free you from it and release you to a life of love-motivated obedience.

If your husband is being persecuted for righteousness' sake, instead of becoming angry and bitter, you can rejoice and be glad because you are in good company with Jesus and with the prophets before you (Matt. 5:10–12)! When your husband is depressed and wants to give up, when his conscience is confused by all the slander, when he thinks that he must have done something wrong for his ministry to fall apart like this, remind him that this suffering is a badge of true ministry, and it is a privilege to suffer with Christ! Sometimes God removes our distractions, the things we think we need for joy, so that we can come to see their worthlessness and his supreme value. He alone is our source of joy.

SEEK COUNSEL

Seek counsel from a fellow pastor or his wife (or both) or a biblical counselor. My husband had trained hundreds of counselors, but he was humble enough to know that he needed one—not to figure out some hidden solution but to speak the same truths. When he couldn't see and he couldn't feel, his counselors could see and feel for him. They could remind him of God's promises and hold him accountable to obey. Men from our local church sat with him, comforted him, assured him that he was saved, gave advice, and prayed. This also gave me a chance to get out for the short breaks I needed. They were sharing our burden and so fulfilling the law of Christ (Gal. 6:2). Don't be afraid to seek help.

Your counselor may need to help you to *see your blind spots*. Sin is deceitful, which is why we need one another (Heb. 3:13). Sometimes as Christian leaders, we have to work harder to find people who will talk straight with us. Your counselor can help you to *make a plan to overcome the pattern of sin that you are struggling with*. You may need to seek forgiveness, go back and be reconciled, or do other hard things in order to take care of your sin, but God will strengthen you for the steps of obedience. If your own sin is not the cause of this depression, your counselor can still help you to know how best to handle the trials you are facing in a God-honoring way.

FIGHT THE FIGHT

Be aware that depression is a spiritual battle for your very life. There is more to your struggles than you can see. Scripture says that you are wrestling against the rulers, authorities, cosmic powers, and spiritual forces of evil in the heavenly places (Eph. 6:12). Satan is our adversary and wants to destroy us when we're down. Jesus said that he is a murderer and the Father of Lies (John 8:44). Satan is telling you that you are done and that God has abandoned you and that everyone would be better off without you. Perhaps you believe that your sins are too bad for God to still love you. *Don't believe Satan's lies.* God has a plan for you that involves this suffering. He will bring you through! That is his promise found in 1 Corinthians 10:13: God is faithful and will provide a way of escape.

READ YOUR BIBLE AND PRAY

Spend time with the Great Counselor. Take time each day to get into God's Word with pen and paper at hand to note any wonderful truth that he impresses on your mind (Ps. 119:18). This forces you to be definite and more personal in what he wants to say to you. *What is in this text that causes me to want to respond in obedience and praise?* Take comfort from the promises of hope that abound and cling to them even when they do not seem to be true. God's Word is ultimate truth—an antidote to distorted negative thoughts leading to hopelessness. Journal the lessons you are learning.

Dig into the biblical accounts of godly men who experienced the depths of despair. From the oldest recorded Scripture, you can read about Job's response to his severe testing. Who can blame him when he says that he longs for death and searches for it more than hidden treasures (Job 3:20–26)? We hear Moses pleading with God to kill him because his burden is too great (Num. 11:14–15). Elijah defeats the prophets of Baal and then collapses in exhaustion and asks God to take his life (1 Kings 19:3–4). Jonah gets angry at God and says, "O LORD, please take my life from me, for it is better for me to die than to live" (Jonah 4:3).

Yet even in their misery, these men knew that God was the author of life and he alone could give and take it. To long for death at God's hands is understandable, but planning suicide is a sin that we must run from. We must remind ourselves that taking our own lives is murder. Have a loved one help to prevent you from sinning in this way.

In each of the Bible accounts, we also see how God met these men where they were, both physically and spiritually. He brought them out of their doubts through faith in his promises to continue serving him. Jeremiah's eyes were a fountain of tears, and his heart was faint (Jer. 8:18–9:1). But in the midst of his sad lament, he gives one of the greatest expressions of hope found in the Bible. Let this key of promise bring you out of the dungeon of despair.

> The steadfast love of the LORD never ceases;
>> his mercies never come to an end;
> they are new every morning;
>> great is your faithfulness.
>
> . . . .
>
> For the LORD will not
>> cast off forever,
> but, though he cause grief, he will have compassion
>> according to the abundance of his steadfast love;
> for he does not willingly afflict
>> or grieve the children of men. (Lam. 3:22–23; 31–33)

As you read the promises in God's Word, put them in your own words and post them around your house. "Jesus Loves Me!—Perfectly, Sacrificially, Eternally, Extravagantly"; "God's forgiven a debt I could never pay!"; "I'm his!"; "God is faithful!"; "Jesus went to hell for me to make me his perfect bride!"; "Jesus' blood gives me victory over my accuser!" Set reminders for yourself.

POUR OUT YOUR SOUL

Voice your sufferings to God. Let him turn them into praises! He already knows what you are going through. You don't have to suffer in silence. When we don't even know how to express the agony of our souls, we open the Psalms to find that David has gone before us. God allowed this man after his own heart to go through every kind of trial and to record the full range of his emotions in song to bring light into our darkness!

Sometimes David confesses that he cannot see God. He lays bare his doubts, his fears, his anxieties, his anguish, and his sin, and God pulls him up out of the miry pit and sets his feet on a rock, making his footsteps firm. God puts a new song in his heart, a song of praise to his God (Ps. 40).

The psalms of lament are for you to use as templates for your pleas to God. You can pray them back to him and include your own lament, and, like David, follow it with your expression of trust, specific petitions in your trouble, and vow of praise or shout of praise to conclude. Let them inform your heart, which is sad and weighed down. Use a journal to record your responses. Some of these psalms of lament are 3, 5, 6, 7, 13, 32, 44, 60, 69, 74, 77, 79, 80, 83, 85, 88, 90, 123, 130, 137, and 142.

We used the "Shepherd Psalm"—Psalm 23—to sooth and comfort our hearts every night before seeking sleep. When you think you're in the valley of the shadow of death, it is comforting to know that your Shepherd is there with you.

Add to your journal things for which you can praise him every day. Do it to glorify God, not to raise your spirits. He is worthy. You can be like Paul and Silas, who sang in the prison cell. Use songs written by other Christians who have experienced God in suffering. The great Reformer Martin Luther often wrote about his struggles with depression. He recognized that Satan had a role in it, being the "accuser of our brothers" (Rev. 12:10) who causes believers to dwell on their past sins. Luther's great hymn has encouraged Christians for more than four hundred years. "A Mighty Fortress Is Our God" assures us that although our ancient Foe—Satan—is crafty, the Man of God's own choosing—Christ Jesus—will win the battle for us.

Choose a good hymn to read or sing every evening before you sleep. Put on praise music and sing along. As you pour out your heart before the Lord in psalms and hymns and spiritual songs, you will find comfort. We read the Puritan prayers and devotions from *Valley of Vision* on a nightly basis as another source of comfort. In it we are given the prayer, "Lord, let me find thy light in my darkness, thy life in my death, thy joy in my sorrow, thy grace in my sin, thy riches in my poverty, thy glory in my valley."[5] The way down is the way up.

A VIEW BEYOND SELF

Ask God for his strength to look outside yourself. Even in your depression, you can pray for and reach out to someone else on a daily basis no matter how you feel. It could be a phone call, visit, or note of encouragement. If

203

the love of Christ is in us, we will love one another (1 John 4:7). You may be surprised by the joy that you receive from giving to others. If your husband is the one in depression, you will also need that same strength to minister to his needs 24/7. I stepped back from teaching and my other ministries to care for my husband. I can tell you that God's grace and strength will sustain you as it did me. You will not even consider it a sacrifice to make your husband your first ministry—your beloved life's partner and dearest earthly treasure.

THE BRIDE OF CHRIST

Access the help of your church. Keep going to church even when you dread the thought of the next person asking you how you are doing. Although you feel like withdrawing, you need to seek fellowship with other believers, both at church and in your daily life. The church is God's provision for this very purpose (Heb. 10:24). This is where you will find strength and encouragement to persevere as others share the comfort they have received from the Lord (2 Cor. 1:4). Allow those who have been through this valley to tell you their stories to enlighten your way, just as I am doing with you.

You need help, support, and prayers from the whole church family. This we received in abundance, from meals to cards and notes of encouragement. It is important to be transparent and let the elders know exactly where you are. You will especially need lots of help if you are in postpartum depression and have children to care for. We received sacrificial help from our grown children and extended family who traveled across the country and from as far as South Africa to lend support.

DO YOUR DUTY

Fulfill your responsibilities as much as you can. Live a structured life. When you don't think that you can do what is necessary, ask God for the strength (Phil. 4:13). When you don't know what to do, do the next thing. Pulling back from meaningful work and activities only adds to depression and complicates the problem. God will give you perseverance. Don't forget to give your body periods of needful rest.

My husband went back to teaching as soon as he could. He had to learn that he had a new normal and needed to take precautions against relapse. He has to set limits for himself to guard and care for his health. But he is fully restored, and we thank God every day for the privilege of serving him and sharing with others how God's grace got us through.

Dear friend, above all, don't give up. Someday you too will be able to share your journey with others and bring them hope. God can bring beauty out of ashes as you persevere together. May your joy be wrapped up in knowing God. You are his blood-bought child. By faith thank him for this trial and ask him for his resurrection power to see you through. He understands what you are going through. He was here, and he is with you now. And it's so amazing . . . Jesus said in that same conversation with his disciples about dying to self, "If anyone serves me, the Father will honor him" (John 12:26). Can you imagine being honored by the Father for dying to self and living for his glory? He is the one who chose me, redeemed me, and kept me. He will glorify me in heaven. He has done anything through me that was for his glory by his Spirit, and he's going to reward me! What a giving God we serve!

> Weeping may tarry for the night, but joy comes with the morning (Ps. 30:5)!

Your sister in Christ,

MARY

STUDY QUESTIONS

God treats us as saints, sufferers, and sinners. In that respect, examine your life in these three areas.

1. As a *saint*: God wants to confirm you. Are you preaching the gospel to yourself every day? Are you reminding yourself of your continual

need for Christ because of your sin but seeing Christ's sinless life, work on the cross, resurrection, and intercessory work for you as sufficient? Read Romans 8 several times and list all that you have in Christ, from "no condemnation" to "no separation." Use this to guide your thoughts at your darkest times.

2. As a *sufferer*: God wants to comfort you. What suffering are you experiencing right now? (Physical suffering? Depression? Rejection? Financial loss? Misunderstanding? Standing alone? Cruel treatment?) What would dying to self and accepting God's will look like in your situation? In what ways would it allow you to truly share in the suffering of Christ and know him more intimately? Read 1 Corinthians 4:9–13 and 2 Corinthians 11:23–33; 12:9–10. List your sufferings like Paul does and boast about them as they display Christ's power in your weakness.

   a. Use Psalm 142 as your own psalm of lament. Read it several times. Does this express how you're feeling? If so, write out your own lament followed by your expression of trust, specific petitions in your trouble, and a shout of praise at the conclusion. Get your husband to pray with you for the specific petitions. Rely on God's promises rather than your feelings.

   b. Write a "thank you" for the privilege of knowing Christ in a deeper way through your suffering. Ask him to help you to grow in your trust of him—that he is *love*, and he is *good*; that he will do only what is best for you; and that he is powerful enough to bring life from dying to self.

3. As a *sinner*: God wants to confront you. In what area of your life do you need to appropriate Christ's resurrection power in conquering a particular sin? Talk about this with your husband or your biblical counselor to sort out your feelings and help you to deal with an offense against your Father in heaven. Make a plan for change by putting off the sin and putting on likeness to Christ through his resurrection power.

RECOMMENDED RESOURCES

Bridges, Jerry. *Trusting God: Even When Life Hurts*. Colorado Springs, CO: NavPress, 1988.

Fitzpatrick, Elyse M. *Because He Loves Me: How Christ Transforms Our Daily Life*. Wheaton, IL: Crossway Books, 2008.

———. *Comforts from the Cross: Celebrating the Gospel One Day at a Time*. Wheaton, IL: Crossway Books, 2009.

Piper, John. *When the Darkness Will Not Lift: Doing What We Can While We Wait for God—and Joy*. Wheaton, IL: Crossway Books, 2006.

Somerville, Mary. *One with a Shepherd: The Tears and Triumphs of a Ministry Marriage*. The Woodlands, TX: Kress Christian Publications, 2005.

Welch, Edward T. *Depression: A Stubborn Darkness*. Greensboro, NC: New Growth Press, 2004.

CHAPTER FOURTEEN

Loneliness and Bereavement: Common to All, Unique to Some

Shannon Baugh Onnink

I commend this letter on loneliness and bereavement to you without hesitation. As Shannon's second husband, I am not a pastor, and consequently I have a different perspective on life within the ministry. I stand on the outside, looking in on ministerial lives. Unquestionably, it is a life of immeasurable blessing, but it is also a life of trial. The Lord has clearly given Shannon an extra measure of grace to deal with sorrow. You will find that she has a voice of wisdom on the matter.

PETER ONNINK

Sister in Christ,

Grace and peace to you from God the Father through our Lord Jesus Christ.

You are embarking on a journey of unknowns, a journey that will be filled with blessings and joy but also with sorrows and disappointments. As you start out as a helpmeet to your husband, loneliness may seem silly. However, Christ prepared his disciples, and I follow his example.

For me the first year of ministry presented itself as a season of struggle. My husband was busy with the demands of the pastorate. I felt like a single parent, struggling to maintain sanity with small children while trying to be a hospitable pastor's wife. The busyness of my husband, and my being alone so much, caused struggles with loneliness. Later my husband was called to Haiti. This call meant extended times of separation and a move to a foreign country. My struggles with loneliness through this were intense and selfish. I have walked the path of loneliness through differing stages as a minister's wife, missionary wife, and widow. To a small degree I have some understanding of loneliness.

LONELINESS DEFINED

What is loneliness? The dictionary tells us that loneliness is feeling "sad from being alone."[1] It may cause thoughts such as, "No one knows the troubles of my heart. No one understands how hard this is." Loneliness can come from thinking too much about yourself and not thinking of others. Loneliness can come also from a difficult providence or calling. Some never struggle with loneliness, but many face it often.

We tend to forget who our Savior is. We forget the ostracism he faced while on earth. As Isaiah describes, "He was despised and rejected by men; a man of sorrows, and acquainted with grief" (Isa. 53:3). He had no one who understood him. His disciples could not comprehend his words, only understanding after his death. He was the companion of fishermen, harlots, tax collectors, and outcasts. He was in great demand to work miracles while being under constant scrutiny. His enemies were always waiting to ensnare him. People loved him not for who he was but only for what he did. They loved getting their bellies filled and seeing signs. He was rejected by his people, the Jews. Seldom did he have times of quiet rest, but he did withdraw and pray. He knew weariness, exhaustion, hunger, and temptation. He knew separation from his Father. Christ bore these burdens on our behalf, as Scripture teaches: we have a High Priest who "has borne our griefs and carried our sorrows" (Isa. 53:4). "He knows our frame; he remembers that we are dust" (Ps. 103:14). He wants us to "draw near . . . in full assurance of faith" (Heb. 10:22–24).

We should consider the calling of a pastor's wife in light of Christ's example. If our Lord suffered hardship, so will we. We are not asked to endure what he did, but our testing will strengthen, purify, and sanctify us into his image. It should not surprise us when trials come (1 Peter 4:12).

We will discuss loneliness under three headings: causes, cures, and comforts. First, let us consider some of the causes.

CAUSES

Isolation

Having been involved in seminary communities over the years, I have heard of pastors' wives being discouraged from making friends in the congregation. For their own protection and the protection of their husband's ministry, they are told to keep everyone at arm's length. There is some practical wisdom here, but wisdom should weigh all in the light of Scripture. It seems obvious that this advice could, and often will, lead to loneliness due to self-imposed rules of separation.

As we think through this advice, let us look to the ultimate ministerial example of Christ in Scripture. Did Christ keep from having close companionship with people? It is clear that he was not aloof. He openly embraced. He shared his private moments. He poured himself out in relationships. In sheer exhaustion he still made himself available to the people (Matt. 15:29–39). He shared himself openly even though he was misunderstood,

211

contradicted, and called a devil (Mark 3:22). Christ was sinless, though, and we are not.

So let us look at the apostle Paul, who called himself the foremost of sinners (1 Tim. 1:15). He opened himself up to getting hurt. Remember, John Mark and Barnabas went separate ways from Paul. He loved those men but was divided from them. Paul laid himself bare to people, suffering the pain of rejection and division. He ended up in a prison cell, writing letters to encourage others when very little encouragement came to him. With this in mind, let us be careful about holding back from relationships. This practice can hurt us, make us lonely, and rob us of opportunities to share Christ among those in our congregation.

In my counsel to you, I would like to add a caution as you diligently seek to follow our Savior's example. As the wife of a pastor, you should be friendly to all. Joy, patience, and love should characterize all your interactions. You should *be* a friend. This does not mean, however, that you can have friendships on equal terms with all people. Exercise wise caution when selecting those in whom you confide. Look for a true friend who loves the Lord supremely, respects your position as pastor's wife, understands the demands of your time, and prays with you.

Perfection

Most every day I put on a little bit of makeup. I want to cover my blemishes and those wrinkles that seem to be taking over. I have found that as Christian women, we do the same thing, both emotionally and spiritually. Before we go to a Bible study, church service, or prayer meeting, we cover those things in our lives that might make us appear less than perfect. We can yell at the children and then talk to the friend at the door in a perfectly composed manner. Our houses may be messy, but when company comes, everything is perfect. No one is fooled. We all know that others have trials, troubles, messy homes, anger, and sorrows, but we still pretend. We might be hiding a heart full of loneliness with a shallow veneer. God has made us to be social creatures. We are not islands of self-sufficiency. We are living, breathing humans with needs for love and friendship. Life has many joys that we should share and troubles that can be eased by companionship. For most of us, transparency does not come easily. Who are we really fooling in our cover-up efforts? Is God fooled? Certainly not! You can encourage others and yourself by being transparent.

Burdens

Demands of ministry may cause loneliness. Pastors have busy lives and long hours. Dinner might be interrupted, delayed, or missed. A couple might need immediate help. There may be a death or a suicidal young woman. There may be unexpected guests brought home. Family time may become difficult.

Pastors are expected to be there for the congregation. A pastor can be so burdened by the cares of his flock that he is exhausted mentally, spiritually, physically, and emotionally. There is no time for his dear wife who has waited to see him. Just think of her day . . . she awakens to find a sick child, the toilet is clogged, the dog runs away, a huge medical bill comes in the mail, the phone keeps ringing, a red crayon colors the laundry, the dishwasher breaks, and she hits her head on the cabinet. It is comical to consider in print, but dear sister, we all have these days. We all desire at times to go back to bed and start over. It is easy to grow discouraged, wanting so much to have your husband's attention. But he comes in preoccupied and overburdened with care. You do not want to make his day worse, so you bear your burdens alone. Loneliness is nearby and can take root.

Change

Being married to a pastor may mean that you move often and find it hard to make friends and leave them. Adjusting to a new place and congregation can be a cause of loneliness. You are the outsider. Your congregation may have people who have grown up together and have a lifetime of memories together. They can be insensitive to the fact that they are excluding you.

213

God may call you to foreign missions. He certainly called many Bible heroes to less than ideal situations. Jeremiah was the weeping prophet. Jonah was sent to deliver the message of repentance to those he hated. Moses could think of almost every reason why he should not return to Egypt. When Isaiah was called, he was willing to go but asked God how long. These men seem to have known some of the demands that the call of God would have on them.

The prophets of old were not treated well. They were lonely men. In Lamentations we read, "I am the man who has seen affliction under the rod of [God's] wrath" (Lam. 3:1). These words echo the lonely path of the prophet. The apostles certainly were not called to places of comfort either. Their record is one of beatings, rejection, prison, and death. As we are called to walk with our husbands in places of difficulty, let us remember these men and be encouraged.

I found loneliness profound on the mission field. Leaving our church was heartrending. Moving to a place where I did not speak the language, understand the culture, or desire to be was difficult. The Lord directs changes in our lives that may bring us to the very ends of ourselves in loneliness. These changes can be places to which he takes us or places from which he removes us. Just as he directed the paths of the prophets and apostles, sending them where he willed, he will direct our path. Following King Jesus has a great price. It has been this way down throughout time.

Rejection

There may be times in the ministry when your husband comes under attack. This is heart-wrenching for the pastor and will deeply affect his wife too. Lamentably, there are sad occasions when the church divides. There are attacks from within and without, and even the very people you have loved can turn on you. These can be seasons that are very lonely. You may also find yourself rejected by your own family. The cause of Christ has been known to cause division, even as Jesus said, "I have not come to bring peace. . . . I have come to set a man against his father, and a daughter against her mother" (Matt. 10:34–35). Guard your heart against loneliness and bitterness.

Loss

Loneliness often accompanies sickness and loss. As we struggle through an illness that keeps us from the fellowship of God's people, we can grow discouraged. It may be cancer, recovery from childbirth, or a broken leg that prevents fellowship. We may be called to walk the valley of loss; indeed, we will all taste the bitter cup of death as people we love are taken away.

Thought Patterns

Sinful thought patterns that are not mortified can cause loneliness. Many sinful, selfish thoughts fill our heads: "These people do not care about me. My husband does not love me like I love him. He only wants me to be his cook, cleaner, and need-fulfiller. Why can't my husband be thoughtful? Does anyone care that I am here alone? I have to do all the work by myself." These are examples of thoughts in seed form, which, if left unchecked, can fester and cause loneliness. Any thoughts that concentrate on ourselves, and not what God has called us to think on, can be poison to the soul. Not only can they contribute to loneliness, but they can be the cause of many sins, such as anger, bitterness, gossip, slander, and adultery. Would you willingly drink arsenic? No! You would be repulsed by the poison. Recognize these sinful thoughts as poison and flee them.

Having addressed some causes, let us now consider some cures. Struggles can be very difficult, and so in no way do I want to diminish the hardship, making it sound like there is a 1 + 1 = 2 solution. I recall many dark hours of feeling alone and full of sorrow, and I know that the struggles with loneliness are multifaceted. We have to address ourselves, our expectations, the world, and the Devil—quite an impressive list of adversaries. We would be foolish indeed if we thought there was an easy solution.

CURES

Rest in Christ

God blesses those who are obedient. He gives joy, and he answers prayer. He gives grace and his mercy is new every morning (Lam. 3:23). He always forgives the sins of his children and offers himself as a companion. He calls us friends and brothers and seals his love and friendship with the blood of sacrifice, securing unconditional love and acceptance. "He brought [us] to the banqueting house, and his banner over [us] was love" (Song 2:4). Here begins the combating of our thoughts and feelings of loneliness as we gaze at Christ. We think on him and consider his finished work. Sing psalms and hymns to him. Read poetry exalting him. Cultivate and guard your relationship with him. He is referred to in the Psalms as a shield, buckler, rock, fortress, stronghold, protection, comfort, and stay to our souls. Here is sure comfort and strength as we rest in our God.

A few years ago, I went on my dream vacation to Maine. While there I wanted to see lighthouses. I am intrigued by their lonely beauty. They occupy desolate, rocky regions, showing sailors the way to avoid and the way to follow. Most lighthouses are not visible from the land; they are out in the water, visible to ships. We took the opportunity of an airplane tour, and there they stood in the midst of the pounding waves and rocks, shining their lights. They are a poignant reminder of Christ. He stands amidst the turmoil and tempests of our lives and reminds us to follow him. He will keep us safe. You are not alone. "Come to [him] . . . and [he] will give you rest" for your weary souls (Matt. 11:28).

Consider loneliness as a tempestuous ocean filled with danger to your soul, and think of Christ as the light shining in the darkness, guiding you to safety. Of course, you must pass through the waters (Isa. 43:2), but you do not pass alone. He is with you to guide you and protect you. He loves you with an everlasting love (Ps. 136:23). We start to find our way out of the darkness of loneliness by looking to Christ. He gives buoyancy to our souls when they are in danger of drowning, and he saves us. Christ's work on the cross and the redemption he purchased for us are far richer and deeper than just our salvation. He has purchased the Comforter to abide in us. He has purchased fruits of the Spirit to uphold us. He has purchased wisdom and raiment of grace for us to wear, which is always sufficient for the day. Meditate on Christ and what he has done. Spend time learning in the school of Christ. Know your Savior and his love for you, and that knowledge will be a lighthouse to even the most afflicted soul.

The Word

Hide God's Word in your heart. "Keep your heart with all vigilance, for from it flow the springs of life" (Prov. 4:23). Many of our struggles start in seed form and grow into a huge tree of trouble, simply because we did not remove the small seedling of sin before it took deep root in our souls. John Owen says, "Sin aims always at the uttermost. . . . Be killing sin or it will be killing you."[2]

I am sure you have all spent some time pulling weeds. They are much easier to remove from the ground while the roots are tender and the plant is small. Let the roots dig deep, and pulling it becomes more difficult. Much more effort is needed to remove older weeds than the young, tender ones. So also it is with our sins. Be quick to weed out those sins that would harm your spiritual growth and harden your heart. This means watching over your thoughts and being careful to feed yourself with thoughts that glorify God, rather than thoughts that feed loneliness. You could supplant the thought that you are alone with the more truthful thought that you may feel alone, but God is always with you. We intentionally "put off" sinful thought patterns, seeking to "put on" holiness through the Word of God (Eph. 4:21–24).

Keep an arsenal of God's Word at your disposal, ready to do battle. The old practice of canning is almost obsolete, but it used to be part of the yearly routine to plant, harvest, and put up food for the winter. Women would spend days canning food for storage. When the winter came, their families would be well supplied. The Proverbs 31 woman is "not afraid of snow" because she has made provision (v. 21). Let us be wise and not be afraid of the winters of loneliness, because we have minds prepared with the food of God's Word.

Prayer

Are you having daily times of prayer? Do you expect to know the friendship of God if you do not avail yourself of him? Do you expect blessing and comfort if you do not talk to him? He desires, even commands, that you pray. This is a discipline that is often neglected. Carve out time each day for prayer. Jesus did this amidst the many distractions he had. Why would we think ourselves above the same need?

We are told in Hebrews 7:25 that Christ, our great High Priest, "always lives to make intercession" for his people. Why do we neglect such an example? Make prayer a priority. Talk to the Lord. He can fill your heart and satisfy your soul, sustaining you in the most sorrowful seasons of life.

Good Theology

Good theology helps us to be more than conquerors through the storms and trials that come our way. For instance, consider the doctrine of immutability. God never changes; he was the same yesterday, is the same today, and will be the same tomorrow. God sets an everlasting love on you. That will never change. Nothing can separate you from the love he has for you in Christ Jesus. These truths come alive when we know that God is steadfast, immovable, unchangeable, and immutable.

Related to God's immutability is his sovereignty. It also is a doctrine that brings great comfort. Our God is not a weak, impotent God of human making. He is the omnipotent, omniscient God of the universe. He has ordered all and is in control of all. He never sleeps or slumbers (Ps. 121:4). He has numbered the very hairs on your head (Matt. 10:30). The smallest detail is under his control. His sovereign plan will never fail. His love will never change. He is God.

A Strong Marriage

Guard your marriage. Your husband is one of the best friends you will have this side of heaven. Fit in coffee or a late-night trip to the ice cream store. If finances are tight, go for a walk or sit on the back porch talking. It is easy to grow apart as life gets complicated, so you need to be diligent, letting nothing come between you. Regarding intimacy, do not deprive one another in the marriage bed. Intimacy symbolizes and reminds you of your love, while keeping you from temptation.

Godly Friendships

Seek to be very wise as you prayerfully establish friendships. You may want to keep in touch with some other pastors' wives or friends from seminary. In your church, there may be wise older women in whom you can confide. Be careful in your choice. Choose those who will confront your sin and encourage you from God's Word. Ask them to pray with and for you. You do not have to confide everything, but be comfortable enough to share your struggles.

COMFORT

I hope that the cures mentioned above will be sufficient to provide comfort for you. My desire here is to share with you how we can help the body of Christ. Samuel Rutherford said, "The secret formula of the saints: when I am in the cellar of affliction, I look for the Lord's choicest wines."[3] Take from your sorrows and struggles the best comforts, and use them in helping others. We should glean from trials the lessons God has ordained for us. As we seek to sanctify our struggles for Christ's glory, let us remember to use these struggles as impetus to reach out to others. We are not to be self-centered but other-centered. Paul wrote, "Let each of you look not only to his own interests, but also to the interests of others" (Phil. 2:4).

As we seek to have the mind of Christ, who emptied himself for those he loved, we can use lessons learned to encourage people. What else do you think Paul means when he spends so much time in 2 Corinthians 1 telling us about the God of comfort and then telling us to comfort others with the comforts we have received? I want to challenge you to become aware of those around you. We can tend to be isolated and self-absorbed. If you are struggling with loneliness, could the women in your church be struggling with the same thing? Could you be like Esther, put in this place at precisely this moment to help the people of God (Est. 4:14)? I would assert, yes! God does nothing by accident but works everything out in a most wise, sovereign plan. Do not be stingy with the comfort of God. He is never stingy with you. Share the comforts and spend them all liberally, for he has showered comfort on you.

Think of the young mom with children. She doesn't want to get out of bed in the morning. The dishes are piled up, and there is much work to be done. She would rather spend the day watching television or reading romance novels in an attempt to cover her loneliness. What about the widow? She knew the love and affection of a man for many years. Now she goes to bed by herself each night, missing him more deeply than her heart can even communicate. Shopping and cooking for one is no fun. Her house, once shared with the man she loved, now echoes the silence of loss and death. There is the cancer patient, staring death in the face as disease ravages her body. She is struggling spiritually, not wanting to face each day as it brings more pain. She struggles to persevere through the hardship and loneliness. What about the wife whose husband is always gone and busy? He has very little time for her, and her heart aches. Then there is the mom whose nest is empty. She finds her home, once bustling with activity, very quiet. Loneliness has many faces. Look for these women, and share with them. Show the love and comfort of God. We do not have to look sad on the outside to be a brewing cauldron of sorrow. You cannot alleviate all the pain, but you can pray with, and for, these women. You can give them a smile, a hug, and a gentle word, use a Bible verse that has blessed you, or send a short note of encouragement.

After the death of my husband, it was as if the Lord opened my eyes to see more clearly the pain around me. Death had awakened me from my slumber. I had spent years in ministry, trying to help others, only to realize that I had never really known the depth of their pain. It was as if walking the valley of sorrow showed me how dark the human experience could really be. My readings in *Morning and Evening* by Charles Spurgeon encouraged me to use the urgency of grief as a catalyst for activity to help others. In doing for others and taking my eyes off my own pain, I found much peace and joy. I did not find the need to wallow in self-pity. I found that self-pity disabled and paralyzed me. I was encouraged and taught by letters from women who reached out to me. I was humbled by the realization of how callous I had unwittingly been. I was taught many lessons by the gracious hand of God in sorrow.

As William Cowper wrote,

The path of sorrow, and the path alone,
Leads to the land where sorrow is unknown;
No traveler ever reached that blessed abode,
Who found not thorns and briars on his road.[4]

This little couplet reminds us of the ultimate end of our sorrows. Be assured, dear Christian sister, that sorrow will come to an end and that heaven awaits. We always have hope, no matter how dark and dreary each day may seem. As the apostle Paul wrote, "We do not lose heart. . . . for this light momentary affliction is preparing for us an eternal weight of glory beyond all comparison" (2 Cor. 4:16–17).

This does not mean that our afflictions are light but rather draws a comparison to glory, which is no comparison at all. Glory will be so much better. Picture our afflictions as the moon and our glory as the sun. The sun outshines the moon and makes the moon's light seem but a very poor reflection. We endure, we encourage, we love, we serve, and we are conquerors in Christ as we hope in him.

Think of your Savior, robed in all his splendor. Angels surround him in his court, ever singing his praises. At his feet are the kingdoms of the

221

earth. He is the lover of your soul. He is the Savior who came to redeem you. Think of seeing your King of Kings. Think of him extending nail-scarred hands to embrace you. The trials of today don't compare. We shall see Jesus! Does not your heart rise in doxology to him? Let the clouds of loneliness dissipate in the radiance of his love.

Entering ministry is an adventure. I hope in some small way that I have encouraged and helped to prepare you. The life of a pastor's wife can be most rewarding. It can also be solitary. I encourage you, dear sister, to think about how God has sovereignly ordained these dispensations in your life. Remember your Savior. Consider how to respond to these providentially ordered circumstances and how you can bring him glory. For his glory is our chief end (WSC 1).

Your sister in Christ,
SHANNON

STUDY QUESTIONS

1. List some of the ways that Christ endured sorrows. How can this encourage you?

2. Which causes of loneliness do you identify with? List some of the wrong thoughts you have and a Bible verse to correct them. For example: I cannot do this anymore. I am so sad and lonely. Correction: Philippians 4:13: "I can do all things through Christ who strengthens me." And Christ was "acquainted with sorrows" (Isa. 53:3) yet he persevered. I can too.

3. How can doctrine help us when we are lonely and struggling? Think particularly of God's sovereignty and immutability.

4. List three cures for loneliness. List a verse that you can memorize which will help to prepare you to combat loneliness or to encourage others who are lonely. One of my favorites is, "For we do not have a high priest who is unable to sympathize with our weaknesses, but

one who in every respect has been tempted as we are, yet without sin" (Heb. 4:15).

5. Have you been encouraged by others? List practical ways you can share that comfort with others.

RECOMMENDED RESOURCES

Bonar, Andrew. *Letters of Samuel Rutherford*. Edinburgh, UK/Carlisle, PA: The Banner of Truth Trust, 1905.

Cook, Faith. *Grace in Winter*. Edinburgh, UK/Carlisle, PA: The Banner of Truth Trust, 1989.

Elliot, Elisabeth. *The Path of Loneliness: Finding Your Way through the Wilderness to God*. Ann Arbor, MI: Servant Publications, 2001.

CHAPTER FIFTEEN

The Lord's Day: A Hard Day's Rest

"Sissy" Floyd Pipa

Reformed theology is not merely a system of thinking but has always included an approach to living. There is a Reformed piety that springs directly from Reformed thinking. Foundational to this piety is the concept that the Lord's Day is the Christian Sabbath, which we are to sanctify by acts of public and private worship as well as Christian service. As R. L. Dabney wrote, "The sacred observance of one day in seven is God's appointed means for the cultivation of piety: when piety vanishes, orthodoxy necessarily follows it in due time."[1] The church today suffers greatly from the neglect and profanation of the Lord's Day.

My wife's letter grows in the soil of forty-one years of loving and keeping the Sabbath. This letter blends a brief biblical and theological foundation with practical suggestions. It is our prayer that God will continue to reform his church in her Sabbath observance and use this letter to encourage pastors' wives who labor with their husbands in this endeavor.

REV. DR. JOSEPH A. PIPA JR.

Dear sister in Christ,

I have been thinking for weeks about what I would like to relate to you as you contemplate your responsibilities as a pastor's wife. It would have been helpful for me to have had someone in whom to confide when I married and moved into the little white house next to our church. My husband had spent years preparing to become a pastor, yet I was thrust—with little preparation—into my role as a pastor's wife on our wedding day. As I have reflected on my life, I realize I could have done a far better job had I possessed, at the time, the wisdom that I have learned over the years through God's grace. However, when I become discouraged by my mistakes and inadequacies, I have found comfort in reflecting on God's character: his sovereignty in all things, his mercy, wisdom, and power. He often uses the weakest and most insignificant things of this world to accomplish his purposes.

When I met the man who was to become my husband, I had never thought about marrying a minister and becoming a "pastor's wife." I was rather naive. I did not realize that a congregation could, at times, place unreasonable expectations on the pastor's wife. Nor did I understand how a pastor's wife affects her husband's ministry. She can be a help to him, or she can damage his ministry.

Joseph Pipa was in his senior year at Reformed Theological Seminary (RTS) in Jackson, Mississippi, when he stopped by my family's farm on a lovely day in November 1970. On this particular weekend, God brought Joseph into my life. Here was the man who would teach me the sustaining beauties of the Reformed faith and prove himself capable of loving me despite my difficult battle with Crohn's disease.

Although Joseph knew that I was a Christian, he did not know how deficient I was in biblical knowledge. Through the illuminating work of the Spirit and Joseph's patient teaching over many months on the doctrines of grace, covenant theology, and the Lord's Day, I came to embrace the Reformed faith with passion. As this system of doctrine took shape within my mind and heart, I felt as if I had been transported into a strange new world. Everything was different. I was drawn to the beauty of God reflected in Reformed worship. There was substance to the preached Word and in the songs we sang. For the first time, I heard the comprehensive attributes of God extolled in prayer. The Reformed faith elicited from me a response similar to that which I had experienced at conversion. God was bigger and brighter than the sun; Santa Claus died; and the thick, invisible page separating the Old and New Testaments disappeared. I could better comprehend God's sovereignty in all things. I could rest in the knowledge that my affliction was designed by my heavenly Father and that "for those who love God all things work together for good, for those who are called according to his purpose" (Rom. 8:28).

After graduating from RTS in May 1971, Joseph was called as pastor of Tchula Presbyterian Church, a rural congregation located not far from my parents' home. We were married in August and settled into the manse that was our home for the next six and a half years. Looking back, I see God's wisdom and kindness in placing us with this congregation. My mother was near when I needed help. Our church was supportive, and we enjoyed the slower pace of life that this small congregation afforded. I was able to read and study, to regain a measure of health needed to manage two pregnancies, and to start learning how to be a pastor's wife.

From the beginning I was committed to my husband's philosophy of ministry. The Westminster Confession of Faith and catechisms served as the church's standard of orthodoxy and as tools to teach scriptural truths in a systematic way. Central to my husband's ministry were expository preaching,

227

prayer, discipleship, evangelism, and pastoral visitation. Furthermore, the Ten Commandments were used to reveal sin and the need for the Savior and to teach God's people the necessity of obedience.

When I came to the Reformed faith, I began to filter what I observed around me through God's holy precepts. I saw how God's law served as a magnifying glass to expose sin. I saw particularly how our culture had diminished God's holiness through the profane use of God's names and expressions of his character, in the veneration of Santa Claus, and by the trite commercialization of the second person of the Godhead, e.g., images of Christ on t-shirts or in coloring books. As antinomianism took hold within the church, what remained of our Sabbath traditions gave way to the world.

Today many professing Christians are working and playing on the Lord's Day and failing to fulfill their duty to worship God corporately. Because of their disobedience, they are causing harm to their souls, their posterity, and the culture.

As your husband seeks to address the issue of the Lord's Day with his congregation and to teach his people to love and obey all God's commandments, you will be called on to help him to model for the congregation a biblical approach to Sabbath keeping. This task will be a vain pursuit unless you have a desire for God's glory, a willing heart, a scriptural conviction of the fourth commandment, and a belief that there are great blessings promised to those who love and keep his commandments. It is my hope that my letter will be of some use and encouragement to you in this matter. Since practical issues regarding the Sabbath will flow from our theology, let me begin by giving a few reasons why keeping the fourth commandment is still required of us today.

First, the Sabbath, along with marriage and work, was instituted by God at creation. These three creation ordinances are binding on all humanity and "to violate [such] ordinances . . . is to attack the authority of God as our creator in the most fundamental sense."[2] At creation God declared that marriage is sanctified and is to be between one man and one woman

(Gen. 2:18–25; WCF 24), that godly labor is prescribed and honorable (Gen. 1:28; 2:15; WCF 4), and that the Sabbath is blessed and set apart for the purposes of rest and worship (Gen. 2:1–3; WCF 21). These three creation ordinances are God's cornerstones for an ordered society and must be protected by civil laws.

The best example to illustrate that the Lord's Day is a perpetual creation ordinance takes place before God gave the Ten Commandments. The familiar story found in Exodus tells of God's providing manna for his people in the wilderness. God gives specific directions regarding how this gracious provision is to be collected. When some of the Israelites disobey God's commands and go to gather on the Sabbath, he responds:

> "How long will you refuse to keep my commandments and my laws? See! The LORD has given you the Sabbath; therefore on the sixth day he gives you bread for two days. Remain each of you in his place; let no one go out of his place on the seventh day." So the people rested on the seventh day. (Ex. 16:28–30)

Second, the fourth commandment is a binding moral law. God relates this commandment to his work of creation:

> Remember the Sabbath day, to keep it holy. Six days you shall labor, and do all your work, but the seventh day is a Sabbath to the LORD your God. On it you shall not do any work, you, or your son, or your daughter, your male servant, or your female servant, or your livestock, or the sojourner who is within your gates. For in six days the LORD made heaven and earth, the sea, and all that is in them, and rested the seventh day. Therefore the LORD blessed the Sabbath day and made it holy. (Ex. 20:8–11)

Two passages in the New Testament clearly reveal Christ's view of the perpetuity of the Law. The first in found in Matthew 22:36–40, in which a Pharisee purposes to test Christ by asking him which he considers to be the greatest commandment. Christ declares, first of all, that man is to love God with the entirety of his being. He then adds that man is to love his neighbor as he loves himself. These two injunctions summarize the two tables of the Law. Christ ends with the declaration, "On these two commandments depend all the Law and the Prophets" (Matt. 22:40).

The second passage is from Matthew 5:17–19, in which Christ testifies in the Sermon on the Mount that he had not come to change the Law or Prophets. He came instead to fulfill them. He concludes with sobering words regarding those who would nullify or teach against any part of the Law. They would "be called least in the kingdom of heaven" (Matt. 5:19). We learn from these two passages that the Ten Commandments continue to direct our obedience today.

Finally, evidence for New Testament Sabbath keeping is illustrated in Isaiah 56:2–5, by the beautiful promise given to the eunuch who would delight and keep the Sabbath. Here, God promises to give the eunuch, who could not have children, an everlasting memorial name within God's house. We know this promise refers to the New Testament church because in the old dispensation a eunuch was not allowed into the assembly of the Lord (see Deut. 23:1).

If we are convinced of these arguments regarding the Lord's Day, how do we put our convictions into practice? To answer this question, I will refer to a paragraph in the Westminster Confession of Faith, which forms the pattern for how our family approaches the Sabbath (21.8). Each section of the paragraph has been paraphrased in order to frame my remarks to you. Scriptural references that are cited in the Confession are as follows: Exodus 20:8; 16:23, 25–26, 29–30; 31:15–17; Isaiah 58:13; Nehemiah 13:15–22; Matthew 12:1–13.

The Sabbath is holy to the Lord, when men prepare their hearts. Because public worship is the focus of the Sabbath, it is our duty to prepare ourselves for this great privilege by worshipping the Lord each day. We should draw aside to read his Word, pray, sing his praises, confess our sins, and meditate on God's attributes, his names, his works of creation and redemption, and the glories of heaven. Daily family worship will also serve as a means of preparing our hearts and those of our children for the Sabbath.

During periods when you feel you have no time for yourself, I would encourage you nevertheless to read God's Word and pray even for a brief time. When you become discouraged, knowing that you have failed to love God as you should, remember that God is willing to forgive you and that he will give you grace.

Order their affairs before the Sabbath. If we are to use the Sabbath as God has instructed, we will need to make preparations well in advance. Preparing for the Lord's Day should begin on Monday morning with a plan for how we will accomplish our duties during the week. The family's goal is to have all work finished by early Saturday evening. Food will be organized for the next day. Clothes, including socks and shoes, are ready. Bags with Bibles are packed. The car has fuel and is clean. After dinner, family worship, and baths, a good night's sleep is in order so that everyone will be rested for the Lord's Day.

Remember that Proverbs 31 teaches that an industrious, God-fearing woman brings honor to her husband and is respected by her children. As you prepare to draw aside from your normal routines on the Lord's Day, you should do so with a good conscience, knowing that you have managed your time well during the week and have performed your duties to the best of your strength and abilities.

Observe a holy rest all the day from their worldly works, words, thoughts, and recreations. This injunction in the Confession is based on God's conditional statement regarding what his people must do in order to receive spiritual blessings: "turn back your foot from the Sabbath, from doing your pleasure on my holy day, and call the Sabbath a delight and the holy day of the LORD honorable . . . honor it, not going your own ways, or seeking your own pleasure, or talking idly" (Isa. 58:13).

Scripture teaches that we are to honor the Lord's Day by turning aside from our regular work, pleasures, thoughts, and conversations (Isa. 58:13–14). The Sabbath was designed to promote our spiritual well-being and the spiritual well-being of others, for physical and mental rest, and for the worship of God. (A rest in the afternoon is often necessary to prepare us for evening worship.) The Sabbath was not designed for watching television, playing sports, pursuing hobbies, or studying for school. Such activities dishonor his day and give rise to idle words and thoughts.

For example, we sought to teach our children to obey God's Word by showing them how his day was to be structured differently. We did not allow our children to play with their neighborhood friends on the Lord's Day but guided them in how they spent their time. Our children had their "special" toys, puzzles, music, and books, which were set aside for their use on Sundays. We took them for walks, reviewed their catechism, watched their Bible story "performances," and enjoyed being together as a family.

Your home will be the place where members and visitors of the congregation will observe your Sabbath practices. They will take part in family worship, observe what you do or do not do on the Lord's Day, and notice the difference in the way you approach them in conversation. When you have visitors in your home, you and your husband will be responsible for guiding the course of conversations in which you are involved and, at times, will have to graciously shift discussions about sports, hobbies, current movies, and so on, to appropriate topics.

As we strive for obedience to God's commandments, we can become overwhelmed and discouraged. At such times, we must turn to our dear Savior who knows our every weakness, remembering that he has kept every one of God's perfect laws for us. Only in Christ can we find peace of conscience, rest for our souls, and the strength to obey. Remember too that God accepts our every feeble attempt to obey him through Christ's perfect work of obedience.

And use the whole day for public and private worship. We have looked at the necessity of preparing our hearts and ordering our affairs so that our full attention on the Sabbath is on the worship of God. At this point, I would speak, very briefly, of the important role family worship plays in Sabbath keeping and of your responsibility in overseeing your children's participation in public worship. You and your husband will not only help to model family worship for families in the congregation, but also be their source of encouragement as they train their children for public worship.

Daily family worship is essential to training our children "in the discipline and instruction of the Lord" (Eph. 6:4) and necessary for preparing them for corporate worship. Within the family circle, our children hear for the first time God's Word read to them and learn that God made them. We patiently teach our little ones how to listen and sit quietly as the Bible is being read. We teach them to confess their sins, to pray for specific needs, and to thank their heavenly Father for answered prayers.

In family worship we practice the songs for public worship. We help our children to memorize the Apostles' Creed, the Lord's Prayer, and the Ten Commandments. In order to engage their minds and hearts for worship on the Lord's Day, we explain the order of worship to them and what we expect of them according to their abilities. As they mature, we will build on this instruction.

For example, our children should know the significance of the "call to worship." We should remind them that the congregation is being called into the presence of God and that we are—in a spiritual sense—gathering with the mighty host of heaven to worship our Creator! We should often remind them that God has promised to meet with his people in corporate worship in a way that is far superior to how he meets with us in family or private worship. They should know why they put coins in the offering plate. At the end of the service, they should look to the minister when the benediction is being proclaimed and receive this blessing with joy and thankfulness. By the time our children reach adulthood, they should be able to show from Scripture why each element of worship is included in the service.

When your family assembles with the congregation for worship on the Lord's Day, your goal, apart from your own worship, will be to help

233

your children focus on what they are doing in the service. To minimize distractions during the service, your children should be taken to the restroom with plenty of time to be seated afterward and to settle quietly. They should not be allowed to leave the service except when you are convinced that there is a true emergency.

Before the service you will have already given your children instructions. Those who can read should quickly review the order of worship. They should bookmark the Scripture texts and hymns and have their sermon notebooks ready. (A simple outline of the sermon printed in the bulletin is useful in helping our children to listen and take notes. Your children should be expected to discuss the sermon to some degree with the family either at lunch or during family worship.)

If your children are very young, you will need to sit where they will be the least distraction to others. If you will be alone in managing your children, you may need to seek someone from the congregation who is free to help you. If you have teenagers, they should sit with you, or, if necessity arises, with those who will oversee their participation in the worship service. Along with wandering thoughts, there are many distractions to challenge our worship.

And perform deeds of necessity and mercy. Although God calls us to cease from our regular work, deeds of necessity and mercy must be performed on the Lord's Day. Just as pastors must "work" on the Lord's Day, there are others who must work as well. For the pastor's wife, Sunday can be one of the busiest days, especially when she has young children. She will prepare meals, wash dishes, accompany her husband to visit members who are ill, ensure that her husband has time to review his sermons, and show frequent, gracious hospitality to others.

Sunday is an excellent day to have guests in our homes to enjoy Christian fellowship and to provide for those who are lonely, discouraged, or away from home. As I mentioned previously, when we open our homes, we have the privilege of modeling family worship and Sabbath keeping to those who are unfamiliar with such practices and to discuss with them why we approach Christian living as we do. We have the opportunity to share the gospel with the lost and to provide occasions for our church members to fellowship with one another.

The most important deeds of necessity and mercy that you perform on the Sabbath will be for your family. You serve and honor your husband on the Lord's Day by being prepared for the day. Your labors free him to pursue his many responsibilities without worry and undue distractions. If you have children, you should let your energies go toward taking care of their needs, instructing them in the ways of the Lord, and helping them to delight in the Sabbath.

In the midst of a busy Sabbath, how can we ensure that we and our children will delight in the day? Ultimately, the enjoyment of the day can come only by the Holy Spirit's work in our hearts. He alone can give us true delight in his day. As we are obedient to God in keeping the Lord's Day holy, God promises in Isaiah 58:14 that we "shall take delight in the LORD," that we will have victory over sin and Satan, and that we will find enjoyment in the covenant blessings that are ours in Christ.[3]

If we are to delight in the Sabbath, we must have a proper attitude toward the day. We must not complain and become embittered because of all the preparations that must be made. If we find that our attitudes are wrong, we must begin by searching our hearts to see if worldliness is perhaps the root of our problem. We may need to evaluate how we are spending our time during the week or to adjust our schedules. We may need more rest. To regain our zeal and strengthen ourselves spiritually, we will need to go to his Word and be reminded of God's promises to us and to our children. To those who love him and keep his commandments, God promises that he will show his steadfast love to thousands—to thousands of generations (Ex. 20:6). What more could we desire?

The Sabbath should be remembered not as a day marked by a list of things we cannot do but as a "special" day marked by what we can do. Service to others, music, delicious food, heartfelt worship, time with

235

our family, good books, and Christian fellowship should distinguish our Sabbaths.

Approach the Lord's Day creatively to make lasting memories for your family. Whatever you choose to do in this "creative" vein will depend on factors such as the ages of your children, your schedule, and your energy. The following are ideas to help you to think of ways you may want to approach the Lord's Day in your home.

Begin the first day of the week somewhat differently. Play Christian music when the children awake to remind them that the Lord's Day has begun and that they are to turn their thoughts to the events of the day. This is the day they will go to Sunday school and worship God with their family and friends.

Set the breakfast table for the children with colorful napkins and their "special" Sunday china—inexpensive bowls and plates found at a garage or estate sale. If there is time the day before, arrange a few flowers for the table. In the morning the children will look forward to their special breakfast—cereals with fresh fruit, fruit breads or muffins from the freezer, or a breakfast casserole or baked oatmeal made the night before.

If the family has a long drive from church in the evening, pack a "sack supper" for the family to eat on the way home. The older children can help with the preparations on Saturday. Include special treats or juice boxes. When you arrive home there will be time for a bedtime story and no kitchen to clean.

Start a "Sabbath Box" for your children's Christian-themed toys, puzzles, and games. Musical instruments such as triangles, small drums, and so on could be included for the children to use for "musical performances" of songs they have learned to sing. These items, along with Bible-story coloring books and art supplies specified for Sunday projects, will be used only on Sundays. Christian movies and audio materials will be kept together and used with discretion. Bible storybooks and other Christian literature should be within easy reach and used throughout the week.

Collect dress-up clothes for the children to use on Sunday afternoons to portray characters from the Bible or church history. Our children enjoyed having company on Sundays for lunch, especially when our guests had children. After the meal and family worship, all the children would go upstairs, dress in costumes, and after a brief time of practice, would come downstairs to perform a Bible-story "play" for the adults.

Double recipes when you cook. Freeze the extra portions for those Sundays when your schedule is hectic. Bake muffins and breads for the freezer to serve at breakfast. Keep baked cookies in the freezer to serve when you need a quick dessert.

Plan "impromptu" lunches for Sunday hospitality. Buy what you will need for making sandwiches and salad and let your guests help with the last-minute preparations.

Set aside part of the afternoon for yourself. Take time to read. Use part of the afternoon to encourage Christian friends by letter, Skype, or e-mail. Send brief messages or cards to missionaries your church supports. Plan a short visit with a friend in your congregation who has little time during the week for fellowship because of work.

While there will be many demands on you and your husband, be sure to take time to enjoy your children on the Lord's Day. Spend time reading to them, going for walks, or perhaps making greeting cards together for people for whom the family has been praying. Plan with your husband how often you will open your home to guests and how you will spend the time together as a family on your "free" Sundays.

It has been a pleasure to write to you, although the task set before me has been a humbling one as I have had to reexamine my own heart and practices by God's Word. My desire to love and keep the Lord's Day, however, has been renewed as well as my faith and trust in God's goodness and wisdom. It is my hope that this letter may be of some use and encouragement to you as you labor with your husband for Christ's kingdom and God's glory.

In his love,

"Sissy"

STUDY QUESTIONS

1. What are the three perpetual creation mandates?

2. What story from Exodus illustrates that the Sabbath ordinance was required of God's people before they had received the Ten Commandments?

3. How does Isaiah 56:4–5 show that the fourth commandment is applicable to the New Testament era?

4. What are the hindrances for your keeping the Sabbath as taught in Isaiah 58:13 and in Exodus 20:8–11?

5. What are the three blessings that God promises in Isaiah 58:14 to those who keep the Sabbath?

RECOMMENDED RESOURCES

Beeke, Joel R. *Family Worship*. Grand Rapids: Reformation Heritage Books, 2002.

McGraw, Ryan M. *The Day of Worship: Reassessing the Christian Life in Light of the Sabbath*. Grand Rapids, MI: Reformation Heritage Books, 2011.

Murray, Iain H. *Rest in God and A Calamity in Contemporary Christianity*. Edinburgh: Banner of Truth Trust, 2010.

Pipa, Joseph A., Jr. *The Lord's Day*. Ross-shire, UK: Christian Focus Publications, 1997.

Shishko, William. *Helps for Worship*. The Committee on Christian Education of the Orthodox Presbyterian Church, 2008.

The Westminster Confession of Faith (with proofs). Chapter 21: Of Religious Worship and the Sabbath.

The Westminster Larger Catechism 178–196.

The Westminster Shorter Catechism 98–107.

Watson, Thomas. *The Ten Commandments*. Edinburgh: Banner of Truth, 1965.

Particular Circumstances

CHAPTER SIXTEEN

Habitual Sin in the Life of My Husband: Now What?

Janie Street

Sexual sin has devastating effects on marriages, families, and churches. When a husband violates the purity of his marriage through sexual sin, he leaves his wife grieved and hurt. My wife has too often counseled women in this situation as she has sought to point them to the hope and healing that only biblical truth can provide. Encouragement of this kind is important because often emotions are overwhelming, and it is easy to make hasty, sinful responses when marital trust has been violated in this way. The counsel of this chapter has been framed by theological truth and will provide immeasurable help and encouragement in making wise decisions to the pastor's wife who has experienced this pain.

REV. DR. JOHN D. STREET

Dear sister in Christ,

This is a letter I wish I didn't have to write. But, because sin is a part of everyone's experience, it is necessary to address certain difficult situations that might become a part of your life experience as the wife of a minister of the Lord Jesus. Whatever help you glean from this letter, I hope you will use it to find encouragement in your marriage, if needed, and that you will help other pastors' wives you know who may find themselves in this difficulty.

It is, most assuredly, a delicate subject. I am speaking of the possibility of your pastor-husband falling into sexual sin. Although the very thought of this is agonizing, you may find yourself in need of this type of biblical counsel and comfort. If not at this time, please read my letter and use it to help another sister in Christ who may be in need.

The most often occurring sin of this nature would seem to be pornography, particularly Internet pornography. Although any sexual sin is very serious, biblically speaking, viewing pornography is not a marriage-ending sin. The teaching on divorce and adultery in Matthew 19:9 is informative at this point. The Greek word *pornea* does not transliterate to *pornography*. It means "immorality," and the context of this passage supports its interpretation as *physical* marital unfaithfulness because it is linked with the statement, "and marries another" (Matt. 19:9). In a similar train of logical thought, if pornography were "grounds for divorce," i.e., marriage-ending sexual sin, then anyone who had entertained lustful thoughts of a sexual nature without the use of pornographic material could also be divorced on that basis, and there is no teaching in Scripture to support that conclusion. The point is that Scripture strongly indicates that divorce was permitted by Moses due to the physical act of immorality with another human being. This puts pornography in a less incriminating category than illicit physical union with another.

Obviously, sexual sin is found in other manifestations than pornography. It would not be profitable for me to mention all the ways that our husbands might fail sexually. The purpose of my writing to you is not to address sexual sin in a comprehensive way, but rather to help you respond in the most loving and biblical way possible should the problem arise. Though the pain of this trial will be intense, your greatest need will not be sympathy and a shoulder to cry on—although those things are important. What will carry you through your darkest moments and days will be God's love and truth and direction found in his Holy Word. These things I hope to convey to you, dear friend.

Let me initially address a few crucial points. First, even though you are married to a sinner (he is too, you know!), you should not allow yourself to be controlled by an irrational fear that his failure is just around the corner . . . lurking, waiting to attack you and your marriage! Sexually explicit images abound in our world. Your husband is human and will be tempted to sin, just as you are, but if he truly loves the Lord his God with all his heart and soul and mind and strength and his neighbor as himself, he will fight that temptation, resist the Devil, and flee! Don't allow the fact that he might be feeling the pull of temptation to devastate you, anger you, or turn you into a suspicious, untrusting wife. He needs your confidence in him as a help against the onslaught of temptation.

Second, trust between husband and wife in marriage is a very good thing and makes provision for two sinners to be sanctified. Let me explain what I mean. As you trust your husband, he uses the grace shown in that trust to bolster him during times of temptation. The same strength is yours as your husband graciously trusts you. However, trust between husband and wife is only as strong as the people are. In other words, marital trust is limited because it is one flawed human trusting in another flawed human. While it is important to build trust between each other, trust in God is of greater priority and importance. You can and must trust God completely, without reservation or fear, because he has commanded you to and because he will never fail you. He is completely trustworthy. He will never sin against you. He will never violate his covenant with you, his chosen one. And beyond that, he can be trusted to carry you through the most difficult days of your life. Trust, for the believer, when it is rightly placed, is placed first and foremost in the One most steadfast and unfailing—our great God and Savior! When you trust him, you will know peace in the most trying of times. So trust your husband, but in your trusting, trust God completely and without reservation.

Third, most women whose husbands sin against them in this way find a way to blame themselves for his failure. *Perhaps if I were more beautiful . . . if I did not carry extra weight from the childbearing years . . . if I had seen this sooner, I could have done something.* No wife is sinless and without her share of fault in the problems of married life. A godly wife, though imperfect, should always strive to be the kind of wife who seeks to be aware of her sins against her husband, to be quick to confess them and repent of them. Here's the unexpected truth: even if a wife lives in this godly pattern, what she may not realize is that most often a husband's sin of a sexual nature is bound up in himself—in what he thinks about himself, what he desires, and how he responds if life does not give him what he was hoping for. For a man, temptation to sin sexually is often unrelated to his wife at all. It is most often a sinful acting out of a physically pleasurable experience as a reward for some disappointment or unfulfilled desire or perhaps an escape from the unpleasantness that life in a fallen world inevitably brings. In regard to you, his wife, he has failed to reserve the beautiful gift of sex as an expression of love for the wife of his youth. Instead he has turned it into a self-indulgent expression of his displeasure and often anger with the things in life that he hates, that he wishes he could change, that he lacks control over.

So to you, his wife, I say: You won't be perfect, but do be a faithful wife. Love the Lord your God with all your heart, soul, mind and strength and your neighbor (husband) as yourself. Discipline yourself for the purpose of godliness. Daily serve your family in love. Repent quickly when you sin, reconciling with those you sin against. Live in loving submission and reverence toward your husband. If you live a godly life in this way and your husband sins sexually, recognize it as *his own sin* that he must deal with before his God.

Fourth, depending on the nature of your husband's sexual sin, the church leadership may become involved in your situation. In some cases, sexual sin will immediately disqualify a minister from continuing in his position. Given that this letter is written to women of various church backgrounds, I will not attempt to define what the parameters are by which this will be judged. If your husband is unwilling to confess his sin before the elders of his church (or even you), I would urge you to seek the counsel of a godly pastor and his wife, perhaps who are outside your church, whom you trust to give you direction that comes from obedience to Scripture. A word of caution, however, is that you respect the office of elder that your own husband holds. Do not set forth an accusation against him merely on the basis of suspicion alone. Wait until what is kept in secret is revealed. Pray that if there is disqualifying and dishonoring sin of this nature, God will bring it to light. Do not be quick to jump to conclusions. Follow Matthew 18 principles and ask your husband first. Contacting an elder or talking with a sister or girlfriend before you lovingly confront him is a sinful violation of God's teaching on how to handle another believer's sin.

Having said this, I want to urge you to find your help and direction from God's all-sufficient Word. It is at a time like this when you, feeling so completely overwhelmed, may be tempted to listen to other voices—voices that shout to you from the culture around you, Christian and non-Christian alike. Let me give you a few examples.

THE VOICE OF VICTIMIZATION

Because you are not to blame for your husband's impurity and sexual sin, so many are telling you that your complete identity is that of a victim. On one level, I could agree with these well-meaning voices, for indeed you are one who has been sinned against. But the extent to which our culture has defined "victim" cannot be supported biblically. The victimization so commonly referred to today attempts to release the "victim" from any culpability for her own sinful responses. In fact, sin is allowed by and condoned in victims because "they cannot help themselves." The hurt perpetrated on a woman seems to give her rights never before mentioned in Scripture—rights of cold silence, refusal to forgive when repentance is clear, retaliation in "emotional" affairs, etc.

THE VOICE OF MEN-HATERS

When women allow anger against their husbands to control them, they often give a willing ear to feminist men-haters around them. You may have altogether rejected feminism as a philosophy, yet how easy it is to slip into the deceitful comfort of its tenets. We have been subtly taught through the media (movies and TV) and the education system to disdain those who sin against us as if they are less than human and most assuredly beneath us. Feminists will tell you that the "societal crime" of the headship of men in home and society, which was the pattern in the early years of this country, is reason enough for women to hate men. How much more when a man breaks his wife's trust and violates their marriage vows through sexual sin! While it may seem far-fetched for a pastor's wife to react with such disdain for her husband, please know that the human heart is capable of far more sin than we would readily admit.

THE VOICE OF SELF-RELIANCE

"Since your husband has sinned against you, you have every right to be angry. Throw the bum out! Don't ever trust him again. You don't need him! You've got to look out for yourself." Being sinned against in this way will turn us toward a self-protective mentality, making us vulnerable to listening to and believing these kinds of thoughts. What person who burns herself while cooking will not do everything she can to protect herself from having that happen again? How much more will you seek to protect yourself from the anguish of this marital trial? And that self-protection will lead you to many a sinful response to your husband's sin.

THE VOICE OF WELL-INTENTIONED HELPERS

"My husband is a pastor. He knows God's Word—and still this happened. I've been reading my Bible and praying ever since this happened, and still I am extremely distraught! I guess what we really need is professional help." And so you turn to a Christian counselor, desperate for biblical help to reconcile the problems you face. You want to be selective here as some Christian counselors support the victimization mentality—not recognizing how it can hinder the counselee from owning up to his or her responsibility in the problem. As a compassionate caregiver, any Christian counselor will seek ways to protect Christian women from further anguish, but you should choose one who will teach you to stand up under this affliction with the strength of God, rather than flee lest any hurt come your way again. You will benefit the most from counsel that encourages you to live in obedience to Christ, regardless of the suffering that at times will accompany such obedience. As you and your husband seek counseling, be sure to look for true biblical counseling. We are blessed to live in a country where there are many good Christian counseling organizations. One that I recommend contacting is a parachurch organization called NANC (National Association of Nouthetic Counselors) at www.nanc.org. On its website you will find a list of certified biblical counselors according to their location.

With these warnings ringing in your ears, you might wonder how you will ever find your way through this trial without losing your faith in the process. Again I urge you, turn to the Word of God! Turn away from that which the world teaches, and find comfort, strength, and hope in obedience to the God who loves you and is rescuing his beloved children.

From Titus 2:3–5, we know that older women are to teach younger women to love their husbands. Oh, how we will need to know how to love our pastor-husbands in the middle of this trial! Let's see how God's Word will instruct and encourage us to do this.

Knowing how to love your husband during a time such as this is crucial. For where in Scripture does it ever say that we are to love our husbands only if they never sin against us in this devastating way? What terms and conditions are put on that command to love him? If the Scripture puts no conditions on it, then we must not! But how can you as his wife love him when he has so violated his vows to you and the Lord? You may at this time be hurt, brokenhearted, even angry. Yet God calls you to pour out love and mercy to your life partner. If he confesses his sin to you and repents, you are required by God to forgive him (Luke 17:3). Difficult as that may seem, it is God's calling on your life (Eph. 4:32). At this point, you will have to examine your own heart as to your willingness to love and forgive him. Perhaps for you this is not a high hurdle to clear. Or you may find yourself languishing in self-pity and anger. How you respond to your husband's sin, how you react, how you allow the hurt and anger to control you, how you get from the anger and depression to loving him—this is what the remainder of this letter is about.

I will begin by reminding you of how Christ reacted when he was mistreated and horribly sinned against. You need only read of the crucifixion and the events leading up to it to know how Christ who is God was treated while living among the creatures he would die to redeem. While much of the bad stuff we experience in life comes because we are sinful people, we realize that Christ suffered through no fault of his own. We should not even have to look at how he handled people sinning against him—for no one should ever sin against Christ. And he did not bring it on himself by sinning against others. Though he was sinless, people did and continually do sin against him. In this way, Christ becomes our help and example. God made him who knew no sin to be sin on our behalf, so that we might become the righteousness of God in him (2 Cor. 5:21).

Christ took the sins his own people had committed against him and, instead of retaliating in anger, paid the penalty for those sins—so that the sinners would no longer bear the guilt and punishment for their sin. You will not be able to take marital sin and pay the penalty for that—taking your husband's sin completely on yourself. However, you will be able to recognize that Christ did so, and having done so he enables you to set aside your anger and indignation and truly love the forgiven one, who in this case is your husband. In Christ there is a way for you to forgive one who has sinned against you. "Be kind to one another, tenderhearted, forgiving one another, as God in Christ forgave you" (Eph. 4:32).

Second, although your husband's sexual sin is *his sin*, you must resist the temptation to revile him and persecute him—to self-righteously condemn him—as though you are not a sinner yourself, as though you do not also daily receive from God the forgiveness that is in Christ Jesus (Matt. 18:21–35). No matter the magnitude of his sin, you must realize the weightiness of your sin before a holy God. Daily recognition of your undeserved cleansing and forgiveness by God will soften your heart toward your husband. You should have a holy pity on his weakness and a desire to come alongside him and strengthen him wherever appropriate.

Third, I recognize that in all likeliness you will not feel like doing this. In fact, you may have very little motivation deep down in yourself to love your husband who now disgusts you. Your feelings are in the exact opposite direction of love, forgiveness, and compassion. Do not expect your feelings to be the motivation for loving your husband. Just being a Christian will not drive off the bad feelings that tend to rule you. You will have to "take every thought captive" and live according to the calling of God on your life.

You know you have been called to love. Let's find out what that calling means. We'll look at Ephesians 4 so that we can examine the context of Ephesians 4:32 and see just what it means to "forgive as Christ forgave."

The apostle Paul wrote to the Ephesian Christians about walking in a manner worthy of their calling and immediately instructed them on how to treat one another—how to love one another. There is a connection here. So many times we think that our calling is bound up in our individual salvation—what God has done for us and how we respond to him. But throughout the New Testament, your calling as a redeemed child of

God is bound up in your place in the body of Christ. Jesus is the Good Shepherd, and he places you in his sheepfold with the other sheep—not by yourself. The body of Christ is the church—and we are placed into his body and given a function and a calling to be unified and to act as one. See how Paul teaches this:

> I therefore, a prisoner for the Lord, urge you to walk in a manner worthy of the calling to which you have been called, with all humility and gentleness, with patience, bearing with one another in love, eager to maintain the unity of the Spirit in the bond of peace. There is one body and one Spirit—just as you were called to the one hope that belongs to your call. (Eph. 4:1–4)

According to these verses, we have been called to five distinct callings:

1. Humility
2. Gentleness
3. Patience
4. Bearing with others in love
5. Eagerness to maintain the unity of the Spirit in the bond of peace

I hope you notice a lack of victim mentality in these verses. You will see no support of hatred of men here. Paul does not wax eloquent on how to list all the ways in which your husband has hurt you and then devise a plan to make sure it never happens again—common counsel that Christian "professionals" peddle. In fact, the list above is very helpful in answering the tough question before you: how can I love my husband? It helps you to answer:

- What do I do now?
- How do I respond to my husband's sin?
- What about me and my damaged reputation?
- How could he sin in this way against me?

In very practical application of God's powerful truth to change lives, this is what this might look like in your thinking and responding:

- Because God has called me to humility, I will not think more highly of myself than I ought to think but rather consider my husband more important than myself (Phil. 2:1–11), recognizing that Christ gave this example. In humility I will recognize that my God has forgiven me a multitude of sins that I committed thoughtlessly, carelessly, and willingly against him when I took no thought for his glory time after time after time. Because God has faithfully forgiven me, how can I not forgive my husband?

- Because God has called me to gentleness, I will refuse to be harsh with my husband. I will seek through a "gentle and quiet spirit" (1 Peter 3:1–6) to influence him toward repentance and righteousness. I will "let no corrupting talk come out of [my mouth], but only such as is good for building up, as fits the occasion, that it may give grace to those who hear" (Eph. 4:29).

- Because God has called me to be patient, I will obey God's command to be patient with all men and not insist that my husband be perfect *right now!* Oh, how my flesh wants to see a multitude of fruits of repentance and lavish devotion toward me, but my calling is to patience. As I reflect on how long-suffering God has been to me, I will soften my heart toward my husband and extend never-ending patience.

- Because I have been called to show tolerance in love, I will live with my husband without hating him during the time that God is sanctifying him in this area. I will seek to know him better, to understand him, and to help him so that my love for him is a blessing to him and ultimately glorifying to God.

- Because I have been called to diligence in preserving the unity of the Spirit in the bond of peace, I will not seek to serve my fears and self-love by protecting myself from any further hurt from my husband but will joyfully fulfill my calling to unity and peace, both in my marriage and in the body of Christ.

I hope you can see from this application that God does not just give us commands but shows us how to obey them as well. With the help of the Spirit of God through your faithful application of the Word of God, you will be able to love your husband during these difficult days and weeks and months. You will be no longer a victim but a beloved child of God who is learning to love when it is difficult. You will no longer be tempted to hate men but will learn that a lover of your husband is humble, gentle, and patient. You will not run and hide in fear, protecting yourself from further harm, but will diligently pursue God's agenda—unity of the Spirit in the bond of peace.

May God's blessing be on you, dear friend, as you walk worthy of your calling in Christ. And may his Word comfort, strengthen, and bless you in the days ahead.

Living in his grace day by day,

Your sister in Christ,

JANIE

STUDY QUESTIONS

1. God's calling for you as a wife is to love your husband (Titus 2:4). Jesus said that all believers are to love their neighbors as themselves (Mark 12:31). Think carefully on these two questions before answering:

   a. In what ways am I loving myself (e.g., protecting myself, believing the best about myself, and so on)?

   b. Am I willing to love my sinful husband as I already love myself? Look at the ways you show love to yourself. Are you ready to begin loving your husband in those ways?

2. Biblical love always seeks the best for the other person (Phil. 2:3–4; Rom. 12:13–21). Write down five new ways that you will seek to

bless your husband this week—things you were not already doing for him. Begin to implement these. One proof that you truly love your husband is when your heart is full of gratitude for him. Take some time to examine your heart. Is it full of bitterness? Or do thoughts of gratitude come easily and joyfully to mind when you think of him? Be prepared to repent and be thankful!

3. Perhaps your husband has sinned against you, but you have also sinned against him. Confess your sins to God and then to your husband. Humble yourself before him because this is well pleasing to God. Be ready to forgive any sins that he repents of to you. Memorize Ephesians 4:32, and repeat it often throughout the day, with an emphasis on the phrase "as God in Christ forgave you."

RECOMMENDED RESOURCES

Fitzpatrick, Elyse. *Women Counseling Women: Biblical Answers to Life's Difficult Problems.* Eugene, OR: Harvest House Publishers, 2010.

Kendrick, Steven, and Alex Kendrick. *The Love Dare.* Nashville, TN: B&H Publishing Group, 2008.

Peace, Martha. *The Excellent Wife: A Biblical Perspective.* Bemidji, MN: Focus Publishing, Inc., 1999.

Tripp, Paul David. *What Did You Expect? Redeeming the Realities of Marriage.* Wheaton, IL: Crossway Books, 2010.

Ministering in a Different Culture: Aliens and Strangers

Pam Schweitzer

"Schweitzer, the best thing that ever happened to you was the day you got married." My staff platoon commander at Quantico, not otherwise known for his perceptive interpersonal observations, had never been more right. The Bible says "it is not good for man to be alone," but this was especially true for me. Not good. However, with my marriage to Pam came a new day. I found not only the married bliss and family life I had always prayed for, but also the dedicated practical help that enabled me to serve effectively in my vocation, first as a Marine officer and now as a minister of the gospel in England. In this work we are not a "great team"—we are one flesh, to the glory of the all-wise God.

REV. DR. WILLIAM M. SCHWEITZER

255

Dear sister in Christ,

Whether at home or abroad, the duty of the minister's wife is "to minister to Christ's servant."[1] Ministering to one's husband is, of course, the calling of every wife (Prov. 31; Titus 2). However, ministers are a special category of Christian men ordained for the purpose of gospel ministry. Jonathan Edwards writes, "There are two kinds of persons that are given to Christ, and appointed and devoted of God to be his servants, to be employed with Christ, and under him, in his great work of the salvation of the souls of men; and they are angels and ministers."[2] The minister's wife has the privilege of loving and serving a man who has been given the "angelic" office of bringing souls to salvation. Some of these ministers—and their wives—are called to minister in faraway lands, often in places where the darkness is far greater than at home. In such situations, we should not be surprised when opposition and trials arise. Those of us who are called to this peculiar work will face special difficulties as well as receive particular blessings.

We must first be able to see these blessings and difficulties in the light of eternity. It is only when we look through this lens that we can have the right perspective on every circumstance we face. We believe that our "light momentary affliction" in this world is "preparing for us an eternal weight of glory beyond all comparison" (2 Cor. 4:17–18).

It is easy to write such things but more difficult to put them into practice in our lives. God has designed us with the purpose of serving others. But we know from Genesis 3 that this service is cursed (Gen. 3:16). Our obedience to the principles of Titus 2 is cursed: it has become hard labor. To love our husbands, to love our children, to be self-controlled, pure, working at home, kind, and submissive to our own husbands that the Word of God may not be blasphemed (Titus 2:4–5) is not going to come naturally. All this is further complicated by life abroad.

SPIRITUAL BATTLE

In maintaining an eternal perspective as ministers' wives, we must recognize first and foremost the spiritual battle unfolding around us. As

Christians, we constantly live under the threat of the Evil One and all his minions. "For we do not wrestle against flesh and blood, but against the rulers, against the authorities, against the cosmic powers over this present darkness, against the spiritual forces of evil in the heavenly places" (Eph. 6:12).

We are in a spiritual battle. But some places are more dangerous than others in the wars of this earth, and the same is also true of the spiritual realm. We should expect that ministers of the gospel and their families will be particular targets of the Evil One.

When we enter the ministry life, we enter the front line of a combat zone. Those who proclaim liberty to the captives present a serious threat to the one who has been holding them captive, and we must expect opposition from him. Satan's spiritual stronghold is obvious, almost tangible, in places where the gospel has never been preached. However, we are more likely to come appropriately armed and ready in such situations. In lands where Christianity was once the dominant force, the opposition is just as real, but it will be subtler. If we are not mindful of this, our defenses will be down, our weapons rusty, and our prayers weak. But this must not be so. "Be sober-minded; be watchful. Your adversary the devil prowls around like a roaring lion, seeking someone to devour" (1 Peter 5:8). Our adversary prowls about seeking to devour God's people everywhere. If he can bring down one who preaches, it would be a great victory for him.

THE REALITY OF SATAN'S EFFORTS

As we prepared to move to our current ministry assignment, Satan attacked in a way that we had not expected. While it was our shortest move, it would prove the most difficult. About a week before the move, I became ill with a terrible flu. I continued to nurse an eight-month-old baby. The flu began to spread, and one by one each member of the family became ill, some before the move, some during, and some after. Then came the secondary infections—an infected finger, infected throats, ears with temporary hearing loss, and the worst, a strange lump along the baby's jaw. It seemed to go away with antibiotics but then returned with renewed vigor. For the first time, a member of our family was admitted to the hospital overnight, remaining there for five days until God mercifully brought an end to the trial.

Since this move, I have heard many similar stories from those moving into gospel ministry. Initially, each trial seemed to be merely physical, something experienced by every family at some time or another. But the timing and severity of the trial coinciding with the move has since alerted us to the spiritual nature of such trials. Moving abroad for the purpose of proclaiming the gospel means moving into enemy territory. It is only natural that Satan will attack. He cannot harm God's people, but he can scare us. He can discourage us. He can lead us to despair. He can lead us to doubt the call. Satan knows the power of the gospel. He knows the power of the Word of God. He knows that it has the power to turn people from darkness to light, from his kingdom to God's kingdom. Therefore, we must "resist him, firm in [our] faith, knowing that the same kinds of suffering are being experienced by [our] brotherhood throughout the world" (1 Peter 5:9).

We are not alone; our brothers and sisters in the ministry throughout the world undergo similar trials, often much worse. We must be sober-minded and watchful as Satan will try to impede the construction of Christ's church. He will do this by attacking those who build, preach, and teach with the authority of Christ. Let us not be downcast by this knowledge, but let us take courage and claim the promise of Christ when he says, "I will build my church, and the gates of hell shall not prevail against it" (Matt. 16:18).

MULTIPURPOSE TRIALS

Trials are multipurpose in nature. First, God brings trials for our humbling. While in the hospital, I was reminded by our minister: "Humble yourselves, therefore, under the mighty hand of God so that at the proper time he may exalt you, casting all your anxieties on him, because he cares for you" (1 Peter 5:6–7). Were we ready to take up the call of the ministry?

Was I really ready to be a minister's wife? In all honesty, no, I was not. We needed this trial for our humbling. I needed this trial. It was not enough just to experience it or even enough to see its spiritual element. We had to realize that we needed to be "clothed with humility" if we were to be of use in the ministry. We needed to put on humility day by day like our clothing.

Unless we humble ourselves under God's mighty hand, we will not be sober-minded and watchful as Peter exhorts us to be. Whatever our culture, we take pride in who we are and where we have come from. We often think that we have a great deal to offer and that other cultures are ready and waiting to receive what we have to offer. Satan is very pleased to make use of our pride as a means to accomplish his purposes. He wants us to esteem ourselves above others because he knows that this is a stumbling block to the gospel and to the unity of the church. We cannot expect people to receive a gospel of grace when we come clothed in pride.

Satan is very powerful, but his power is very small when compared with the power of God's grace at work in us. The Lord will bring about trials and difficulties for our humbling so that we may serve him to his glory in our given context.

Second, God brings trials so that we might truly know that our sufficiency is from him.

> Not that we are sufficient in ourselves to claim anything as coming from us, but our sufficiency is from God, who has made us sufficient to be ministers of a new covenant, not of the letter but of the Spirit. For the letter kills, but the Spirit gives life. (2 Cor. 3:5–6)

God has made our husbands sufficient ministers of a new covenant, one that gives eternal life. Ministers' wives along with their husbands may be tempted to think of themselves as self-sufficient. At times, the roles to which we are called will set us apart from others. We may be tempted to trust in our own sufficiency. Throughout the time of our family illness, we could do very little for ourselves and what we could do seemed pathetically small. We were dependent on other people. We could barely lift our heads to read God's Word. It was weeks before we could sing properly again. Trials may be of an all-encompassing sort for a distinct period of time, or they may be ongoing thorns in the flesh such as Paul experienced. Either way, as ministers' wives we will know trials and thorns in order that we may also know the truth of these words: "My grace is sufficient for you, for my power is made perfect in weakness" (2 Cor. 12:9).

Third, God brings trials to test our faith. Just as our bodies require exercise to maintain and increase strength, so our spirits require trials to do likewise. In the midst of a trial, we cannot always see its end. Its purpose may be veiled from sight. We may know that it is for our good and for the glory of God, but our hearts grow weary.

It takes faith for our husbands to take up the call to the ministry and for us as their wives to serve with them. For those who are called abroad, we must exchange the familiar for the foreign. Not only will the ministry itself serve to test our faith, but daily living—where to buy food, how to find transport, even how to communicate—will try us as well. Therefore, we do well to remember that "without faith it is impossible to please him, for whoever would draw near to God must believe that he exists and that he rewards those who seek him" (Heb. 11:6).

MINISTERING ABROAD IN THE HOME

Strangers and Pilgrims

First, we must recognize the difficulties of living between cultures. We will never truly become one of the natives of our host country, no matter how many years we live there, no matter how fluently we speak the language (or the accent), no matter how thoroughly we understand the culture. We may even be granted citizenship or "unlimited leave to remain." But we will always to some degree remain true to our first nationality and culture. At the same time, we will also find that our experience abroad has irreversible effects on us. We see ourselves differently. We see our home culture differently. There is a degree of separation from our homeland that is more than physical. Our home culture begins to seem more foreign to us. People from churches back home may come to help us from time to time. They expect us to be as they are, to think as they think, to react as they react. Sometimes we do, but sometimes we do not. We have changed. It can be stressful to negotiate between those from our home culture while in our place abroad. Moving between these two worlds can be emotionally and mentally draining.

Second, we are separated from our extended family. Grandparents will not get to spend much time with their grandchildren. We will not always be able to attend family gatherings; indeed, we may become so absorbed in managing the care of our husbands, families, and homes abroad that we even forget things that are happening back home. The time difference affects our ability to keep in touch and, before we know it, months have passed. If our extended families are Christians, they may understand, but it will still be hard. If they are not Christians, it may further distance our relationships with them. They might make us feel guilty. They might even become angry with us. This may be spiritual opposition as well. Cling to God's Word, his promises, his calling. Trust his sovereign purpose even in this, and pray that it would be to the good of their souls.

Third, we leave behind friendships. Things will happen in each of our lives that will change us. Time will pass before we can communicate. When we do write or speak or see one another again, there will be more to say than can be said. Those at home carry on with their lives while we are just trying to make our way in a new environment. We feel as if we have no friends at all. Over time, however, we will form new relationships, and we will know the riches of the fellowship of the saints both at home and abroad.

Fourth, we may have to surrender the privilege of owning our home. Most of those who minister abroad find themselves renting accommodation in their new country. When we return on furlough, we may no longer have a "home" to return to. We will find ourselves living with family, friends, or strangers in houses, hotels, or campers. But the God of all grace provides for all our needs according to his riches in glory. This entire world will soon melt with fervent heat, and this includes our homes (whether rented or owned), as precious and necessary as they may seem to us now. Perhaps if God has called you to minister abroad, it is part of his process of weaning you from the world and preparing you for the next.

Hospitality in Our Homes Abroad

When we are called abroad, our homes may become the secondary meeting place of the church. Although we will typically rent a building for Sunday services, we may need to open our homes for other gatherings throughout the week. Our husbands will need a study. Guests will need a place to stay, and because we are abroad, we may have more guests than usual. Privacy for our own families will be at a premium. With so many things going on, it will seem impossible to keep things very tidy. Hospitality requires humility as well as love. Perhaps that is why hospitality is one of the marks of every Christian (Rom. 12:13; 1 Peter 4:9), but it is particularly important for those in ministry (1 Tim. 3:2; Titus 1:8).

We wives enable our husbands to be hospitable. We clean, we cook, we bake, and we wash. If possible, we recruit the help of our children in the process. Providing food and shelter should not be denigrated. We are not Platonists. When we minister abroad, food can be a means of communicating love to people before we have the language skills or the cultural savvy to say the right things. Our cooking becomes a hybrid as it serves the tastes of our family as well as those of the foreign culture.[3] Although the visible burden of hospitality may be on the wife, we should see it as a one-flesh demonstration of love to every tribe, tongue, and nation that God brings through our door.

However, amidst the stresses and strains, the home of those who minister abroad knows great blessings. Our perspective on the world has enlarged. We can see the world not only from the sight of our homeland, but also from that of the new land we have come to embrace. Most significantly, we have a constant reminder that this world is not our home, but we are strangers and pilgrims here (Heb. 11:13–16). It is good for us not to feel at home in this world, for God has prepared for us the new heavens and the new earth where we will dwell with him forever as the bride of Christ. "He did not create us primarily to make us happy and comfortable here in this life. That is not our highest calling."[4] A sense of being unsettled reminds us that this world is not our home.

TREASURE IN HEAVEN

In most cases, ministering abroad means raising support for the work. When embarking on the prospect of missionary work, we found the idea of going around from church to church "begging" (as we saw it) repulsive. Truly, it is not easy work. But we soon began to see the benefit of such labor. As we go into battle on the front lines, not only do we need to be in prayer, but we need churches and individuals to do likewise. Matthew 6:19–21 reminds us that "where your treasure is, there your heart will be also." This principle means that those who support you financially will be inclined to pray more earnestly for you; their hearts will be where their treasure is.

Even still, could we not just send out a letter or an e-mail explaining the need rather than having to travel from church to church? In a word, no. Churches and individuals want to meet the people they are investing in. Keep in mind that they will be investing in the spread of God's kingdom in a part of the world they may never see and for the sake of a people they may never meet until glory. We must be the means of communicating God's work in that land. As we serve God primarily abroad, we serve him at home as well in making his glory known. And so we must travel about. We must send prayer updates. It can seem weary and daunting, but it is necessary and God-glorifying work.

MINISTERING ABROAD WITH CHILDREN

Our faith in God's calling us to minister abroad must sustain not only us, but also our children. Some children readily embrace a foreign culture while some are more hesitant. When we first came abroad, our children were four, two, and two months. To no one's surprise, the baby was quite adaptable as long as her basic needs were met. The other two were young and still quite dependent, but they were more aware of the change than we had expected. They were thankful to have each other. Still, they missed their friends, they missed familiar places, and most of all, they missed our church family. It was not until we were once again part of the fellowship of the saints at a good church that they began to feel at home.

Another thing we noticed was that our oldest child developed a bit of a stutter. This could have been his age, but it was hard not to believe that it bore some relationship to our move abroad. His younger sister then seemed to imitate him. While serving in an English-speaking country has advantages, one disadvantage is that you suddenly question your native tongue. Words, intonation, accent, sentence structures—all these ways of speaking that have been with you since birth—seem a little odd. As hard as this might be for the parents, it seems to have an even greater impact on the children.

At such times, we may be tempted to think we are damaging our children by ministering abroad. If only we were back home, this trial for our children would not be happening. Yet we can never know what other things might have befallen us were we at home or in some other place. While we must protect them, we must also help them to live in a fallen world with all its imperfections. We must help them to live in the light of eternity. We must help them to see that trials are for their good and are given to us so that we will depend on God.

Ministering abroad may challenge how we educate our children. Christian schools may not exist, homeschooling may be a completely foreign concept (or illegal), and the children might not have the language skills or spiritual maturity to cope in a state school. As we face these challenges, doubt, despair, and discouragement may creep into our hearts. We are tempted to grow anxious. We must remember that the God who called us to minister abroad also gave us our children, and he will ensure that their needs are perfectly met (Matt. 6:25–33). As we surrender our anxieties and commit ourselves to prayer, our children will see the peace of God, which surpasses all understanding, guarding our hearts and minds in Christ Jesus.

MINISTERING ABROAD WITH OUR HUSBANDS

Ministering abroad may also mean that there is more work placed on our husbands. At first, there will be fewer people to share in the labor. Our husbands may be the webmasters, and we may be the secretaries. Our husbands may have to do some of the diaconal work until deacons are appointed. We will share in their burdens and try to lighten their load. We will do whatever it takes to keep the doors of the church open, because we know that "faith comes from hearing, and hearing through the word of Christ" (Rom. 10:17).

Because our husbands' labor is greater, our work as helpmeets will be greater. Living abroad may require our husbands to travel back and forth between countries for various reasons. It will be too impractical to go as a family, but we must hold things together at home. We must maintain discipline for that little one who tries to see what he can get away with in Daddy's absence. We will have to remind an older child of his responsibilities. We will carry on the instruction of God's Word.

As we minister with our husbands, we may be tempted to compare ourselves with other women. Everyone seems to have it easier. Those at home seem to have an easier situation amidst familiar conveniences and comforts. In our adopted lands, the women in our churches seem to lead orderly lives because they are completely at home in their surroundings. Meanwhile, we feel as if we live in permanent chaos. We think that we are the only wives who must give ourselves to keeping our husbands afloat.

At this point, I return to the spiritual battle. The ministry at times will be mentally, emotionally, and physically exhausting. As we face exhaustion, we will become more vulnerable to the attack of the Evil One. Satan has no greater victory than to bring down a minister of the gospel. As we minister on the front lines of the battle, we must keep putting on our spiritual armor (Eph. 6:13). If we use it in our own strength, it will not be effective. But when we pray, we acknowledge our dependence on God in all ways. We must put on each piece with prayer and use each piece with prayer (Eph. 6:18).

In this spiritual battle, our primary focus should be prayer. We call on the power of the Holy Spirit to make his Word efficacious through our husbands. A shepherd of the flock is in an exposed position and therefore needs a special measure of prayer. Satan is not at all threatened by the priest of the Roman Catholic church on the corner. He rejoices in the minister of the neighboring church where one cannot speak the name of Jesus because it may offend. Satan casts his fiery darts at shepherds who faithfully feed God's sheep. Sheep cannot simply be fed once and expect to grow; there must be an ongoing nourishing through the ministry of the shepherd.[5]

Our husbands' natural tendency will lean toward pride. Pride leads to a host of other sins. As strong as our husbands may seem, we must remember that they are weak, earthen vessels that are vulnerable to breaking if not upheld in prayer. Therefore, we must pray for our husbands to discern their own weakness and to know that the surpassing power belongs to God and not to themselves (2 Cor. 4:7).

If we are to pray with the urgency demanded, we must have a high view of the proclamation of God's Word. Our husbands need supernatural courage and strength as they prepare and preach his Word. In Ephesians, Paul requests such prayer for himself "that I may declare it boldly" (Eph. 6:20). Likewise, our husbands must preach with boldness. Boldness is not arrogance but assurance in the truth of the gospel they bring. We must pray that God would guard their lips from error and that our husbands would speak as they ought: "For I decided to know nothing among you except Jesus Christ and him crucified" (1 Cor. 2:2).

Our husbands serve as ambassadors for Christ. They have no message of their own, nor do they preach of their own authority. They are not at liberty to give their own opinions or worldly wisdom (1 Cor. 2:4–5). Our prayer should be that our husbands' preaching would lead people away from the wisdom of men and to the saving and sustaining power of God. To do this, our husbands must "not shrink from declaring . . . the whole counsel of God" (Acts 20:27), the mystery that was once hidden but is now revealed.

It will be our labor of love to persevere in prayer for our husbands. If they are to preach the Word in season and out of season, we must pray in season and out of season. As we pray for them to be sober-minded, to endure suffering, to do the work of an evangelist, to fulfill their ministry (2 Tim. 4:5), we will fulfill our ministry as well.

Our prayers will do them the greatest good. Moreover, we will become more "one flesh" with them; they suffer no lack, so we suffer no lack wherever God calls us to serve. When suffering comes, we will endure it with them. Together we will trust that the preaching of the Word and prayer will bring about the salvation of souls and prepare the bride for the Bridegroom. Truly, our labor as one flesh can know no greater joy.

CONCLUSION

Ministering abroad may be a short-term stay or a lifelong calling. We may remain in one country, or we may move about. We may see abundant fruit from the ministry, or we may not live to see anything beyond the sowing of seeds. Whatever our situation, however arduous our labor, when our time of departure comes, may we be able to say, "I have fought the good fight, I have finished the race, I have kept the faith" (2 Tim. 4:7).

With love,
Your sister in Christ,
PAM

STUDY QUESTIONS

1. What is the wife's function in regard to her husband's ministry?

2. What is the wife's function in regard to her family?

3. Why might it be difficult when people from your home country come to visit you abroad?

4. Why might spiritual warfare be more prominent on the mission field?

5. How can ministering abroad help us gain a heavenly perspective?

RECOMMENDED RESOURCES

Edwards, Jonathan. *The Life of David Brainerd*. Edited by Philip E. Howard Jr. Grand Rapids, MI: Baker Book House, 1992.

Henry, Matthew. *A Way to Pray*. Edited by O. Palmer Robertson. Edinburgh: The Banner of Truth Trust, 2010.

Owen, John. *Communion with God*. Abridged by R. J. K. Law. Edinburgh: The Banner of Truth Trust, 2008.

Roberts, Maurice. *Great God of Wonders*. Edinburgh: The Banner of Truth Trust, 2003.

CHAPTER EIGHTEEN

Campus Ministry:
Life at the Crossroads

Kathy Wilcke

A good woman I found; a faithful wife of nineteen years I have been given. Out of the Lord's divine knowledge and eternal goodness, he gave me Kathy. She has taught me more of his tender mercies than any other I have known. It is an immeasurable privilege to be molded for eternity with her. Kathy's tireless love of our five children and her infectious hospitality have indeed glorified the name of Jesus in the places where we have sojourned. May his renown be visible in the lives of many who know him because they have known her. A sojourner by grace with you,

REV. CLINT WILCKE

Dear sister in Christ,

It is a great privilege to watch the Lord work in the lives of young women entering into the role of campus ministry, partnered with their husbands. Having served in this capacity for a number of years, I feel compelled by the Holy Spirit to share with you some of the experiences and life lessons that God has taught me. His kindness in allowing me this opportunity to share my experience with you does not imply that I have always lived according to the principles that I discuss. As Paul wrote, "Not that I have already obtained this or am already perfect, but I press on to make it my own, because Christ Jesus has made me his own" (Phil. 3:12).

Surely God gives us experiences to share with others for the edification and encouragement of the body so that we may learn from one another's successes and failures. You have heard the old adage, "Do as I say, not as I do." The following counsel is based on lessons I have learned, not necessarily ones that I have lived.

First of all, your relationship to God the Father and the Lord Jesus Christ is paramount and trumps every discussion of experience and principles. Time spent daily in God's Word and in prayer leads to obedience to God and his commands. Christian friends with whom you can confess your sin and be mutually encouraged are a gift beyond measure. That being said, I want to write about some circumstances you may face as your husband takes his job as a campus minister!

YOUR RELATIONSHIP WITH YOUR HUSBAND: UNIQUE CHALLENGES

There will be unique challenges in your new role as wife and ministry partner. In the book coauthored by J. Ligon Duncan and Susan Hunt titled *Women's Ministry in the Local Church*, Hunt quotes fifth-century patriarch John Chrysostom, who wrote, "If [the husband and wife] perform their proper duties, everything around them acquires firmness and stability."[1] The students under your husband's care will recognize the beauty of the husband-wife relationship as you both "perform your proper duties." Your students are not yet married, and they are looking to the closest Christian married couple for proof that the gospel is real. Your marriage is a picture of Christ and the church, and you do not want to deceive them by the way you live. You will be watched and analyzed. Of course, you will not be perfect, and the students need to see grace and forgiveness at work. All of life is ministry, including your marriage.

Paul David Tripp says it beautifully in *Broken-Down House*: "Marriage involves a flawed person, in a comprehensive and interdependent love relationship with another flawed person, in the middle of a fallen world, but with a faithful God."[2] Because this is the unchangeable reality of every marriage, there is not a day when ministry is not required. You and your spouse are not yet the persons God created you to be. By his grace, God has drafted you both into his service and called you to be tools of restoration in the other's life.

What about My Needs?

It is important to be content with the income your husband receives as a campus minister. Be thankful for how he provides for you, and do not constantly want for more. Carefully manage your household finances by not spending more than he earns. If it appears inadequate, take your burdens to the Lord, and he will provide for your needs. Your husband must never be made to feel inadequate because his income does not meet your expectations.

> But godliness with contentment is great gain, for we brought nothing into the world, and we cannot take anything out of the world. But if we have food and clothing, with these we will be content. But those who desire to be rich fall into temptation, into a snare, into many senseless and harmful desires that plunge people into ruin and destruction. For the love of money is a root of all kinds of evils. It is through this craving that some have wandered away from the faith and pierced themselves with many pangs. (1 Tim. 6:6–10)

The same is true for the campus to which your husband has been called. It may not meet your idyllic expectations, but refrain from saying, "I will never go there!" A wise woman once told me, "God's people are everywhere." When God calls your husband to a campus, you must trust that he will provide for you in that place. Be open to the Spirit's direction because you have no way of knowing the future and what God has in store for you. Be willing to leave what is comfortable and trust God with the circumstances.

I have grown to appreciate Paul's words in Acts 17:24–28.

> The God who made the world and everything in it, being Lord of heaven and earth, does not live in temples made by man, nor is he served by human hands, as though he needed anything, since he himself gives to all mankind life and breath and everything. And he made from one man every nation of mankind to live on all the face of the earth, having determined allotted periods and the boundaries of their dwelling place, that they should seek God, and perhaps feel their way toward him and find him. Yet he is actually not far from each one of us, for
>
> "in him we live and move and have our being."

Remember, you are a missionary wherever you live. The place God is calling you to serve may not be a "destination," but his people are there!

Young, Pretty Girls?

In the middle of our time in campus ministry, one of the students' mothers asked me, "How do you feel about your husband being around all these young, beautiful girls all the time?" I did not know how to answer and simply shrugged it off. On pondering the question, however, I remembered a comment I had read by a pastor friend. He had asked his new session to give him a secretary who was old and ugly! This request came from a man who had lived many years as a Christian minister and knew that Satan still roamed around like a roaring lion, no matter a pastor's age and stage of ministry. We are never immune to the schemes of the Devil, and we are always prone to wander.

Do not believe for a second that your marriage is immune to falling apart. It is in the areas of apparent strength that our prideful hearts most often fall, even in areas where we thought we were untouchable. Satan is at work to destroy your marriage, so it is vitally important that your communication is honest and open about such topics. It is a fact of life that campus ministers will be around young, beautiful, single women. Pray that your marriage will be honored among all of them and that your husband will keep a kingdom mindset and minister to young men and women out of a pure heart. Also keep your own heart and eyes pure, as you cannot judge others without being careful to see your own sin. "Why do you see the speck that is in your brother's eye, but do not notice the log that is in your own eye?" (Matt. 7:3).

I have read about countless ministry couples losing their witness and their families to the sin of adultery. We cannot deny the reality of sin and temptation and have to be vigilant about protecting the covenant we make before God and witnesses. But we are also not to be slaves again to fear and should trust in the One who is able to keep us from falling. As you and your husband grow closer to Christ, you will grow closer to one another. He is "able to keep you from stumbling and to present you blameless before the presence of his glory with great joy" (Jude 24).

Examples from My Garden

One of my newfound hobbies is gardening, and I have come to learn that there are many spiritual life lessons to be found in nature. The following premise is taken from an article by J. R. Miller, "How to Live a Beautiful Christian Life," which was written in 1880. God places us in the life circumstances that will most effectively cause us to be spiritually nourished and grow in Christian virtues. Even in my short tenure of gardening, I have learned that not all plants and bushes are created equally. I have planted bushes in the ground and realized after several days of watching them continually wilt that they are not actually sickly plants but just need more

273

shade from the sun. After a year of no fruit on a vine or no flowers from a bush, I have realized that such plants need more sun, and so I dig them up and replant each one in a place where it is most likely to flourish. The new ground allows for necessary growth and fruit bearing. This principle applies to how God directs our lives. Our purpose is to bring him glory and reflect his character. In order to do this, he will plant us in the places where we will be most sanctified and he will be most glorified.

The spiritual lessons gleaned from my gardening experiences don't stop there! Every day, I look at my fledgling butterfly garden, which I planted on a hill in hard clay soil. Amazingly, some of the plants are still alive, albeit barely! I have often thought of my marriage relationship and our ministry in light of my garden. I do not want to find satisfaction in the mere existence of my plants, our marriage, or our ministry. I do not want to be satisfied with their survival; I want to see them thrive! I desire to be a helpmeet for my husband in such a way that he feels free to do his work heartily unto the Lord and that he blossoms in his calling as a husband, father, and pastor. Tend to your marriage, cultivate your relationship, and the fruit will bring glory to God, spilling over into every other area of ministry.

> Do not be deceived: God is not mocked, for whatever one sows, that will he also reap. For the one who sows to his own flesh will from the flesh reap corruption, but the one who sows to the Spirit will from the Spirit reap eternal life. And let us not grow weary of doing good, for in due season we will reap, if we do not give up. (Gal. 6:7–9)

YOUR RELATIONSHIP WITH THE STUDENTS: UNIQUE CHALLENGES

For the most part, the college students to whom you minister will be engaged in the same activities and share a relatively narrow age range, from eighteen to twenty-four years. They will be making decisions that will affect and set the course for their future adult years. You and your husband have the privilege and responsibility of influencing those decisions by allowing them to see you doing normal, married, adult things. Because you are fairly close to them in age, you will be tempted to want to stay on their level of youth, both physically and spiritually. But you have the opportunity to grow in front of them, and I exhort you to continue on in your spiritual journey, bringing them along with you. Paul encouraged the Ephesians by reminding them that Jesus gave certain men gifts

> to equip the saints for the work of ministry, for building up the body of Christ . . . so that we may no longer be children, tossed to and fro by the waves and carried about by every wind of doctrine, by human cunning, by craftiness in deceitful schemes. Rather, speaking the truth in love, we are to grow up in every way into him who is the head, into Christ, from whom the whole body, joined and held together by every joint with which it is equipped, when each part is working properly, makes the body grow so that it builds itself up in love. (Eph. 4:12, 14–16)

Your maturity will help them to grow. How they see you living out the gospel will influence them for years to come.

Do not flippantly encourage dating and marriage among the students. The decisions they make regarding a future spouse will affect countless other people: future children, and their friends, parents, grandparents, and other relatives. It is not a "college decision" but a lifelong decision with lifelong implications. Of course you will pray with and for them and rejoice with them when the time comes to marry. However, do not persuade them to choose a spouse solely on the basis of your recommendation. God, the perfect matchmaker, was at work even before the foundation of the world. Trust him to do it, and give advice only when you are asked!

YOUR RELATIONSHIP WITH YOUR CHURCH: UNIQUE CHALLENGES

Church membership is another area with unique challenges. You are married to a minister, but he is not on staff at a church. You yourself will

275

join a particular church for worship, edification, involvement, service, and oversight, but it may not be permissible for your husband to join a church given his unique calling.

You will have to share your husband with lots of different churches, and you may not be able to spend much time worshipping together on the Sabbath. You may also be required to travel together to other churches. This will curtail your involvement and presence at the church you have joined. The benefit of this arrangement is that it enables you to see the larger body of Christ and to be encouraged by it. You need to be supportive of your husband's ministry when he asks you to join him on preaching engagements or to visit others who support his work on the college campus.

There can be jealousies among churches about which particular church you join and with whom you spend the most time. Be sensitive to that fact, and seek to share the ministry with as many people as possible. However, for your own edification, join a church where your soul is fed and where the Holy Spirit is clearly leading you.

Encourage students to become part of a local body of believers in a local church. Let them see you using your gifts in your church. You will be modeling Christian living as you involve yourself (and any children) in the life of the local church.

I have found that the church had fewer expectations of me as a campus minister's wife than it would have of a "normal" pastor's wife. That is not an excuse to avoid using your spiritual gifts. You are called to use them for the mutual encouragement of the body of Christ. It is, however, a perk of the job, and I would encourage you to enjoy this season of ministry.

Please note that your students are not your peers. You will need friends in your new town, and I encourage you to start praying for the Lord to provide you with godly, sweet friendships. Pray for friends with whom you can live out the Christian experience. All our relationships are meant to sanctify us. Some are more enjoyable than others. I have

276

known wonderful times of refreshing friendship, as well as very dry and lonely times in ministry. Seek to be a friend by treating others the way you would like to be treated, and trust the Lord to provide. God is able to give us the good gift of friendship if we will only ask. Use the lonely times to draw closer to the Lord. Oftentimes, the fewer human distractions we have, the more possible it is to find quality time in meditation, reflection, and communion with God. But you cannot stay there, because we were created for relationships!

Finally, dear sister, stay on your knees during every season of ministry.

Be sober-minded; be watchful. Your adversary the devil prowls around like a roaring lion, seeking someone to devour. Resist him, firm in your faith, knowing that the same kinds of suffering are being experienced by your brotherhood throughout the world. And after you have suffered a little while, the God of all grace, who has called you to his eternal glory in Christ, will himself restore, confirm, strengthen, and establish you. To him be the dominion forever and ever. Amen. (1 Peter 5:8–11)

Sweet sister, enjoy this season! Engage in conversations, games, exercise, Bible study, and prayer. Relax, be yourself, love the Lord Jesus, love your husband, love your local church, and love every single student who comes into your home. You will not know, until you reach the other side, what invisible things God had planned for your time at the university.

It is the LORD who goes before you. He will be with you; he will not leave you or forsake you. Do not fear or be dismayed. (Deut. 31:8)

Now to him who is able to do far more abundantly than all that we ask or think, according to the power at work within us, to him be glory in the church and in Christ Jesus throughout all generations, forever and ever. Amen. (Eph. 3:20)

Your sister in Christ,

KATHY

STUDY QUESTIONS

1. Consider Christ's saving work in your life and where your soul would be apart from the grace of God. How will that help you to love the students under your care?

2. What motivates you to serve Jesus every day? Is it your material blessings or his eternal salvation? Meditate on Hebrews 13.

3. Think of creative ways that you can be a helper to your husband in his calling.

4. How will you consider the interests of others above your own? Will you fight for your own rights or lay down your life for the sake of the next generation?

5. Consider how much value you have put on other people's advice in your life. How much value do you think a college student will put on your advice? How freely do you think you should offer advice? Find Scripture proofs for your answer.

RECOMMENDED RESOURCES

Fitzpatrick, Elyse. *Helper by Design: God's Perfect Plan for Women in Marriage.* Chicago, IL: Moody Publishers, 2003.

Hughes, Kent R., and Barbara Hughes. *Liberating Ministry from the Success Syndrome.* Wheaton, IL: Tyndale House Publishers, Inc., 1987.

Hunt, Susan. *Spiritual Mothering: The Titus 2 Model for Women Mentoring Women.* Wheaton, IL: Crossway Books, 1993.

————. *Your Home a Place of Grace.* Wheaton, IL: Crossway Books, 2000.

MacDonald, Gail. *High Call, High Privilege.* Peabody, MA: Hendrickson Publishers, Inc., 1998.

Peace, Martha. *The Excellent Wife: A Biblical Perspective.* Bemidji, MN: Focus Publishing, Inc., 2005.

Notes

Preface

1. Isn't it interesting to note that when God first introduced the *imago dei*, it is as male and female together, not as Adam first with Eve created second?

2. J. I. Packer, *A Quest for Godliness: The Puritan Vision of the Christian Life* (Wheaton, IL: Crossway Books, 1994), 262.

3. Ibid.

Chapter One: Priorities

1. James Anderson, *Memorable Women of Puritan Times*, vol. 2 (Morgan, PA: Soli Deo Gloria, 2001), 229–30.

2. Ibid., 46.

Chapter Three: Humility

1. Stuart Scott, *The Exemplary Husband: A Biblical Perspective* (Bemidji, MN: Focus Publishing, 2000), 187.

2. Arthur G. Bennett, ed., *Valley of Vision: A Collection of Puritan Prayers and Devotions* (Carlisle: The Banner of Truth Trust, 2002), 193.

3. Halcyon Backhouse, ed., *Collected Letters of John Newton* (London: Hodder & Stoughton, 1989), 237.

Chapter Five: Expectations

1. Gail MacDonald, *High Call, High Privilege* (Peabody, MA: Hendrickson Publishers, Inc., 1998), 150.

2. Elisabeth Elliot, *Keep a Quiet Heart* (Ann Arbor, MI: Servant Publications, 1995), 155.

3. John Piper, "The Renewed Mind and How to Have It" (sermon), *desiringGod.org*, August 2004. Emphasis in original. http://www.desiringgod.org/resource-library/sermons/the-renewed-mind-and-how-to-have-it.

Chapter Six: Hospitality

1. "Hospitality," *TheFreeDictionary.com*, accessed February 11, 2013, http://www.the freedictionary.com/hospitality.

Chapter Seven: Friendships over the Long Haul

1. Joseph Parry, BrainyQuote.com, retrieved June 19, 2013, http://www.brainyquote .com/quotes/quotes/j/josephparr227774.html.

Chapter Eight: Respecting My Husband

1. Quoted by David McCullough, *John Adams* (New York: Simon and Schuster, 2001), 171.

2. *Webster's Seventh New Collegiate Dictionary*, s.v. "respect."

3. Nancy Wilson, *The Fruit of her Hands* (Moscow, ID: Canon Press, 1997), 41–42.

Chapter Nine: Sharing My Husband

1. Amy Carmichael, *His Thoughts Said . . . His Father Said* (Fort Washington, PA: CLC Publications, 1958), 39.

2. Amy Carmichael, *Rose from Brier* (Fort Washington, PA: CLC Publications, 1973), 50.

Chapter Eleven: Conflict within the Church

1. John C. LaRue, "Forced Exits: A Too-Common Ministry Hazard," Your Church, March/April 1996, 72.

2. John C. LaRue, "Profile of Today's Pastor: Ministry Preparation," Your Church, March/April 1995, 56.

3. Ron Allchin, "Faith Motivation Versus Feeling Motivation," counseling homework. The Biblical Counseling Center, Arlington Heights, IL.

4. Ken Sande, *The Peacemaker: A Biblical Guide to Resolving Personal Conflict* (Grand Rapids: Baker Books, 2004), 35.

Chapter Twelve: Ministry Moms

1. Notes on Titus 2, *ESV Study Bible* (Wheaton, IL: Crossway Bibles, 2008), 2349.

2. The names of those interviewed in this chapter have been changed.

3. "Geoffrey Allen," text message to author, June 15, 2012.

4. Walter J. Chantry, "The High Calling of Motherhood," *The Reformed Reader*, accessed July 16, 2012, http://www.reformedreader.org/rbb/chantry/motherhood .htm.

5. "Chrissa," August 25, 2010 (11:12 p.m.), comment on "Duty before Family?," *Being a Pastor's Kid: Life from the Front Pew* (blog), June 16, 2005, http://pastorskids.typepad .com/being_a_pastors_kid_life_/2005/06/duty_before_fam.html#comments.

6. "April Moore," e-mail message to author, June 20, 2012.

7. "John Hedman," e-mail message to author, June 12, 2012.

8. Barnabas Piper, "Sinners in a Fishbowl," *Ligonier Ministries*, July 1, 2012, http:// www.ligonier.org/learn/articles/sinners-in-a-fishbowl/. Used by permission.

9. Ibid.

10. "Christina Mendez," e-mail message to author, June 12, 2012.

11. "John Hedman," e-mail message to author, June 12, 2012.

12. "Beth Hallisey," e-mail message to author, June 21, 2012.

13. Ibid.

14. Barnabas Piper, "Sinners in a Fishbowl," *Ligonier Ministries*.

15. "John Hedman," e-mail message to author, June 12, 2012.

16. "Leslie Thurner," e-mail message to author, June 15, 2012.

17. Gene C. Fant Jr., "First-Person: Be Kind to PKs," *Baptist Press*, August 2, 2005, http://bpnews.net/bpnews.asp?ID=21336.

18. Fred T. Garmon, "The Pastor and Conflict Management," *Faith Library*, accessed July 17, 2012, http://faithlibrary.cc/index.php/christian-sermons/sermon/the_pastor_and _conflict_management/.

19. "April Moore," e-mail message to author, June 20, 2012.

20. "Beth Hallisey," e-mail message to author, June 21, 2012.

Chapter Thirteen: Depression

1. American Psychiatric Association, *Diagnostic and Statistical Manual of Mental Disorders 2*, 4th ed. (Washington, DC: American Psychiatric Association, 1994), 327.

2. John Piper, *When the Darkness Will Not Lift: Doing What We Can While We Wait for God—and Joy* (Wheaton, IL: Crossway Books, 2006), 25.

3. Edward T. Welch, *Blame It on the Brain: Distinguishing Chemical Imbalances, Brain Disorders, and Disobedience* (Phillipsburg, NJ: P&R Publishing, 1998), 126.

4. Edward T. Welch, ed., *Depression: A Stubborn Darkness* (Greensboro, NC: New Growth Press, 2004), 212.

5. Arthur G. Bennett, *Valley of Vision: A Collection of Puritan Prayers and Devotions* (Carlisle, PA: The Banner of Truth Trust, 2007), 1.

Chapter Fourteen: Loneliness and Bereavement

1. *Merriam-Webster's Dictionary and Thesaurus*, 2007 edition, s.v. "lonely."

2. John Owen, *The Works of John Owen,* vol. 6 (Edinburgh: The Banner of Truth Trust, 1995), 9, 12.

3. Samuel Rutherford (n.d.), BrainyQuote.com, retrieved July 26, 2012, http://www .brainyquote.com/quotes/quotes/s/samuelruth185289.html.

4. William Cowper, *Epistle to an Afflicted Protestant Lady in France* (Vancouver, BC: Regent College Publishing, 2007) 116.

Chapter Fifteen: The Lord's Day

1. R. L. Dabney, *Lectures in Systematic Theology* (Grand Rapids: Zondervan Publishing House, 1972), 374.

2. Ryan McGraw, *The Day of Worship: Reassessing the Christian Life in Light of the Sabbath* (Grand Rapids: Reformation Heritage Books, 2011), 10.

3. Joseph Pipa, *The Lord's Day* (Fearn, UK: Christian Focus Publications, 1996), 13.

Chapter Seventeen: Ministering in a Different Culture

1. Maurice Roberts, *Great God of Wonders* (Edinburgh: The Banner of Truth Trust, 2003), 91.

2. Jonathan Edwards, "Christ the Example of Gospel Ministers," in *The Works of Jonathan Edwards, Volume 25: Sermons and Discourses, 1743–1758,* ed. Wilson H. Kimnach (New Haven and London: Yale University Press, 2006), 344.

3. Incidentally, I regularly look to my husband's insight for what to make for particular guests and occasions. This again makes our hospitality a one-flesh effort.

4. Maurice Roberts, *The Happiness of Heaven* (Grand Rapids: Reformed Heritage Books, 2009), 85.

5. WSC 1:88. Q. *What are the outward means whereby Christ communicateth to us the benefits of redemption? A. The outward and ordinary means whereby Christ communicateth to us the benefits of redemption, are his ordinances, especially the Word, sacraments, and prayer; all which are made effectual to the elect for salvation.*

Chapter Eighteen: Campus Ministry

1. J. Ligon Duncan and Susan Hunt, *Women's Ministry in the Local Church* (Wheaton, IL: Crossway Books, 2006), 35. I am grateful to Susan Hunt for her faithfulness as a pastor's wife, mother, Bible study teacher, and director of women's ministries and for her commitment to the next generation in the many books she has written. I heartily recommend studying her books for guidance in your role as a wife.

2. Paul David Tripp, *Broken-Down House* (Wapwallopen, PA: Shepherd Press, 2009), 194.

Contributors

Betty Jane Adams has been married to Jay for sixty-two years. Together they have journeyed through his pastorates, graduate school, seminary teaching, counseling, and writing ministries. They have four children, thirteen grandchildren, and one great-granddaughter.

Donna Ascol has served alongside her husband-pastor, Tom, for thirty-three years. A pediatric nurse, she launched her second career as a homeschooling mother with the birth of the first of her six children. Donna finds her greatest joy in serving her family as wife to her husband, mom to her children, and Noni to her granddaughter, Emi.

Sarah Ascol is the eldest of six pastor's kids. She is a private homeschool consultant and founder of One Room Learning, an educational center for homeschooling families. In her spare time, Sarah enjoys coaching basketball, singing opera, and playing with her niece. Sarah blogs at tckteacher .wordpress.com.

Mary Beeke is the wife of Dr. Joel Beeke and the mother of Calvin (wife Laura), Esther, and Lydia. She has served as a registered nurse and an elementary school teacher and has her MAT in Learning Disabilities from Calvin College. Since 1989, she has been a homemaker and a pastor's wife.

Lynn Crotts has been a believer since high school. She graduated from Liberty University, where she met her husband John. After he attended The

Master's Seminary, they moved to Georgia in 1995 to serve at Faith Bible Church. They are grateful to be raising four children.

Barbara Davis is the daughter of a Kansas farmer and a graduate of Sterling College, Sterling, Kansas. She has worked as an elementary teacher and has served as the wife of a pastor-professor. Barbara is the mother of three sons, an addict of college sports, and a quilter of thirty years.

Joan Hamilton was raised in Edinburgh and studied geography at Aberdeen University. After teaching primary school for six years, she married Ian, a Presbyterian minister. Together they have four children and one granddaughter.

Shannon Baugh Onnink became a Christian during college. She married Matt Baugh and had five covenant children while serving in Mississippi and in Haiti. Matt died while working in Haiti. Since then, she moved to Illinois, married a second time, and has been blessed with two more children. She stays busy with home, church, and Hope for La Gonave. Her chief delight is her Savior, Jesus Christ.

"Sissy" Floyd Pipa was born in 1946 in Cleveland, Mississippi. She graduated from Delta State University in Art Education. In 1971 "Sissy" married Joseph A. Pipa Jr. They have two children and eight grandchildren and live in South Carolina, where her husband is president of Greenville Presbyterian Theological Seminary.

Shirley Rankin is married to her high school sweetheart and has been blessed with three wonderful children. She and her husband have lived in seven states and spent four years in Scotland during his studies. In addition to staying busy as a mother and pastor's wife, she works part-time as an assistant in a law firm in Houston, Texas.

Sue Rowe has been a pastor's wife for almost forty years. She leads women's Bible studies and speaks at women's events. Sue is a NANC-certified biblical counselor with Trinity Presbyterian Church, Statesboro, Georgia, where her husband, Craig, serves as a pastor and directs the biblical counseling ministry. Craig and Sue have four children and ten grandchildren.

Pam Schweitzer is a native of South Glens Falls, New York. She graduated from William Smith College and married in 1997. Pam served eight years as a Marine wife, three years as a graduate student's wife in Scotland, and the past five as a minister's wife in England; her husband Bill is the church-planting minister of Gateshead Presbyterian Church. They have six children.

Mary Somerville has directed a ministry of evangelism and discipleship of teen moms with Young Life for fourteen years. She authored the book *One with a Shepherd: The Tears and Triumphs of a Ministry Marriage* and holds an MA in counseling from Trinity Evangelical Divinity School. Mary is an adjunct faculty member at The Master's College, California. She is married to Bob, and together they have two children and seven grandchildren.

Catherine J. Stewart, a native of Northern Ireland, is a pastor's wife living in Savannah, Georgia. She and her husband, Neil, have five children whom they homeschool. Before moving to the United States in 1999, she received a degree in theology from Queens University, Belfast.

Janie Street has been married to her pastor, Dr. John Street, for over thirty-five years. They have four children and five grandchildren. Janie is a former piano teacher, but has retired to help her husband manage his very busy teaching, writing, and traveling schedule. Her other ministries include discipleship of younger women, teaching discipleship classes, and occasionally speaking at women's meetings.

Margy Tripp and her husband, Tedd, have been married for forty-five years, during which time she has served in ministry as a pastor's wife and Christian educator. The mercy of Christ, and the fullness of his power, has energized her to study his Word and to share the freedom and joy of the gospel to others.

Kathy Wilcke has been married to Clint for twenty years, and they have five children. She has served alongside her husband in youth ministry, seminary, campus ministry, and church planting. The Wilckes are currently on mission among the flock of Christ Covenant Church in Hernando, Mississippi.

Noelle Wilkerson is a pastor's wife and homemaker in Columbia, South Carolina. She and her husband, Jim, have six children. She loves the service of her family and the particular church where God has called her. Her main interests are reading, knitting, traveling with Ian, and welcoming people into their home.